Contents

PART 2 Accelerating Literacy Development Through Easy-Reading Materials

PART 3 Communicating Children's Successes to Parents

Overview of the *Extra Support Handbook*

The questions and answers that follow will provide you with an overview of the *Extra Support Handbook.*

What is the *Extra Support Handbook*?

- The *Extra Support Handbook* is a collection of resources that will assist teachers in providing extra support to any child who needs it.
- The activities, suggestions, and ideas in the handbook can be used to help children who are reading below grade level participate in the regular classroom activities for *Invitations to Literacy* and will move them toward on-grade-level reading.

How is the *Extra Support Handbook* used?

- It is intended that these resources be used in small-group settings and that they be used in addition to the regular classroom activities of *Invitations to Literacy.*
- All children, regardless of their reading ability, will benefit from being integrated into the regular classroom and exposed to the rich, exciting, and varied literature that appears in their *Invitations to Literacy* grade-level anthologies.

Which children will benefit from the activities in the handbook?

- Children who consistently need support to read books written at their grade level
- Children who are reading one or more years below their designated grade level
- Children in Title 1/Chapter 1 programs

Which teachers will find the resources in the handbook helpful?

- Reading resource teachers in regular or resource classrooms
- Teachers working with small groups in regular or inclusion classrooms

How much time is needed to provide extra support?

- Using the resources with children in a small-group setting for 20–30 minutes each day will help most children participate successfully in regular classroom activities and move them toward on-grade-level reading.

For which selections and skills is extra support provided?

- Big Books and major literature selections in children's anthologies
- tested comprehension skills
- Watch Me Read Books
- tested phonics/decoding skills
- easy books

What support is provided for reading the Big Books?

Before Reading Options

- **Activating Prior Knowledge** Children discuss information that they individually and collectively have that will help them read and understand a selection.
- **Picture Walk** As children are guided through the selection, they are provided with advance information about characters, events, and selection vocabulary.
- **Oral Language Development** Children discuss and use groups of related words that they will meet in the selection.

Reading Options

- Prior to participating in the shared reading of the Big Book selection, children listen to an Audio Tape or to a teacher read aloud a portion of the Big Book. This prereading prepares children for the shared reading experience.

After Reading Options

- Included among the options are activities for helping children reread to develop fluency, participate in a language experience activity, practice using the Think About Words strategy, and practice reading high-frequency words.

What support is provided for reading the major selections in the anthologies?

Before Reading Options

- **Activating Prior Knowledge** Children call to mind information that will help them read and understand a selection and then listen to a selection summary that incorporates key vocabulary.
- **Picture Walk** As children are guided through the selection, they are provided with advance information about characters, events, and selection vocabulary.
- **Activity and Selection Master** Children and teachers complete a selection master together that children can use for support when they read the selection.

During Reading Options

- **Guided Reading** Prior to reading in the whole-class setting, children are guided through the reading of a portion of the selection. Children unable to read on their own, read aloud with the teacher.
- This guided prereading provides advance information about the important aspects of a selection and offers opportunities to clarify parts that are confusing.
- Guiding children up to the most exciting part of the story instead of through the complete story will provide the support and motivation most children need to read in the whole-class setting, and prevents them from giving away surprise endings to classmates not involved in the prereading.

After Reading Options

- Additional experiences with the literature are provided through activities that guide children in thinking critically about the selection, rereading for fluency, and using the Think About Words strategy.

What are the different ways that the activities in the handbook can be used to support the activities in the Teacher's Book?

- It is recommended that the prereading and guided reading activities from the handbook prepare children for participating in activities from the Teacher's Book. The activities may, however, be used in other ways. For example:
  - Children might listen to the complete selection before participating in the shared reading in the whole-class setting.
  - Children might be guided through a portion of the selection and read the remainder of the selection cooperatively with a partner.
  - Children who need them may participate in the guided reading activities in the handbook after first reading the selection in a whole-class setting.

What support is provided for the tested skills?

- While the Teacher's Books include formal skill lessons, minilessons, and reteaching lessons for each tested skill, activities in the handbooks provide additional practice for those skills.
- Working with children in a small-group setting will provide opportunities to identify the skills children understand as well as the skills for which they need additional instruction and practice.

What support is given for reading the Watch Me Read books?

- Watch Me Read books, which are available for each theme, include previously taught high-frequency words and phonic elements. An instructional plan that includes coaching and guided reading is available for each book.
- The Watch Me Read plan can also be used to determine which children would benefit from additional phonics instruction.

What additional phonics support is provided?

- Lessons provide additional phonics and decoding activities related to the Watch Me Read books.

What support is provided to keep beginning readers from falling behind?

- Included in the handbook is a five-day instructional plan for providing children with additional practice in reading and writing. This five-day plan is based on Houghton Mifflin's *Early Success* program, a program that incorporates all the characteristics of successful intervention programs.

What support is provided for the independent reading of easy books?

- The handbook includes a variety of ideas for motivating children to read independently, including suggestions designed to help them develop the ability to read smoothly and easily.

Where will the easy books come from?

- In the *Extra Support Handbook* is an annotated bibliography of easy and very easy books that have been carefully selected to provide children with a wide range of literature.
- Also included is a bibliography of books from Rigby's *Literacy Tree Program.*
- A collection of cost-effective ways to acquire easy reading materials is provided as well.

How does the handbook involve families?

Too often, the families of children reading below grade level hear only about the problems their child is experiencing. Included in this handbook are suggestions for

- communicating children's successes to their families
- helping children experience success as they read at home with their families

What additional resources are included in the handbook?

- A complete description of many of the strategies and techniques used in the handbook
- Selection Masters (described above) at the back of the handbook for easy access
- Generic Masters—a story map (for fiction) and a main idea form (for nonfiction)

PART 1 Support for the Program Literature

Prior Knowledge/Background Building Choices

Three options that provide children with background for understanding the selection. One or more of these activities should be used prior to children listening to or reading the selection.

Activate Prior Knowledge

- Prompts children to think about and discuss what they already know about the main concept of the selection and to discuss it.

- A summary of the selection, which includes selection vocabulary, is read aloud to children.

Picture Walk

- Guides children through the illustrations, providing them with an overview of the selection, a backdrop for building background, and a discussion of selection vocabulary.

Pages 3–23 of

Annie, Bea, and Chi Chi Dolores

Use **BEFORE**  Introduce *the* Literature

OPTION 1

Activate Prior Knowledge

Read aloud the title. Tell the children that this is a story about some animal friends and what they do in school. Explain that keeping track of what these animals do will help the children learn their own ABCs.

Invite children to share what they know about the alphabet—what the letters are, how they are shaped, the sounds they stand for, and so on. Encourage children to come to the board and write any letters they may know.

Point out that this is an alphabet, or ABC, book. Have children describe other ABC books they have seen. (If you have any of these alphabet books on hand, let children show them to the group as they talk about the books they know.) Then share and discuss the following pages.

Page 5 Point to *A a* on the page and have children identify the letter. Then ask them where else they see *a* on the page. Help children identify *a* in the words *all* and *aboard*, and have them say the words with you.

Page 9 Point to *D d*, and name this letter for children. Talk with them about what the animals in this picture are doing. Then ask children to point out the word on this page. Say the word *drawing* with them and have them point out the letter *d* in that word.

Page 12 Have children identify the letter at the top of this page if they can. Then ask them to point out where else they see that letter on the page. Tell children that the word on this page is *giggling*. Ask if they see anyone on this page who is giggling. Have children point out those characters.

Page 16 Continue with the letters *j* and *k* and the words *jumping* and *kicking*.

(Underlined words are key words in the selection.)

Ask children if any of the things they have seen the animals do in this selection are things they themselves do in school. Invite children to share other things they like to do in school.

OPTION 2

Picture Walk

Display the book cover and read aloud the title. Point to the first letter of each name in the title and have children identify it. Write those letters on the board and explain the A-B-C-D pattern to children. Then guide them through the illustrations, incorporating the key words. Point to each word in the Big Book as it is discussed.

DISPLAY

all aboard	follow
buddies	giggling
counting	hopping
drawing	icky
erasing	

Pages 4–5 Point to the picture of the school bus. Ask children what the animals in the picture are doing. Talk with children about where they think the animals are going. Encourage children to share the reasoning behind their ideas. Point to *Aa* and read *all aboard*. Help children see the letter *a* at the beginnings of those words.

Pages 6–7 Ask children where they think the animals are now and encourage them to explain their ideas. Then ask children what the friends are doing on page 7. Explain that these friends are buddies. Point out the letter *b* in the word *buddies*.

Page 8 Ask what the animals are doing on this page. Have children point out details that help them see that the animals are counting. Then point out the *c* in *counting*.

Use the same technique to discuss pages 9–15.

18 Off We Go—See What We Know!

Prior Knowledge/Background Building Choices, continued

Oral Language Development

- Interactive opportunities for children to expand their understanding of related words from the selection.

Reading Choices

Two options by which children hear a portion of the selection read aloud. In either case, children listen only up to the most exciting point of a story or to an appropriate stopping point in a nonfiction selection. Then, when children join in whole-class instruction, they will be motivated to read to find out the ending of a selection and they will not be tempted to give away the selection climax to their classmates.

Read Aloud for Interest

- The teacher reads aloud. A listening experience in which children participate in discussing and responding to the selection.

Use Audio Tape

- Children listen to the designated portion of the Audio Tape.
- A purpose for listening is provided. Discussion points follow up on the purpose and ask children to make predictions about the rest of the selection.

 Oral Language Development

Explain that this selection includes many words that tell about what Annie, Bea, Chi Chi Dolores, and the others do at school. As you display pages of the Big Book, point to and read aloud each of the following words, and ask volunteers to tell or act out what Annie and her friends are doing.

Page 11–follow the leader	**Page 15**–icky
Page 12–giggling	**Page 26**–untangling
Page 13–hopping	**Page 27**–vamoose

Use BEFORE Interact *with* Literature

 Read Aloud for Interest

Pages 4–23 Read aloud the title and the names of the author and the illustrator. Discuss the cover illustration. Then read pages 4–23 to children. As you read, stop periodically to ask children what letter they think will come next.

When you have finished, have children review what the animals do at school. Have children predict what activities the animals might do in the rest of the selection.

 Use the Audio Tape

Off We Go—See What We Know: Annie, Bea, and Chi Chi Dolores

As you display the pages of the Big Book, have children listen to pages 3–23 of the audio tape. Tell them to listen to find out all the interesting things Annie, Bea, and Chi Chi Dolores do in school.

Discussion Points
- Ask children which of the things the animals do are like things they themselves do in school.
- Ask which of these things children enjoy most.
- Encourage children to predict other activities the animals might do in the rest of the selection.

Use AFTER Interact *with* Literature

 Develop Fluency: Choral Reading

Invite small groups to read aloud pages 4–13 together. If children pause or have difficulty reading a word, encourage any group member to read the word aloud for the others to repeat.

Annie, Bea, and Chi Chi Dolores 19

Developing Language

Two opportunities to develop children's use and knowledge of language. The first focuses on helping children become fluent readers; the second is a language experience activity.

Develop Fluency

- An opportunity for children to practice reading fluently and expressively from their selection.

Language Experience

- An activity in which children's responses to a selection are recorded by the teacher so that children may reread them and perhaps reuse them in written materials.
- Engages children in evaluative and creative thinking about the Big Book selection.

Skills Practice

Tested Skills

- Additional practice is provided for tested comprehension skills. This small-group activity provides an opportunity to identify and clarify ineffective or inaccurate practices.

OPTION 3 Oral Language Development

Explain that this selection includes many words that tell about what what Annie, Bea, Chi Chi Dolores, and the others do at school. As you display pages of the Big Book, point to and read aloud each of the following words, and ask volunteers to tell or act out what Annie and her friends are doing.

Page 11–follow the leader
Page 12–giggling
Page 13–hopping
Page 15–icky
Page 26–untangling
Page 27–vamoose

Use BEFORE **2 Interact with Literature**

OPTION 1 Read Aloud for Interest

Pages 4–23 Read aloud the title and the names of the author and the illustrator. Discuss the cover illustration. Then read pages 4–23 to children. As you read, stop periodically to ask children what letter they think will come next.

When you have finished, have children review what the animals do at school. Have children predict what activities the animals might do in the rest of the selection.

OPTION 2 Use the Audio Tape

Off We Go–See What We Know: Annie, Bea, and Chi Chi Dolores

As you display the pages of the Big Book, have children listen to pages 3–23 of the audio tape. Tell them to listen to find out all the interesting things Annie, Bea, and Chi Chi Dolores do in school.

Discussion Points
- Ask children which of the things the animals do are like things they themselves do in school.
- Ask which of these things children enjoy most.
- Encourage children to predict other activities the animals might do in the rest of the selection.

Use AFTER **2 Interact with Literature**

OPTION 1 Develop Fluency: Choral Reading

Invite small groups to read aloud pages 4–13 together. If children pause or have difficulty reading a w... repeat.

OPTION 2 Language Experience

Have the group create its own alphabet book about all the interesting things that happen in school.

- Have children suggest their favorite school-time people, things, and activities.
- Write the words on the board. Then work with children to rewrite the list in alphabetical order, choosing as necessary one item for each letter of the alphabet.
- Let each child choose two entries and make them for the group's alphabet book. Each entry should consist of a letter (capital and lowercase forms), one or more words beginning with that letter, and a picture illustrating that school-time item.
- Read the class's alphabet book aloud, having children say the words along with you.
- Then display the pages around the room or collect and bind them into a book that children look at and read on their own.

Use AFTER **3 Instruct and Integrate**

OPTION 1 Noting Details

Play a game in which children remember details. Display Big Book page 8, asking children to look carefully at the page. Then, after 20 seconds, cover the page and tell children that you'll see how many of them remember the details on the page.

Ask the questions below. After each question, count the number of correct responses to see which question was answered correctly the most often. (Remember to emphasize that you are trying to see which details are remembered most, not to "test" children or their memories.)
- What letter is this page about?
- What is(are) the word(s) on the page?
- How many animals are on the page? *(six)*
- What are the animals counting with? *(beans)*
- *What are the beans going into? (jars)*

Follow the same procedure, using similar questions, for Big Book pages 18, 19, 20, and 21.

OPTION 2 Initial Consonants b, t, g, v, k, m, z

Write the word *box* on the board and read it aloud. Repeat *box* and have children listen for the sound they hear at the beginning of the word. Have a volunteer identify the letter that stands for that sound. *(b)* Then ask children to look through the Big Book to find another word that begins with that sound and letter *(buddies on page 7)*.

Continue in the same way with the remaining initial consonants, using the following key words: *toy* (for *tickling*, page 26); *gum* (for *giggling*, page 12); *vote* (for *vamoose*, page 27); *kangaroo* (for *kick*, page 16); *mud* (for *making music*, page 18); and *zap* (for *zip*, page 32).

20   Off We Go–See What We Know!

Skills Practice, continued

Options for Decoding and Vocabulary Practice

- Additional practice with previously taught phonics skills and high-frequency words, combined with opportunities for guided practice with the Think About Words strategy, provide beginning readers with a variety of strategies for decoding unfamiliar words.

OPTION 3

Think About Words Strategy

Display Big Book page 16 and point to the word *ball.* Then demonstrate how children could figure out this word if they didn't know it.

- **What makes sense** First I'll read the two words that come before this word. Now I know that the word has something to do with kicking.
- **Sounds for letters** When I look at the letters, I see the letter *b* at the beginning. I know that letter. It stands for the same sound I hear at the beginning of the word *buddies.*
- **Picture clues** In the picture on pages 16 and 17, I see that something has gone flying over the animals' heads. It could be a ball, and the word *ball* begins with the same sound as *buddies.* Now I'm pretty sure I know the word. The word is *ball.*

Next, point to the word *races* on page 24 and ask children how they could figure out this word if they did not know it. Discuss the following clues:

- **What makes sense** something to do with running
- **Sounds for letters** *r* (as in *rope*) at the beginning
- **Picture clues** animals running toward a finish line, as in a race

OPTION 4

all, I, jump, run, the, time, up

High-Frequency Words

Write the following high-frequency words on index cards: *all, I, jump, run, the, time,* and *up.* Shuffle the cards, arrange them face down on a desk or table, and have a volunteer select a card. Then have the volunteer read the word aloud and find it in the Big Book. As he or she displays the page in the Big Book, have the group read the word aloud once more.

Annie, Bea, and Chi Chi Dolores **21**

Prior Knowledge/Background Building Choices

Four options that provide children with background for understanding the selection. One or more of these activities should be used prior to students listening to or reading the selection.

Activate Prior Knowledge

- Prompts children to think about the main concept of the selection and to discuss it.
- A summary of the selection, that includes key vocabulary, is read aloud to children.

Picture Walk

- Guides children through the illustrations, providing them with a backdrop for building background and discussing selection vocabulary.

Selection Master

- Helps children organize their thinking about the selection.
- Gives children a preview of the vocabulary and concepts needed for successfully participating in the background activity in the Teacher's Book.

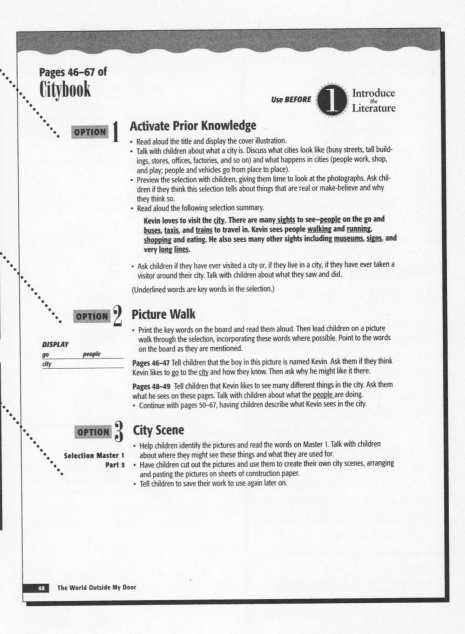

Pages 46–67 of
Citybook

Use BEFORE **1** Introduce the Literature

OPTION 1 Activate Prior Knowledge
- Read aloud the title and display the cover illustration.
- Talk with children about what a city is. Discuss what cities look like (busy streets, tall buildings, stores, offices, factories, and so on) and what happens in cities (people work, shop, and play; people and vehicles go from place to place).
- Preview the selection with children, giving them time to look at the photographs. Ask children if they think this selection tells about things that are real or make-believe and why they think so.
- Read aloud the following selection summary.

   Kevin loves to visit the <u>city</u>. There are many <u>sights</u> to see—<u>people</u> on the go and <u>buses</u>, <u>taxis</u>, and <u>trains</u> to travel in. Kevin sees people <u>walking</u> and <u>running</u>, <u>shopping</u> and eating. He also sees many other sights including <u>museums</u>, <u>signs</u>, and very <u>long lines</u>.

- Ask children if they have ever visited a city or, if they live in a city, if they have ever taken a visitor around their city. Talk with children about what they saw and did.

(Underlined words are key words in the selection.)

OPTION 2 Picture Walk
- Print the key words on the board and read them aloud. Then lead children on a picture walk through the selection, incorporating these words where possible. Point to the words on the board as they are mentioned.

DISPLAY

go	people
city	

Pages 46–47 Tell children that the boy in this picture is named Kevin. Ask them if they think Kevin likes to <u>go</u> to the <u>city</u> and how they know. Then ask why he might like it there.

Pages 48–49 Tell children that Kevin likes to see many different things in the city. Ask them what he sees on these pages. Talk with children about what the <u>people</u> are doing.
- Continue with pages 50–67, having children describe what Kevin sees in the city.

OPTION 3 City Scene

Selection Master 1
Part 5
- Help children identify the pictures and read the words on Master 1. Talk with children about where they might see these things and what they are used for.
- Have children cut out the pictures and use them to create their own city scenes, arranging and pasting the pictures on sheets of construction paper.
- Tell children to save their work to use again later on.

48 The World Outside My Door

Reading Choices

Two options for reading. In either case, children read only up to the most exciting point of a story or to an appropriate stopping point in a nonfiction selection. Then, when children join in whole-class instruction, they will be motivated to read to find out the ending of a selection and they will not be tempted to give away the selection outcome to their classmates.

Read Aloud or Audio Tape

- Students unable to read the selection on their own will benefit from hearing it.
- A purpose for listening is provided. As a discussion point follow up on the purpose and ask children to make predictions about the rest of the selection.

Guided or Assisted Reading

- Guided Reading is provided for students able to read the selection on their own when given strong support.
- Assisted Reading is suggested if, in Guided Reading, it becomes clear that children are unable to decode and comprehend the selection. To be used flexibly. A return to Guided Reading may be desirable if children improve their ability to read and understand the selection.

Reading Segments

- Manageable segments that children can read and discuss.
- Stopping at intervals gives opportunities to clear up confusion or misunderstandings, thus ensuring that children do not become overwhelmed, confused, or lost in the text.

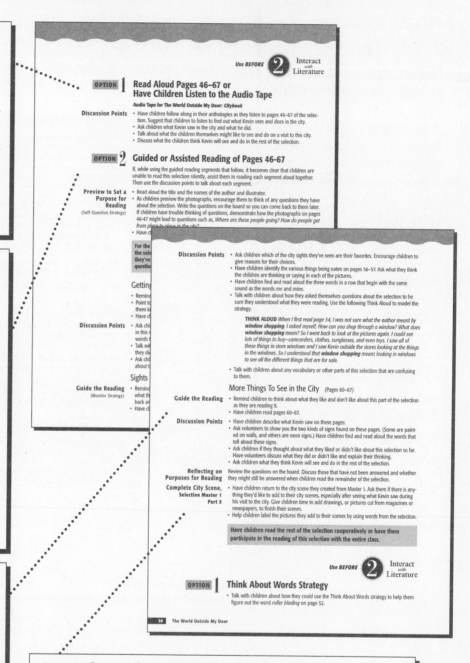

Complete the Selection Master

- Children return to their sheet to complete or revise earlier responses.
- This helps children summarize their understandings and integrate new information.

Developing Critical Thinking, Think About Words Strategy, Developing Fluency

Two activities. The first one is for developing critical thinking skills or practicing the Thinking About Words strategy. The second one develops children's ability to read fluently.

Developing Critical Thinking

- An activity that instructs children in critical thinking and guides them in using their skill in relation to the selection.

or

Think About Words Strategy

- The strategy is modeled and children practice using it within the context of the selection.

Develop Fluency

- An opportunity for children to develop reading fluently and expressively from their selection.

Skills Practice

Tested Skills

Practice is provided for the tested comprehension skills, phonics skills, and strategies. This is an opportunity to identify and clarify ineffective or inaccurate practices.

Discussion Points
- Ask children which of the city sights they've seen are their favorites. Encourage children to give reasons for their choices.
- Have children identify the various things being eaten on pages 56–57. Ask what they think the children are thinking or saying in each of the pictures.
- Have children find and read aloud the three words in a row that begin with the same sound as the words *me* and *mine*.
- Talk with children about how they asked themselves questions about the selection to be sure they understood what they were reading. Use the following Think Aloud to model the strategy.

> **THINK ALOUD** *When I first read page 54, I was not sure what the author meant by* **window shopping**. *I asked myself, How can you shop through a window? What does* **window shopping** *mean? So I went back to look at the pictures again. I could see lots of things to buy—camcorders, clothes, sunglasses, and even toys. I saw all of these things in store windows and I saw Kevin outside the stores looking at the things in the windows. So I understood that* **window shopping** *means looking in windows to see all the different things that are for sale.*

- Talk with children about any vocabulary or other parts of this selection that are confusing to them.

More Things To See in the City (Pages 60–67)

Guide the Reading
- Remind children to think about what they like and don't like about this part of the selection as they are reading it.
- Have children read pages 60–67.

Discussion Points
- Have children describe what Kevin saw on these pages.
- Ask volunteers to show you the two kinds of signs found on these pages. (Some are painted on walls, and others are neon signs.) Have children find and read aloud the words that tell about these signs.
- Ask children if they thought about what they liked or didn't like about this selection so far. Have volunteers discuss what they did or didn't like and explain their thinking.
- Ask children what they think Kevin will see and do in the rest of the selection.

Reflecting on Purposes for Reading
Review the questions on the board. Discuss those that have not been answered and whether they might still be answered when children read the remainder of the selection.

Complete City Scene, Selection Master 1 Part 5
- Have children return to the city scene they created from Master 1. Ask them if there is anything they'd like to add to their city scenes, especially after seeing what Kevin saw during his visit to the city. Give children time to add drawings, or pictures cut from magazines or newspapers, to finish their scenes.
- Help children label the pictures they add to their scenes by using words from the selection.

Have children read the rest of the selection cooperatively or have them participate in the reading of this selection with the entire class.

Use BEFORE **2** Interact with Literature

OPTION **1** **Think About Words Strategy**
- Talk with children about how they could use the Think About Words strategy to help them figure out the word *roller blading* on page 52.

50   The World Outside My Door

...rds in the sentence, I know that this word tells

...letters, I see the letter *r* at the beginning. I ...*r* at the beginning of *run* and *ride*. ...ny word parts that I might know, and I see the

...e pictures. The first word on page 52 is **walk**-...walking. The second word is **running**, and the ...g. This gives me a pretty good idea that the ...these pages. That picture shows someone on ...inline skates. I know that another name for inline skates is **roller blades** and that the name **roller blades** begins with the sound for **r**. I try the word **roller blading** in the sentence, and it makes sense.

Have children explain how they could use the Think About Words strategy to figure out the word *flags*.

OPTION **2** **Develop Fluency: Partner Reading**
Have partners read pages 46–52 together. Have the partners alternate as they read, one reading the pages on the left, the other, the pages on the right. Tell the partners to read the last page, page 52, together.

Use AFTER **3** Instruct and Integrate

OPTION **1** **Noting Details**
- Tell children that much of the fun in a book such as *Citybook* is in noticing the details in the pictures and words. Illustrate this by having children look at the photographs on pages 56–57. Ask them to look carefully at the pictures to find out exactly what is happening. Then talk with children about what they have found. Help them identify all the different things being eaten in the pictures—soda, bagel, ice cream cone, pizza, hot dog.
- Then ask children to look at the pictures to see what these children are wearing. Help them notice that the children are all wearing jackets of some kind.
- Have pairs of children work together to find details to answer these questions:

Page 55: What do you see in these windows?
Pages 64–65: What are the birds standing on?
Page 68: How many people are there in these pictures? How many dogs are there?

OPTION **2** **Consonant Clusters with *l* and *s***
- Point to the word *flag* on page 67 and have children read it aloud with you. Explain that *flag* begins with the same sound as *fly* and *flat*. Ask what letters stand for the beginning sounds in *flag*. Tell children to turn to pages 52–53 of *Citybook* to find and name another word that begins with a consonant and the letter *l*. (*blading*).
- Point to the word *stopping* on page 57 and have children read it aloud with you. Explain that *stopping* begins with the same sound as *step*. Ask what letters stand for the beginning sounds in *stopping*. Have children look for and name a word that begins with the letter *s* and another consonant on page 67. (*statues*)

Citybook   51

Selection Master

Provided for each selection is a master that supports children in the following ways:

- Before reading, children use the master to activate prior knowledge and to build background.

- During reading, children use the master to remind themselves of the concepts and vocabulary important to the selection.

- After reading the portion of the selection covered in Extra Support, children use the master to summarize learnings and to integrate new knowledge.

- During whole-class instruction, children can refer to the master as needed.

- The reproducible masters are in Part 5: Resources, at the back of this handbook.

Name _____

Citybook

buses

taxis

window

signs

statues

flags

220 Selection Master 1: City Scene

Off We Go—See What We Know!

Use *BEFORE* Launching the Theme Activities

Theme Concept

Familiar concepts: alphabet, colors, numbers, animal names and sounds, the five senses.

Materials Suggested For The Theme

• Audio Tapes for Off We Go—See What We Know!

OPTION 1 What We Use in the Classroom

Have children brainstorm a list of things in the classroom that they will use during the year. Encourage children to look around the room and identify items they see. Record the list on the board or on chart paper. (Examples include: desks, chairs, pencils, paper, computers, chalkboard, books)

OPTION 2 A School Tour

Take children on a tour of the school, visiting such places as the cafeteria, the library, and the main office. Try to meet the people who work in those places and have them introduce themselves to the class. Create a chart like the one below that shows where children visited and the names of the people they met.

Places We Visited	People We Met
office	Mr. Jones Ms. Smith
library	Mr. Shelf
cafeteria	Ms. Cook

Annie, Bea, and Chi Chi Dolores

Use BEFORE **1** Introduce *the* Literature

OPTION 1 Activate Prior Knowledge

Read aloud the title. Tell the children that this is a story about some animal friends and what they do in school. Explain that keeping track of what these animals do will help the children learn their own ABCs.

Invite children to share what they know about the alphabet—what the letters are, how they are shaped, the sounds they stand for, and so on. Encourage children to come to the board and write any letters they may know.

Point out that this is an alphabet, or ABC, book. Have children describe other ABC books they have seen. (If you have any of these alphabet books on hand, let children show them to the group as they talk about the books they know.) Then share and discuss the following pages.

Page 5 Point to *A a* on the page and have children identify the letter. Then ask them where else they see *a* on the page. Help children identify *a* in the words <u>all</u> and <u>aboard</u>, and have them say the words with you.

Page 9 Point to *D d,* and name this letter for children. Talk with them about what the animals in this picture are doing. Then ask children to point out the word on this page. Say the word <u>drawing</u> with them and have them point out the letter *d* in that word.

Page 12 Have children identify the letter at the top of this page if they can. Then ask them to point out where else they see that letter on the page. Tell children that the word on this page is <u>giggling</u>. Ask if they see anyone on this page who is giggling. Have children point out those characters.

Page 16 Continue with the letters *j* and *k* and the words <u>jumping</u> and <u>kicking</u>.

(Underlined words are key words in the selection.)

Ask children if any of the things they have seen the animals do in this selection are things they themselves do in school. Invite children to share other things they like to do in school.

OPTION 2 Picture Walk

Display the book cover and read aloud the title. Point to the first letter of each name in the title and have children identify it. Write those letters on the board and explain the A-B-C-D pattern to children. Then guide them through the illustrations, incorporating the key words. Point to each word in the Big Book as it is discussed.

DISPLAY

all aboard	follow
buddies	giggling
counting	hopping
drawing	icky
erasing	

Pages 4–5 Point to the picture of the school bus. Ask children what the animals in the picture are doing. Talk with children about where they think the animals are going. Encourage children to share the reasoning behind their ideas. Point to *Aa* and read <u>all aboard</u>. Help children see the letter *a* at the beginnings of those words.

Pages 6–7 Ask children where they think the animals are now and encourage them to explain their ideas. Then ask children what the friends are doing on page 7. Explain that these friends are buddies. Point out the letter *b* in the word <u>buddies</u>.

Page 8 Ask what the animals are doing on this page. Have children point out details that help them see that the animals are counting. Then point out the *c* in <u>counting</u>.

Use the same technique to discuss pages 9–15.

OPTION 3   Oral Language Development

Explain that this selection includes many words that tell about what Annie, Bea, Chi Chi Dolores, and the others do at school. As you display pages of the Big Book, point to and read aloud each of the following words, and ask volunteers to tell or act out what Annie and her friends are doing.

Page 11–follow the leader
Page 12–giggling
Page 13–hopping

Page 15–icky
Page 26–untangling
Page 27–vamoose

Use BEFORE  Interact *with* Literature

OPTION 1   Read Aloud for Interest

Pages 4–23 Read aloud the title and the names of the author and the illustrator. Discuss the cover illustration. Then read pages 4–23 to children. As you read, stop periodically to ask children what letter they think will come next.

When you have finished, have children review what the animals do at school. Have children predict what activities the animals might do in the rest of the selection.

OPTION 2   Use the Audio Tape

Off We Go–See What We Know: Annie, Bea, and Chi Chi Dolores

As you display the pages of the Big Book, have children listen to pages 3–23 of the audio tape. Tell them to listen to find out all the interesting things Annie, Bea, and Chi Chi Dolores do in school.

Discussion Points
- Ask children which of the things the animals do are like things they themselves do in school.
- Ask which of these things children enjoy most.
- Encourage children to predict other activities the animals might do in the rest of the selection.

Use AFTER Interact *with* Literature

OPTION 1   Develop Fluency: Choral Reading

Invite small groups to read aloud pages 4–13 together. If children pause or have difficulty reading a word, encourage any group member to read the word aloud for the others to repeat.

OPTION 2 Language Experience

Have the group create its own alphabet book about all the interesting things that happen in school.

- Have children suggest their favorite school-time people, things, and activities.
- Write the words on the board. Then work with children to rewrite the list in alphabetical order, choosing as necessary one item for each letter of the alphabet.
- Let each child choose two entries and make them for the group's alphabet book. Each entry should consist of a letter (capital and lowercase forms), one or more words beginning with that letter, and a picture illustrating that school-time item.
- Read the class's alphabet book aloud, having children say the words along with you.
- Then display the pages around the room or collect and bind them into a book that children look at and read on their own.

Use AFTER **3** Instruct *and* Integrate

OPTION 1 Noting Details

Play a game in which children remember details. Display Big Book page 8, asking children to look carefully at the page. Then, after 20 seconds, cover the page and tell children that you'll see how many of them remember the details on the page.

Ask the questions below. After each question, count the number of correct responses to see which question was answered correctly the most often. (Remember to emphasize that you are trying to see which details are remembered most, not to "test" children or their memories.)

- What letter is this page about?
- What is(are) the word(s) on the page?
- How many animals are on the page? *(six)*
- What are the animals counting with? *(beans)*
- *What are the beans going into? (jars)*

Follow the same procedure, using similar questions, for Big Book pages 18, 19, 20, and 21.

OPTION 2 Initial Consonants *b, t, g, v, k, m, z*

Write the word *box* on the board and read it aloud. Repeat *box* and have children listen for the sound they hear at the beginning of the word. Have a volunteer identify the letter that stands for that sound. *(b)* Then ask children to look through the Big Book to find another word that begins with that sound and letter (*buddies* on page 7).

Continue in the same way with the remaining initial consonants, using the following key words: *toy* (for *tickling*, page 26); *gum* (for *giggling*, page 12); *vote* (for *vamoose*, page 27); *kangaroo* (for *kick*, page 16); *mud* (for *making music*, page 18); and *zap* (for *zip*, page 32).

OPTION 3 ## Think About Words Strategy

Display Big Book page 16 and point to the word *ball.* Then demonstrate how children could figure out this word if they didn't know it.

- **What makes sense** First I'll read the two words that come before this word. Now I know that the word has something to do with kicking.
- **Sounds for letters** When I look at the letters, I see the letter *b* at the beginning. I know that letter. It stands for the same sound I hear at the beginning of the word *buddies.*
- **Picture clues** In the picture on pages 16 and 17, I see that something has gone flying over the animals' heads. It could be a ball, and the word *ball* begins with the same sound as *buddies.* Now I'm pretty sure I know the word. The word is *ball.*

Next, point to the word *races* on page 24 and ask children how they could figure out this word if they did not know it. Discuss the following clues:

- **What makes sense** something to do with running
- **Sounds for letters** *r* (as in *rope*) at the beginning
- **Picture clues** animals running toward a finish line, as in a race

OPTION 4 ## High-Frequency Words

all, I, jump, run, the, time, up

Write the following high-frequency words on index cards: *all, I, jump, run, the, time,* and *up.* Shuffle the cards, arrange them face down on a desk or table, and have a volunteer select a card. Then have the volunteer read the word aloud and find it in the Big Book. As he or she displays the page in the Big Book, have the group read the word aloud once more.

One Red Rooster

Use BEFORE **1** Introduce *the* Literature

OPTION 1 Activate Prior Knowledge

Read the title aloud. Point out the cover illustration and have children identify the animal in the picture. Then ask them what roosters are famous for (crowing first thing in the morning) and have children locate details in the picture that might tell them that this is what is happening. Then demonstrate or have children demonstrate the sound a rooster makes.

Invite children to share what they know about farms and the animals that live on them. Then organize a Guess the Animal game. Choose volunteers to imitate the sounds and movements of various farm animals while the rest of the group guesses which animal is being imitated.

Extend the discussion by sharing the following pages with the children.

Pages 4–5 Have children identify the animals on these pages and share what they know about them—their movements, the sounds they make, and what they look like. Encourage children to use color words when describing the animals.

Follow the same pattern as you discuss pages 6–7; 8–9; 10–11; 12–13, 14–15, and 16–17. For pages 8–9, point out the word *bleat* and discuss its meaning with children (a word that names the sound sheep make). For pages 12–15 be sure to point out the words *cats* and *dogs*. For pages 16–17, help children as necessary to identify the donkeys.

(Underlined words are key words in the selection.)

OPTION 2 Picture Walk

Display the Big Book and read aloud the title. Explain to children that this is a counting book in which they will see first one animal, then two of another animal, then three of another animal, and so on. Ask children to tell you about other counting books they have read. Then guide them through the illustrations, incorporating the key words. Point to each word in the Big Book as it is discussed.

DISPLAY

one	five
two	six
three	seven
four	eight

Page 3 Ask children what animal they see on this page and how many there are. As children answer, point to the numeral *1* at the lower left and the corresponding number word *one* on the page. Identify these for children.

Pages 4–5 Ask children what animal they see on this page and how many there are. (two cows) Point to the numeral at the lower left of the page and ask what numeral it is. Then point to the underlined number word *two*. Ask children how two cows might sound.

Continue in the same way for pages 6–17.

Oral Language Development

Tell the children that this selection includes the names of many different animals.

Display Big Book pages 8–9 and point to the words *Four white sheep*. Mention to children that the words *four* and *white* tell about the sheep on these pages. *Four* tells how many sheep there are and *white* tells what color they are. Invite children to think of other words that could be used to tell about the sheep. (*pretty, fluffy, soft*) Write children's suggestions on the board.

Continue in the same manner with the following pictures:

Pages 10–11 dogs
Pages 12–13 cats
Pages 14–15 horses

Use BEFORE **2** Interact *with* Literature

Read Aloud for Interest

Pages 3–17 Read aloud the title and the names of the author and the illustrator. Talk with children about the cover illustration. Then read aloud pages 3–17.

As you read, pause to ask such questions as, "How is this page like the one before it? How is it different? What number do you think will come next? What animals do you think you will see on the next page?" Help children follow along by running your hand under the words as you read. Encourage children to chime in on familiar words.

When you have finished, give children time to talk about which animals were their favorites. Then let them make predictions about the numbers, animals, and animal sounds they will find in the remainder of the book.

Use the Audio Tape

Audio Tape for Off We Go–See What We Know!: *One Red Rooster*

As you display the illustrations in the Big Book, have children listen to pages 1–17 of the audio tape. Tell children to listen for the sounds the different animals make and for the way in which some of those sounds rhyme with other animal sounds.

Discussion Points
• Ask children which animals they like best and why.
• Talk about which sounds on these pages rhyme.
• Ask children to name the animals they think they might see in the remainder of the book.

OPTION 1 ## Develop Fluency: Cloze Reading

Reread the story to children, displaying each Big Book page you are reading. As you read, omit each word that names an animal or animal sound. Encourage children to fill in that word for you.

OPTION 2 ## Language Experience

Help children create their own animal counting book.

- Have them suggest other animals that might be fun to use for their book. They can pick familiar animals from homes or farms, or they can choose animals from other habitats—zoos, forests, jungles, and so on.
- Talk with children about the kinds of information they would like to include for each new animal and the words they will use to tell about the animal—its color, size, shape, habits, activities, and so on. Record children's ideas on chart paper.
- Let volunteers create illustrations for each page of the book.

The pages of the class counting book can be displayed around the room, or if you wish, you can let children take turns taking it home to share with family members.

OPTION 1 ## Inferences: Make Predictions

Read aloud pages 22–23 again and ask children about what they think would come next if there were more pages in this book. Ask them what numeral they would see on the next page (11), if they think they would find a new animal on that page, and how many of those animals they think they would see. Ask children if they can see a pattern to the way the numbers appear in this book. (Each number is one more than the number before it.)

OPTION 2 ## Initial Consonants *c, d, n, p, r, y, f, h, s, w*

Write the letters *c, d, n, p, r, y, f, h, s,* and *w* on index cards. Give each child one or more cards. Then display each page of the selection and have children read it aloud with you. When children hear a word that begins with the sound for a consonant they are holding, have them raise their card. Have children exchange cards and repeat the activity.

OPTION 3 ## Think About Words Strategy

Point to the word *fell* on page 21 of the Big Book. Then model how children could figure out this word if they did not know it.

- **What makes sense** First I'll read the sentence on pages 22–23. From this I know that the word tells about the pigs going to sleep.
- **Sounds for letters** When I look at the letters I see *f* at the beginning. I know the sound for *f*; it is the same sound I hear at the beginning of *fast*.
- **Picture clues** Now I look at the picture. The picture shows the pigs lying on the ground, sound asleep. That helps me know that the word *fell* makes sense in the sentence, since the pigs fell asleep.

Next, point out the word *nine* on page 18. Ask volunteers to demonstrate how they would figure out this word. Help and guide the children as needed.

- **What makes sense** a number that comes after 8 and before 10
- **Sounds for letters** *n* (as in *noisy*) at the beginning of the word
- **Picture clues** nine chicks on the floor

OPTION 4 ## High-Frequency Words

and, cat, dog, fast, one, three, two, went

Write these high-frequency words on the board: *and, cat, dog, fast.* Then lead children on a word hunt. Display and read each page of the Big Book, having children raise their hands when they hear a word that is on the board. As soon as children's hands are raised, stop reading and have a volunteer go to the board and point to the word that was just read. Have children read aloud that word as it is pointed out. When you have finished, play another round, this time with the remaining words.

My Five Senses

Use **BEFORE**

1

Introduce
the
Literature

OPTION **1** ## Activate Prior Knowledge

Begin a discussion of the senses by having children identify various common objects, using only one of their senses.

- Hide an object (a book, for example) under a large piece of cloth.
- Invite a child to figure out what the object is just by touching it.
- Continue with other children and objects.
- Have children use their other senses, one sense at a time, to identify different objects. Use, for example, the sound of chalk on the board for the sense of hearing; a piece of fruit for the sense of smell; a slice of a different fruit for the sense of taste; and a close-up photo of a piece of fabric or food for the sense of sight.
- If there is time, let children experiment, using different senses to identify the same objects. For example, see if they can identify a piece of chalk by smelling it or a piece of fruit by feeling it.

Read the title of the Big Book aloud and ask children if they know what their five senses are. Help children identify the senses. Then explain that this selection is about how people use those senses to know the world and what is in it. Then share the following photographs, talking with the children about how people are using their senses in these pictures:

Pages 4–7 Ask children which sense the child in these pictures is using and what they think she <u>sees</u>.

Pages 8–9 Ask children which sense this child is using and what she <u>smells</u>.

(Underlined words are key words in the selection.)

OPTION **2** ## Picture Walk

Read aloud the title and help children identify the five senses and the sense organs that go with them (sight–eyes, hearing–ears, and so on). Then walk children through the photographs, incorporating the key words. Point to each word in the Big Book as it is discussed.

DISPLAY

eyes	hands
nose	see
mouth	smell
ears	taste

Pages 2–3 Point out the photographs and have children identify their own <u>eyes, nose, mouth, ears,</u> and <u>hands</u>. Then talk with children about how those parts help them know about the world. Ask them what they use their eyes for, what their noses tell them about the world, what their mouth is used for, and so on.

Pages 4–7 Display the pages and ask children what the girl can <u>see</u> with her eyes and how she might feel about the things she sees.

Pages 8–11 Ask children what the girl can <u>smell</u> with her nose. Then ask which things they think she likes to smell, which she doesn't like, and why.

Pages 12–15 Ask children what the girl can <u>taste</u> with her mouth. Discuss which things she likes to taste and which she doesn't like.

Oral Language Development

Explain that this selection contains words for many things that can be seen, smelled, tasted, touched, and heard.

Display Big Book page 15. Point to and read aloud the words *ice cream.* Ask children to name other foods that taste sweet. Continue with these other pages and words:

Page 8 *popcorn* – Ask children to name other snacks that smell good.
Page 11 *garbage* – Have children suggest other things that smell bad.
Page 17 *fire engine* – Ask children to name other things that make loud noises. Let them have fun imitating those sounds.

Use BEFORE **2** Interact *with* Literature

OPTION 1 # Read Aloud for Interest

Pages 1–15 Read aloud the title and author information and talk about the cover illustration. Then read pages 1–15 to the children.

As you read, help children to follow along by running your hand under the words. Pause to ask what else the girl might see with her eyes, smell with her nose, and taste with her mouth.

After you have finished, ask children which senses they have talked about so far. (seeing, smelling, tasting). Then ask what senses they think they will learn about in the rest of the book.

OPTION 2 # Use the Audio Tape

Audio Tape for Off We Go–See What We Know!: *My Five Senses*

As you display each page of the Big Book, have children listen to pages 2–15 of the audio tape. Tell them to listen to find what their five senses can help them learn about the world.

Discussion Points:
- Ask what the girl in the selection does with her eyes, what the next girl does with her nose, and what the third girl does with her mouth. Encourage children to describe each thing the girls see, smell, and taste.
- Ask children which of these things they would like to see, smell, or taste.
- Ask children what they think they will read about in the rest of the selection.

OPTION **1** Develop Fluency: Echo Reading

Read aloud pages 2–11. As you read the text on each page, run your hand under the words. Pause every few words so children can reread the words after you.

OPTION **2** Language Experience

- Have children cut out magazine and newspaper pictures of interesting objects to see, smell, taste, hear, and touch.
- Have children paste their pictures onto sheets of paper.
- Then ask children to describe each pictured object. Encourage them to tell what they see and what the object smells, tastes, sounds, or feels like.
- Record children's responses and help them to read the words back to you.

OPTION **1** Compare and Contrast

Remind children that their senses tell them what objects in the world are like. Display pages 8 and 12 of the Big Book. Point out the popcorn and the watermelon in the pictures and ask children how those two things are alike. (Both are foods, both are fun to eat, and so on.) Then ask how popcorn and watermelon are different. (A kernel of popcorn is small, a watermelon is large; popcorn is dry, watermelon is wet; a bowl of popcorn looks and feels bumpy and lumpy, the outside of a watermelon looks and feels smooth; and so on.)

Help children complete a diagram similar to the one here comparing popcorn and watermelon.

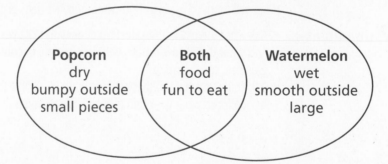

Follow the same procedure to have children compare the dog on page 6 and the horse on page 9.

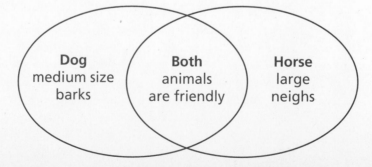

OPTION 2

Initial Consonants *b, g, m, t, f, h, l, s, w, qu*

Make letter cards for these consonants: *b, g, m, t, f, h, l, s, w.* Give each child a card and have him or her look through *My Five Senses* for words that begin with the letter on the card. Children should copy the words they find and share their words with the group.

To review the sound for *qu,* display page 19 of the Big Book and call attention to the boy whispering. Ask children if a whisper is loud or quiet. Write *quiet* on the chalkboard and repeat it several times as children listen to the beginning sound. Remind them that the letters *qu* stand for the sound they hear at the beginning of *quiet.* Have children brainstorm other words that begin with that sound.

OPTION 3

Think About Words Strategy

Point to the word *hands* on page 20. Model how children could figure out this word if they didn't know it.

- **What makes sense** First I'll read the words on this page: *With my _____ I feel finger paints.* From this I know that the word names a part of my body that I use to feel things.
- **Sounds for letters** When I look at the letters I see the letter *h* at the beginning. I know the sound for *h.* It stands for the sound at the beginning of *have.* I think the word might be *hand* since that word begins with the sound for *h* and names a part of my body that I use to feel things.
- **Familiar word parts** I see *s* at the end of the word. I know this means "more than one." So, the word must be *hands.*
- **Picture clues** Now I can check to see if there are any picture clues. Right above this word is a picture of a girl holding out her hands on a finger painting. Now I know that the word is *hands.*

Have children read the words on page 20 to see if *hands* makes sense. Then point out the word *sand* on page 21 and ask volunteers to demonstrate how they could figure it out if they didn't know it.

- **What makes sense** Something about what the girl is doing.
- **Sounds for letters** *s* as in *see.*
- **Picture clues** The picture shows lots of sand.

OPTION 4

a, baby, have, my, our, see, with

High-Frequency Words

Make a set of word cards for the high-frequency words *a, baby, have, my, our, see,* and *with.* Give each child or pair of children a card. Then, using the word cards as guides, have children go through the pages of the selection, one by one, looking for their word(s). When they find them, children should raise their hands and share their discoveries. Children can trade cards and go on a "word hunt" for other words.

Growing and Changing

Use *BEFORE* Launching the Theme Activities

Theme Concept Many things in our world grow and change with time.

Materials Suggested For The Theme • Audio Tapes for Growing and Changing

OPTION 1

Things that Grow and Change and Things that Stay the Same

Begin a discussion with children about how some things grow and change and others stay the same. Encourage children to brainstorm ideas for each category. (Grows and changes: a baby, a seed, a caterpillar; Stays the same: a building, rocks, a fence, a car)

Next, form small work groups and distribute some old magazines to each group. Label two pieces of chart paper, *Things that Grow and Change* and *Things that Stay the Same*. Tack both pieces of chart paper on the chalkboard.

Give children time to search the magazines for examples to put in each category. As children identify each picture, have them cut it out and set it aside. When children have finished, have them paste the pictures in a collage on the chart paper for a classroom display. Then, review their choices with them and talk about how each item does or does not grow and change.

OPTION 2

Create a Concept Map

Create a concept map in which children explore what they can do this year that they could not do when they were two or three years old. List their ideas on the concept map. Discuss how it felt to make those changes. (Examples: tie my own shoes, write my name, ride a bike)

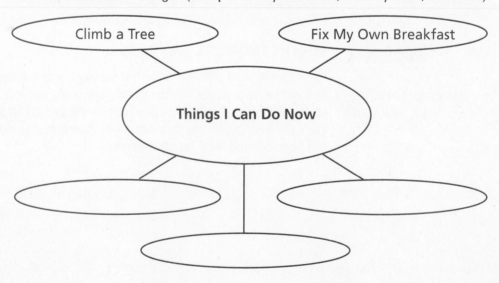

Climb a Tree   Fix My Own Breakfast

Things I Can Do Now

When This Box Is Full

Use BEFORE 1 Introduce *the* Literature

OPTION 1 Activate Prior Knowledge

- Write the names of the months on the board and read them aloud. Ask children to share what they know about the months. Invite them to name a favorite month and talk about the things that are part of that month. Discuss what the weather is like and what holidays, birthdays, and other special occasions come in the month. Ask children to name things they like to do during their favorite month.
- Preview the selection by reading aloud the title and invite children to look at the illustrations. Tell children that keeping track of what happens in this Big Book will help them learn more about the months of the year.
- Read aloud the following selection summary.
  A child puts something different into a <u>box</u> each month. As the months go by, the child adds special things to fill the box. The child puts in a snowman's scarf, a red foil heart, a robin's feather, an eggshell, and even a wild daisy.

(Underlined words are key words in the selection.)

Ask children what things they might like to store in a box like this. Discuss what things they might put in the box for <u>January</u>, <u>February</u>, <u>March</u>, or any of their favorite months.

OPTION 2 Picture Walk

DISPLAY

it	January
is	February
empty	March
but	April
will	May
not	June
for	

Display the cover of the Big Book and read aloud the title and the names of the author and the illustrator. Ask children what the child in the illustration might be thinking as she looks at the box. Explain that in this selection, a child puts something special into a box for each month of the year. Then walk children through the illustrations, incorporating key words where possible. Point to each word in the Big Book as it is mentioned.

Page 5 Invite children to describe the <u>box</u>. Explain that <u>it</u> <u>is</u> <u>empty</u> now, <u>but</u> that it <u>will</u> <u>not</u> be empty <u>for</u> long.

Pages 6–7 Read aloud the word *January* and ask children what is special about this month. If necessary, explain that January is the first month of the year. Then call attention to the scarf and have children describe its size, shape, and how it might be used. Ask children where the scarf is going. (into the box)

Pages 8–9 Point out that the names of the next two months of the year have been added on page 8 and read aloud the words *<u>February</u>* and *<u>March</u>*. Ask children why the child would put a heart in the box for February and why she would put in a feather for March.

Pages 10–11 Point out that the name of another month has been added on page 10 and ask children if they know what that month is. Then ask why the child would put an eggshell in the box for the month of <u>April</u>.

Pages 12–13 Repeat *January, February, March, April* and ask children what month is named next on page 12. Have children find the word *<u>May</u>*. Then ask what month comes after May and have children find the word *<u>June</u>*. Discuss what is going into the box for these months (a daisy, helicopters from a maple tree).

Ask children what month they think will come next. Have them make suggestions about what might go into the box for that month.

OPTION 3 Oral Language Development

- Explain that this selection contains several words that name colors.
- Display Big Book page 8 and point to the word *red*. Explain that this word names the color of the heart. Then have children suggest other things that are red. Organize the children's suggestions into a word web like the one below:

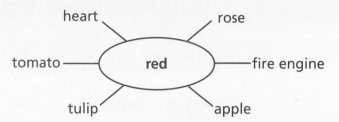

- Continue in the same manner for these other color words from the selection:

> **Page 10** purple
> **Page 23** silver

Use BEFORE **2** Interact *with* Literature

OPTION 1 Read Aloud for Interest

Pages 5–13 Read aloud the title as well as the author and illustrator information on the cover. Then have children describe what they see in the cover illustration.

Read aloud pages 5–13. As you read, help children to follow along by running your hand under the words. Pause to ask questions such as, "What month is it now? What is already in the box? What is being added to the box this month?"

When you finish page 13, ask children which months they have talked about so far. (January, February, March, April, May, June). Then ask what months they think they will read about in the rest of the selection and what objects they think might go into the box.

OPTION 2 Use the Audio Tape

Audio Tape for Growing and Changing: *When This Box Is Full*

As you display the pages of the Big Book, have children listen to pages 3–17 of the audio tape. Tell them to listen to find out what the child puts in the box each month.

Discussion Points
- Discuss what object(s) goes (go) into the box for each month and why the child might have chosen each object.
- Ask what months children will read about in the rest of the selection and what they think the child will put into the box for each of those months.

OPTION 1 **Develop Fluency: Choral Reading**

- Point to the name of each month in turn, from January to December, and have children read it aloud with you. Repeat each name as necessary to help children with correct pronunciations.

OPTION 2 **Language Experience**

- Have children create their own box in which they put drawings of some of their favorite things.
- Ask children to suggest some of their favorite things. (If you wish, have them suggest things in such categories as Favorite Food, Color, Game, Sport, Type of Clothing, Movie or TV Star, and so on.)
- Write the items children name on the chalkboard.
- Read the list of items aloud as children read along with you.
- Give each child a sheet of paper. At the bottom of the paper the child should write the word that names an object he or she would like to put into the box of favorite things. Above it, he or she should draw that object.
- When children have finished, have them take turns putting their words and pictures into a box. Encourage each child to name the item he or she chose and to tell why that item was chosen.
- Help the group decide on a name for the box. Write their suggested name on the box and read it aloud with them.

OPTION 1 **Categorize/Classify**

Remind children that it is often useful to group things that are alike in some way together. Use the following categorizing activity to reinforce this.

- Write the following heading on the chalkboard and read it to children: *Things Found in Nature.* Have children return to the selection and look through the pages for objects that fit in this category. (daisy, feather, helicopters from a maple tree, seashell, sand, red leaf, pumpkin seeds) List children's findings on the board.
- Invite children to suggest other items for this category. Children can draw the items on sheets of paper while you add their names to the list.

Follow up by having children regroup these same items into new categories—animals, plants, things found in water, and so on.

OPTION 2 — Final Consonants *f, s, t, l, (ll), r*

- On the board, draw three large boxes. Sketch a simple outline of a bell in the first box. Inside the bell write the word *bell* and underline the final consonants *ll. D*o the same with *hat* for the second box and *car* for the third.
- Name the pictures aloud, telling children to listen carefully for the ending sounds. Then turn to page 14 of the Big Book and point to the word *seashell.* Read the word aloud and have a volunteer go to the board and point out the picture whose name ends with the same sound. (the bell)
- Continue in the same manner with the following words: *heart,* page 8; *feather,* page 9; *eggshell,* page 10; *fair,* page 16; *silver, star,* page 23; *will, it,* page 24.
- Create two more boxes. In the first, draw a simple house, with an arrow pointing to the roof. Write the word *roof* in the house and underline the final consonant in that word *(f).* Do the same with *trees* for the second box.
- Follow the same procedure as you did for the other final consonants. Use these words: *scarf,* page 6; *helicopters,* page 13; *leaf,* page 19; *seeds,* page 20.

OPTION 3 — Think About Words Strategy

Point to the word *fill* on page 5 of the Big Book. Then use the following to model how children could figure out this word if they did not know it.

- **What makes sense** The first sentence on this page says that the box is empty. The words around this word are *I will _____ it with. . . .* From this I know that the word tells something the child will do to the box. I ask myself what someone could do with an empty box.
- **Sounds for letters** The word begins with the sound for *f.* I see the letters *ll* at the end of the word, so I know it ends with the sound for *l.* The word might be *fill.* Someone might fill an empty box, and *fill* begins with the sound for *f* and ends with the sound for *l.*
- **Picture clues** The picture shows an empty box. It makes sense for someone to be putting things into the box. That makes me think that the word is *fill.* When I read the sentence again, I can tell that the word *fill* makes sense. Now I know that *fill* is the right word.

When you have finished, point to the word *leaf* on page 19. Ask volunteers to tell how they would go about figuring out this word.

- **What makes sense** names something for September, which is a fall month
- **Sounds for letters** begins with *l* as in *look;* ends with *f* as in *scarf*
- **Picture clue** a leaf

OPTION 4 — High-Frequency Words

but, for, is, it, not, will, you

Arrange children in groups of three or four for a word-hunt activity.

- Begin by distributing seven small pieces of paper to each group. Then have the groups copy each of these seven words onto a separate piece of paper: *but, for, is, it, not, will, you.*
- Have the groups look through the selection to find each word. As a word is found, have the child who finds it say, "I see the word _____." Have him or her tell on what page the word was found. When everyone has found the word on that page, have children read aloud the sentence containing the word. The group then turns that paper facedown.
- Continue the activity until all seven words are found in the selection.

The Chick and the Duckling

Use BEFORE **1** Introduce *the* Literature

OPTION 1 ## Activate Prior Knowledge

- Preview the selection by reading aloud the title and inviting children to look at the illustrations.
- Talk with children about ducks and chickens. Ask volunteers to describe each kind of bird. Encourage others to share what they know about ducks and chickens.
- Read aloud the following selection summary.

  A <u>duckling</u> and a <u>chick</u> <u>came</u> out of their shells at almost the same time. As time passed, the chick tried to do everything that the duckling did. When the duckling took a walk, the chick did, <u>too</u>. When the duckling dug a hole, so did the chick. When the duckling caught a butterfly, the chick tried to catch one as well.

  (Underlined words are key words in the selection.)

- Ask children if they have ever acted like the chick or if they know someone who has. Have children share their experiences, and discuss why one person might want to copy another.

OPTION 2 ## Picture Walk

DISPLAY

chick	he
duckling	said
came	

Read aloud the title and explain that *chick* is the name we use for a young chicken. Ask children what they think *duckling* is the name for.

Then walk children through the illustrations, incorporating the key words. Point to each word in the Big Book as it is discussed.

Cover Have children identify which is the <u>chick</u> and which is the <u>duckling</u> in the cover illustration. Talk with them about ways in which the two look alike and ways in which they look different. Then discuss what the chick and duckling are doing in this illustration. Ask children whether they think the chick or the duckling will come out first and why they think so.

Pages 4–5 Ask children which bird they see on these pages and how they know it is the duckling. Explain that the duckling just <u>came</u> out of his shell. Ask children what they think <u>he</u> might have <u>said</u> when he came out.

Pages 6–7 Have children identify the chick and ask them what the chick is doing.

Pages 8–9 Tell children that the duckling is taking a walk. Then ask them where the chick is and what the chick is doing. Ask why the chick might decide to do what the duckling does.

Pages 10–11 Have children locate the chick and the duckling. Then ask them what else they see on the page (dirt, worms). Tell children that the duckling is digging a hole and ask what they think the chick will do.

Pages 12–13 Ask children if they predicted what the chick would do.

Pages 14–15 Ask children if they see something funny in the illustration on these pages. If necessary, explain that the chick and the duckling are both pulling on the same worm.

OPTION 3 Oral Language Development

- Remind children that *chick* is a word we use to name a baby chicken; *duckling* is a name for a baby duck.
- Ask children to suggest special names for other young creatures. Organize children's ideas and suggestions in a list like the one below.

Baby Animal's Name	Grown-Up Animal's Name
puppy	dog
kitten	cat
cub	bear
lamb	sheep
tadpole	frog
kid	goat

- You may wish to have children locate pictures of the various young and adult animals they have named. Talk with children about how the creatures look, how the babies and adults are alike and different, and so on.

Use BEFORE

OPTION 1 Read Aloud for Interest

Pages 4–21 Read aloud the title of the story and discuss the illustration on the cover. Then read pages 4–21 to children. Pause frequently as you read, asking questions such as, "What is the duckling doing now? What do you think the chick will want to do? Do you think the chick will be able to do that? Why do you think so?" Have children read along with you. Help them follow your reading by running your hand under the words. Encourage children to chime in whenever they wish.

Ask children what they think the duckling and the chick will do next. Encourage them to explain why they think this is what will happen.

OPTION 2 Use the Audio Tape

Audio Tape for Growing and Changing: *The Chick and the Duckling*

As you display the pages of the Big Book, have children listen to pages 4–21 of the audio tape. Tell children to listen to find out what happens to the chick and the duckling.

Discussion Points
- Discuss what the chick and the duckling do in this part of the story.
- Ask children what they think the chick might do next and whether he will be able to do it.
- Talk with children about what they think might happen in the rest of the Big Book.

1 ## Develop Fluency: Partner Reading

Have children work with partners to reread the story aloud. One child can read the pages that tell about the duckling while the partner reads the pages that tell about the chick.

OPTION **2** ## Language Experience

Remind children that the duckling pulled the chick out of the water so the chick would not drown. Invite children to make a large thank-you card from the chick to the duckling. Ask children what they think the chick might say to the duckling. Record their suggestions on chart paper and have children read them aloud. Then allow children to add illustrations to their card.

Use AFTER **3** Instruct *and* Integrate

OPTION **1** ## Inferences: Drawing Conclusions

- Remind children that an author does not always tell readers everything about what happens in a story and that readers often have to figure out some things for themselves.
- Display Big Book pages 14–15 and ask children what the birds are doing on these pages. (They are both pulling on the same worm.) Then turn to pages 16–17. Ask children why the chick got the worm. (The duckling let go of the worm so he could catch a butterfly.) Ask children what clues helped them know this. (The picture shows the duckling without the worm in his bill; the words say *"I caught a butterfly," said the duckling.)* Remind children that readers often use clues in the words and the pictures to figure out what is happening in a story.
- Display Big Book pages 24–25 and read the text aloud. Point out that the duckling says he is swimming and that the chick says "Me too!" Turn to pages 26–27 and ask children what clues tell them that the chick cannot swim. (The chick is sinking to the bottom of the pond.) Then discuss with children the clues on pages 28–32 that also tell the reader that the chick cannot swim. (The words and the picture on pages 28–29 tell the reader that the duckling pulled the chick out of the water–the chick did not swim back up and climb out. The picture on page 30 shows the chick looking very wet and unhappy. On page 32, the chick says "Not me!" when the duck goes back in for another swim.)

OPTION 2 Final *b, g, k, ck, m*

- Display page 31 of the Big Book and read the text aloud. Call attention to the word *I'm*. Remind children that the letter *m* stands for the sound they hear at the end of *I'm*. Write the letter *m* at the top of a sheet of chart paper.
- Display and read aloud page 32, pointing to the word *Chick*. Explain that in the middle or at the end of a word, the letters *ck* often stand for the /k/ sound. Write the letters *k* and *ck* at the top of another sheet of chart paper.
- Display pages 10–11 of the Big Book and read aloud page 10. Ask children what the chick will do. Write the word *dig* on the chalkboard and remind children that the letter *g* stands for the sound they hear at the end of *dig*. Write the letter *g* at the top of a chart.
- Have children brainstorm words that end with each of the letters for which you have made charts. Have children work with one ending sound at a time. (For the letters *ck*, encourage them to think of words that have the /k/ sound in the middle as well as at the end.) Record children's responses on the charts and add them to the Word Wall.
- Review the sound for final *b* by having children brainstorm words that end like *tub*. Make a chart of these words for the Word Wall.

OPTION 3 Think About Words Strategy

- Point to the word *found* on page 14 of the Big Book. Model how the children could use the Think About Words Strategy to figure out this word if they didn't know it.

- **What makes sense** First I'll read the sentence. It says: "I _____ a worm," said the duckling. From this I know that the word tells what the duckling did with a worm.
- **Sounds for letters** I recognize the letter *f* at the beginning of the word. It stands for the sound I hear at the beginning of *for, fish,* and *five.*
- **Picture clues** When I look at the picture, I see the duckling tugging at a worm. I can see that he found the worm. Since the word *found* begins with the sound for *f,* the word is probably *found.* To make sure, I'll read the sentence again. The word *found* makes sense in the sentence, so now I'm sure the word is *found.*

Point to the word *out* on page 28 and ask volunteers to explain how they would figure out this word if they did not know it.

- **What makes sense** the words tell about the Duckling pulling the chick
- **Sounds for letters** ends with *t* as in *it*
- **Picture clues** The Duckling is pulling the chick out of the water.

OPTION 4 High-Frequency Words

am, came, he, me, said, too

Print these words on index cards: *am, came, he, me, said,* and *too.* Choose six volunteers and give each one a word. Have each child find his or her word in the selection and read the sentence in which it appears. Finally, have children work together to count the number of times each word appears in the selection. (*am,* 5; *came,* 1; *he,* 1; *me,* 8; *said,* 15; *too,* 7)

Pages 1–13 of
Pumpkin, Pumpkin

Use BEFORE  Introduce *the* Literature

 Activate Prior Knowledge

- Ask children if they have ever planted a seed or grown a plant. Encourage children to share what they know about how plants grow.
- Preview the selection by reading aloud the title and asking children to look at the illustrations.
- Read aloud the following selection summary.

  A boy <u>planted</u> a <u>pumpkin</u> <u>seed</u>. The pumpkin seed <u>grew</u> a tiny <u>sprout</u>. Then the sprout grew into a small pumpkin <u>plant.</u> After a while, a <u>flower</u> appeared. From that flower came a little pumpkin.

  (Underlined words are key words in the selection.)

- Ask children what they think the little pumpkin will need in order to grow and to be healthy. Discuss what children think the boy can do to help the pumpkin as it grows.

OPTION 2 **Picture Walk**

Lead children on a picture walk through the selection, using the following suggestions as a guide. Incorporate key words, pointing to each word in the Big Book as it is mentioned.

DISPLAY

Jamie	planted
pumpkin	seed
sprout	plant
flower	grew

Cover Display the cover of the Big Book and read aloud the title and the name of the author and illustrator. Talk with children about what they see in the cover illustration. Tell them that the boy in the picture is named *Jamie.*

Pages 4–5 Point to the seed on page 4 and ask children what Jamie is holding in his hand. Explain that the illustration on page 5 shows what happened after Jamie <u>planted</u> the <u>pumpkin</u> <u>seed</u> in the ground.

Pages 6–7 Ask children what they see coming from the mound of dirt and why Jamie is so interested in it. Discuss where children think the <u>sprout</u> came from and what might happen to it.

Pages 8–9 Point out the leaves on the pumpkin <u>plant</u> and ask children where they think these leaves came from.

Pages 10–11 Point to the pumpkin <u>flower</u> and explain that this is what <u>grew</u> next. Ask children what they think will happen to the flower.

Pages 12–13 Ask children what they see in this illustration (a small pumpkin and what is left of the pumpkin flower). Talk with children about where they think the pumpkin came from.

Ask children what they think is going to happen to the little pumpkin.

OPTION 3 Oral Language Development

- Display the Big Book cover and point out the large pumpkin in the middle of the illustration. Encourage children to share what they know about pumpkins — what they look like, what people do with them, and so on.
- Write the words *Jamie's Pumpkin* on chart paper or on the chalkboard. Explain that Jamie is a boy who grew a pumpkin and ask children what they think Jamie might do with his pumpkin. Organize their suggestions into a semantic map like the one below.

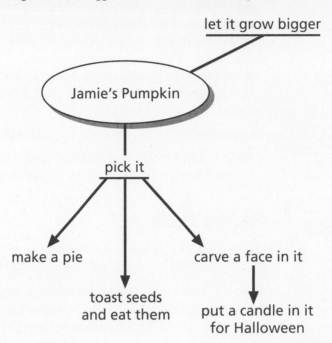

Use BEFORE **2** Interact *with* Literature

OPTION 1 Read Aloud for Interest

Pages 3–13 Read aloud the title and discuss the illustration on the cover. Then read aloud pages 4–13.

Interrupt your reading frequently to ask questions such as, "What is Jamie doing? What has happened so far? What do you think will happen next? What else has grown besides the pumpkin? How do you think Jamie feels about growing the pumpkin? What makes you think that?"

As you read, help children follow along by running your hand under the words. Encourage children to chime in on familiar words.

After you have finished, talk with children about what has happened to the pumpkin plant so far. Ask them how big they think the pumpkin will get.

Use the Audio Tape

Audio Tape for Growing and Changing: *Pumpkin, Pumpkin*

As you display the pages of the Big Book, have children listen to pages 4–13 of the audio tape. Tell them to listen to find out what happens to the pumpkin seed Jamie plants.

Discussion Points
- Ask children what has happened to the pumpkin seed so far in the story.
- Talk with children about what they think will happen to the pumpkin in the rest of the story.

Use AFTER **2** Interact *with* Literature

OPTION 1 **Develop Fluency: Choral Reading**

Choral Reading
Have children reread the story with you as you display each Big Book page. Pause to record each word that names another stage of the pumpkin's growth—*seed, sprout, plant, flower, pumpkin.* When you have finished rereading the story, have children read the names of the stages aloud with you.

OPTION 2 **Language Experience**

Write the following title on a sheet of chart paper: *How Pumpkins Grow.* Then have children share what they have learned from the selection about how pumpkins grow. Encourage them to talk about the stages in which a pumpkin grows and what it looks like at each stage. Record children's ideas on chart paper. Have children read aloud what you have written.

Use AFTER **3** Instruct *and* Integrate

OPTION 1 **Sequence**

- Remind children that we expect things to happen in a story in an order that makes sense. Then have children use the illustrations in the Big Book to identify the order of the stages in which the pumpkin grew (seed, sprout, plant, flower, pumpkin).
- Use magazine and newspaper pictures to create three-part sequences of events. Use these suggestions as well as others you can find:

  A. (1) baby   (2) child   (3) grown-up
  B. (1) egg   (2) chick   (3) chicken
  C. (1) seed   (2) shoot of a vegetable plant   (3) head of lettuce or other vegetable

- Give each child a set of pictures. Have children arrange pictures in an order that makes sense. Encourage them to use their sequence of pictures to tell a story.

OPTION 2 Final Consonants *d, n, p, x*

- Read aloud the text on page 5 of the Big Book and call attention to the word *seed.* Have children say the word *seed,* listening for the ending sound. Ask them what letter stands for the sound they hear at the end of seed. *(d)* Follow a similar procedure with the word *in* on page 23.
- Write the words *seed* and *in* at the top of two columns on the chalkboard. Have volunteers underline the final consonant in each word. Then have children search through the Big Book to find words that end with the same final consonants. Have children point to the words in the Big Book as they find them and write each word in the appropriate column on the board. (final *d: planted, seed, and, picked, scooped, carved, saved*; final *n: pumpkin, in*)
- Next, say *six* several times and ask children to name the letter that stands for the ending sound in *six. (x)* Have children find the word *six* in the Big Book. (page 24) Follow the same procedure with the word *pulp* on page 23.

OPTION 3 Think About Words Strategy

- Read aloud the sentence on page 23 of the Big Book, omitting the word *put.* Then model for children how they could use the Think About Words strategy to figure out the word *put* if they didn't know it.

- **What makes sense** From the sentence I know that this word tells something Jamie did with the pumpkin face. I also know that it is something he could do in a window. I ask myself what could he do with a pumpkin face and a window.
- **Sound for letters** The word begins with the sound for *p* and ends with the sound for *t.* I think the word is *put. Put* begins with *p* and ends with *t,* and Jamie could put the pumpkin face in a window.
- **Picture clues** When I check for picture clues I don't see anything that helps me know what this word is. But when I read the sentence again, the word *put* makes sense. So the word is probably *put.*

Next point out the word *picked* on page 21. Let volunteers model the process for figuring out this word if they did not know it.

- **What makes sense** the word tells what Jamie did with the pumpkin
- **Sound for letters** begins with the sound for *p;* ends with the sound for *ck*
- **Familiar word parts** ending *-ed*
- **Picture clues** The pumpkin has been picked.

OPTION 4 High-Frequency Words

in, out, plant, put, six, then

- Write the high-frequency words on the chalkboard. Then display page 23 of the Big Book and tell children that they can find some of these words on this page. Have children find and point to the words *in, out, put,* and *then.* Then have children read page 23 aloud with you.

The World Outside My Door

Use BEFORE Launching the Theme Activities

Theme Concept **People and animals live in many different environments.**

Materials Suggested For The Theme
- Audio Tapes for The World Outside My Door
- Selection Masters 1 and 2

OPTION 1

What Do We Know About the River, the City, and the Desert?

Write the following words in columns on the chalkboard: *river, city, desert.* Encourage children to brainstorm words that help describe these places. Record their responses on the board under the appropriate headings. (Possible responses: river: wet, water, fish, rocks, plants, animals; city: people, busy, traffic, stores, crowded, loud; desert: sand, cactus, hot, dry, thirsty, camels)

OPTION 2

Make a Collage

Choose one setting—river, city, or desert—for a picture collage. Review with children what kinds of things they might find in that particular setting. Then, provide some old magazines and have children cut out pictures that could go in the collage. Paste the collage together when finished.

My River

OPTION 1 Activate Prior Knowledge

- Remind children that some creatures live on land and some in or near water. Ask children to name some creatures that live on land. Then have them name some water creatures.
- Display the Big Book and read aloud the title and the name of the author-illustrator. Tell children that in this selection they will meet some of the many living things that make their homes in or near a <u>river</u>. Point to the cover and have children identify the living things shown in the illustration (a fish, a plant, a dragonfly). Have children describe each of them —its movements, sounds, shape, colors, and so on. Assign roles to volunteers and have children act out the cover scene. Continue by sharing the following pages with children.
- **Pages 6–7** Point to the illustration and have children name the creature they see. Encourage children to share what they know about turtles. Invite volunteers to imitate the way a turtle walks and the way it pulls its head in and out of its shell.
- **Pages 8–9** Have children identify the creatures they see. Have children share what they know about where and how frogs <u>live</u>. Have volunteers imitate the frogs' croaking sounds and the way they jump and swim.
- Ask children what other creatures they think they might meet in this selection. Encourage them to imitate those creatures. If you wish, turn this into a guessing game in which children try to guess which creature is being imitated.

(Underlined words are key words in the selection.)

OPTION 2 Picture Walk

DISPLAY
this
it's
here
was
where

Guide children through the selection, using these suggestions. Incorporate key words as shown, pointing to each word in the Big Book as it is mentioned.

Cover Display the cover of the Big Book, and read aloud the title and the name of the author-illustrator. Talk with children about what a <u>river</u> is. Explain that rivers come in all sizes, that they can have fast-running water or slow, and that they are home to many kinds of living things. Ask children what they see in the illustration. Talk with them about what is living in and near the water. Explain that fish, plants, and dragonflies all are living things that can make their homes in and near rivers.

Pages 4–5 Point to the illustration and ask children to name the objects they see. Have volunteers point to these things as they are named. Then point to and read aloud the words *<u>Whose</u> river <u>is</u> <u>this</u>?*
Pages 6–7 Have children identify the turtle in the illustration. Point to the words and read them aloud. Explain that the turtle is answering the question *"Whose river is this?"* He is saying that <u>it's</u> his river.
Pages 8–9 Have children identify the frogs. Talk with the children about what these frogs are doing. Ask children how they think the frogs might answer the question *"Whose river is this?"* (*It's <u>our</u> river.*)
Pages 10–11 Have children identify the fish. Then point to the words and explain that the fish are answering the same question as all the other creatures. Tell children that the fish are saying it is <u>everyone's</u> river.
Pages 12–13 Help children identify the eel. Ask them where the eel lives. Tell them that the eel is saying the river is its <u>home</u>.

Pages 14–15 Have children identify the salamanders. Tell children that the salamanders <u>live here too</u>.

Pages 16–17 Have children identify the dragonfly. Explain that the dragonfly is saying it was <u>born</u> in the river.

Pages 18–19 Point out the plants and flowers on these pages. Ask children <u>where</u> these plants and flowers are growing.

Talk with children about why all of these different living things think the river is their river. Ask what other living things might say it is their river.

OPTION 3 **Oral Language Development**

- Tell children that, in this selection, they will meet many of the living things that make their home in and near a river.
- Display the Big Book and point to the illustration on pages 6–7. Ask children to name this creature. Then ask them to imagine that they had to describe this creature to someone who had never seen it. Ask which parts of the body they would talk about and what words they would use to describe those parts.
- Encourage children to think of several different words to describe each of the creature's features. For example, for the turtle's shell, children might offer the words *hard, green, black,* and *beautiful.*
- Continue in the same way with the creatures on these pages:

> **Pages 8–9:** frogs (eyes: *bulging, popping;* legs: *long, green*)
> **Pages 12–13:** eel (body: *long, thin, skinny, snaky*)
> **Pages 14–15:** salamanders (tail: *long, thick;* legs: *stubby, short*)

Use BEFORE ② Interact *with* Literature

OPTION 1 **Read Aloud for Interest**

Pages 4–19 Read aloud the title and the name of the author-illustrator. Then discuss the cover illustration.

Read aloud pages 4–19. As you read, move your hands under the words and invite children to chime in. Pause to ask questions such as, "What creature is this? What is it doing? Do you think this creature believes this is its river, too? Why?"

When you have finished, encourage children to talk about the living things they met in this selection. Let children discuss which ones were their favorites and make predictions about what else they might meet in the remainder of the book.

OPTION 2 **Use Audio Tape**

As you display the illustrations of the Big Book, have children listen to pages 4–19 on the audio tape. Tell them to listen to find out what each different living thing has to say about the river.

Discussion Points
- Have children name the different living things they saw in the Big Book. Then discuss what these things said about the river.
- Discuss what children learned from the selection. Were there facts they did not know before they read the selection? Did anything in the selection surprise them?
- Ask what other living things children think they will read about in the rest of the selection.

OPTION 1 Develop Fluency: Echo Reading

Read aloud pages 4–11. As you read each sentence, pause and have children repeat it after you. Encourage children to speak the words with the same expression and tone that you use.

OPTION 2 Language Experience

- Help children create their own river book. Have them suggest their own favorite living things that make their home in and near a river. Then ask them to draw pictures of their living things on pieces of paper.
- When children have finished, ask them what words they would put on each page. Write their suggestions on the appropriate pages. Then have children read the book with you.

OPTION 1 Text Organization and Summarizing

- Display the Big Book. Read aloud the title and explain that the topic of this selection, or what it is mostly about, is a river. Talk with children about how the title *My River* tells readers this.
- Put the following pyramid chart on the board. Work with children to create a sentence that tells the main idea about this river. Write the sentence in the second box. Then page through the Big Book and have children supply details to complete the chart.

RIVER		
The river belongs to everyone.		
Animals	Plants	People

OPTION 2 Consonant Clusters with *r*

- Read aloud Big Book pages 18–19 and point out the word *grow*. Remind children that when two consonants come together in a word, the sounds for those letters are sometimes so close together that they almost seem like one sound. Ask children what two letters stand for the beginning sounds in *grow*.
- List the consonant clusters *br, cr, dr, fr, gr, pr,* and *tr* on the board. Then write the following known high-frequency words on the board and read them with children. Have children replace the beginning consonant in each word with one of the clusters to make a new word. Have children use each new word in an oral sentence.

see	(free, tree)	and	(brand, grand)
my	(cry, dry, fry, pry, try)	jump	(grump)
will	(drill, frill, grill)		

Think About Words Strategy

- Display Big Book pages 14–15 and point to the word *live.* Then demonstrate how children could figure out the word if they did not know it.

- **What makes sense** First I'll read the sentence on pages 14–15: *We _____ here, too.* From this I know that the word tells something that these creatures do at the river.
- **Sounds for letters** When I look at the letters of the word I see the letter *l* at the beginning. I know the sound for *l.* It's the sound I hear at the beginning of *laugh, light,* and *loud.* This makes me think that the word might be *live, leap,* or *like.*
- **Picture clues** When I look at the picture I see salamanders standing still on rocks in the river. This helps me see that the word *live* makes the best sense in this sentence, *We live here, too.*

Next, point to the word *mine* on pages 26–27. Have volunteers model how they would figure out this word if they didn't know it. Help and guide children as needed.

> **What makes sense** something that the river is
> **Sounds for letters** begins with the sound for *m,* as in *map* and *milk*
> **Picture clues** crayfish, at the edge of the river, acting as if it belongs there

High-Frequency Words

do, here, it's, need, so, this, was, where

- Play a guessing game with the children. Display Big Book pages 22–23 and tell children to find the word you're thinking of. Then tell them that you're thinking of a word that rhymes with *who (do).* When children identify the word, have a volunteer point it out in the book. Then have volunteers read aloud the sentence containing that word.
- Continue with these words and clues:

> **Pages 14–15:** <u>here</u>; rhymes with *clear*
> **Pages 6–7:** <u>it's</u>, rhymes with *fits*
> **Pages 20–21:** <u>need</u>, rhymes with *feed*
> **Pages 22–23:** <u>so</u>, rhymes with *no*
> **Pages 4–5:** <u>this</u>, rhymes with *kiss*
> **Pages 16–17:** <u>was</u>, rhymes with *does*
> **Pages 18–19:** <u>where</u>, rhymes with *there*

Use BEFORE Introduce
the
Literature

OPTION 1 ## Activate Prior Knowledge

- Read aloud the title and display the cover illustration.
- Talk with children about what a city is. Discuss what cities look like (busy streets, tall buildings, stores, offices, factories, and so on) and what happens in cities (people work, shop, and play; people and vehicles go from place to place).
- Preview the selection with children, giving them time to look at the photographs. Ask children if they think this selection tells about things that are real or make-believe and why they think so.
- Read aloud the following selection summary.

  Kevin loves to visit the <u>city</u>. There are many <u>sights</u> to see—<u>people</u> on the go and <u>buses</u>, <u>taxis</u>, and <u>trains</u> to travel in. Kevin sees people <u>walking</u> and <u>running</u>, <u>shopping</u> and eating. He also sees many other sights including <u>museums</u>, <u>signs</u>, and very <u>long lines</u>.

- Ask children if they have ever visited a city or, if they live in a city, if they have ever taken a visitor around their city. Talk with children about what they saw and did.

(Underlined words are key words in the selection.)

OPTION 2 ## Picture Walk

DISPLAY

go	people
city	

- Print the key words on the board and read them aloud. Then lead children on a picture walk through the selection, incorporating these words where possible. Point to the words on the board as they are mentioned.

Pages 46–47 Tell children that the boy in this picture is named Kevin. Ask them if they think Kevin likes to <u>go</u> to the <u>city</u> and how they know. Then ask why he might like it there.

Pages 48–49 Tell children that Kevin likes to see many different things in the city. Ask them what he sees on these pages. Talk with children about what the <u>people</u> are doing.

- Continue with pages 50–67, having children describe what Kevin sees in the city.

OPTION 3 ## City Scene

Selection Master 1
Part 5

- Help children identify the pictures and read the words on Master 1. Talk with children about where they might see these things and what they are used for.
- Have children cut out the pictures and use them to create their own city scenes, arranging and pasting the pictures on sheets of construction paper.
- Tell children to save their work to use again later on.

OPTION 1 ## Read Aloud Pages 46–67 or Have Children Listen to the Audio Tape

Audio Tape for The World Outside My Door: *Citybook*

Discussion Points
- Have children follow along in their anthologies as they listen to pages 46–67 of the selection. Suggest that children to listen to find out what Kevin sees and does in the city.
- Ask children what Kevin saw in the city and what he did.
- Talk about what the children themselves might like to see and do on a visit to this city.
- Discuss what the children think Kevin will see and do in the rest of the selection.

OPTION 2 ## Guided or Assisted Reading of Pages 46-67

If, while using the guided reading segments that follow, it becomes clear that children are unable to read this selection silently, assist them in reading each segment aloud together. Then use the discussion points to talk about each segment.

Preview to Set a Purpose for Reading
(Self-Question Strategy)
- Read aloud the title and the names of the author and illustrator.
- As children preview the photographs, encourage them to think of any questions they have about the selection. Write the questions on the board so you can come back to them later. If children have trouble thinking of questions, demonstrate how the photographs on pages 46-47 might lead to questions such as, *Where are these people going? How do people get from place to place in the city?*
- Have children read pages 46–53 to find answers to their questions.

> For the first section, children's questions are necessarily based on their previews of the selection. Before children read each subsequent section, discuss any answers they've found to their questions, and have children decide if they want to add questions to the list. Then have them continue reading to answer their questions.

Getting Around in the City (Pages 46–53)

- Remind children to use the Think About Words strategy to help figure out unfamiliar words.
- Point to the photos on pages 48–49. Have children identify things in the photos that help them know that this is a city.
- Have children read pages 46–53.

Discussion Points
- Ask children to name the different ways of getting from place to place that they read about in this section. Then have children look back at the pages, and point out pictures and read words that tell about these ways to travel.
- Talk with children about how the Think About Words strategy helped them figure out words they did not know.
- Ask children if any other words or parts of this section were confusing to them and talk about these parts.

Sights in the City (Pages 54–59)

Guide the Reading
(Monitor Strategy)
- Remind children that good readers stop once in a while to make sure that they understand what they are reading. Explain that, if something doesn't make sense, good readers go back and read the words and look at the pictures again more carefully.
- Have children read pages 54–59.

Discussion Points
- Ask children which of the city sights they've seen are their favorites. Encourage children to give reasons for their choices.
- Have children identify the various things being eaten on pages 56–57. Ask what they think the children are thinking or saying in each of the pictures.
- Have children find and read aloud the three words in a row that begin with the same sound as the words *me* and *mine*.
- Talk with children about how they asked themselves questions about the selection to be sure they understood what they were reading. Use the following Think Aloud to model the strategy.

> **THINK ALOUD** *When I first read page 54, I was not sure what the author meant by* **window shopping**. *I asked myself, How can you shop through a window? What does* **window shopping** *mean? So I went back to look at the pictures again. I could see lots of things to buy–camcorders, clothes, sunglasses, and even toys. I saw all of these things in store windows and I saw Kevin outside the stores looking at the things in the windows. So I understood that* **window shopping** *means looking in windows to see all the different things that are for sale.*

- Talk with children about any vocabulary or other parts of this selection that are confusing to them.

More Things To See in the City (Pages 60–67)

Guide the Reading
- Remind children to think about what they like and don't like about this part of the selection as they are reading it.
- Have children read pages 60–67.

Discussion Points
- Have children describe what Kevin saw on these pages.
- Ask volunteers to show you the two kinds of signs found on these pages. (Some are painted on walls, and others are neon signs.) Have children find and read aloud the words that tell about these signs.
- Ask children if they thought about what they liked or didn't like about this selection so far. Have volunteers discuss what they did or didn't like and explain their thinking.
- Ask children what they think Kevin will see and do in the rest of the selection.

Reflecting on Purposes for Reading
Review the questions on the board. Discuss those that have not been answered and whether they might still be answered when children read the remainder of the selection.

Complete City Scene, Selection Master 1 Part 5
- Have children return to the city scene they created from Master 1. Ask them if there is anything they'd like to add to their city scenes, especially after seeing what Kevin saw during his visit to the city. Give children time to add drawings, or pictures cut from magazines or newspapers, to finish their scenes.
- Help children label the pictures they add to their scenes by using words from the selection.

Have children read the rest of the selection cooperatively or have them participate in the reading of this selection with the entire class.

Use BEFORE **2** Interact *with* Literature

OPTION **1** **Think About Words Strategy**
- Talk with children about how they could use the Think About Words strategy to help them figure out the word *roller blading* on page 52.

What makes sense *From the other words in the sentence, I know that this word tells how people go from place to place.*

Sounds for letters *When I look at the letters, I see the letter **r** at the beginning. I know that **r** stands for the sound I hear at the beginning of **run** and **ride**.*

Familiar word parts *Next, I look for any word parts that I might know, and I see the ending **-ing.***

Picture clues *Then I notice clues in the pictures. The first word on page 52 is **walk-ing,** and the first picture shows a child walking. The second word is **running,** and the second picture shows someone running. This gives me a pretty good idea that the last word will match the last picture on these pages. That picture shows someone on inline skates. I know that another name for inline skates is **roller blades** and that the name **roller blades** begins with the sound for **r**. I try the word **roller blading** in the sentence, and it makes sense.*

Have children explain how they could use the Think About Words strategy to figure out the word *flags*.

OPTION 2 Develop Fluency: Partner Reading

Have partners read pages 46–52 together. Have the partners alternate as they read, one reading the pages on the left, the other, the pages on the right. Tell the partners to read the last page, page 52, together.

Use AFTER **3** Instruct *and* Integrate

OPTION 1 Noting Details

- Tell children that much of the fun in a book such as *Citybook* is in noticing the details in the pictures and words. Illustrate this by having children look at the photographs on pages 56–57. Ask them to look carefully at the pictures to find out exactly what is happening. Then talk with children about what they have found. Help them identify all the different things being eaten in the pictures—soda, bagel, ice cream cone, pizza, hot dog.
- Then ask children to look at the pictures to see what these children are wearing. Help them notice that the children are all wearing jackets of some kind.
- Have pairs of children work together to find details to answer these questions:

  Page 55: What do you see in these windows?
  Pages 64–65: What are the birds standing on?
  Page 68: How many people are there in these pictures? How many dogs are there?

OPTION 2 Consonant Clusters with *l* and *s*

- Point to the word *flag* on page 67 and have children read it aloud with you. Explain that *flag* begins with the same sound as *fly* and *flat*. Ask what letters stand for the beginning sounds in *flag*. Tell children to turn to pages 52–53 of *Citybook*. Ask them to find and name another word that begins with a consonant and the letter *l*. (*blading*).
- Point to the word *stopping* on page 57 and have children read it aloud with you. Explain that *stopping* begins with the same sound as *step*. Ask what letters stand for the beginning sounds in *stopping*. Have children look for and name a word that begins with the letter *s* and another consonant on page 67. (*statues*)

Listen to the Desert

Use BEFORE **1** Introduce *the* Literature

OPTION 1

Activate Prior Knowledge

- Ask children if they have ever seen a desert—in real life, in books, in movies, or on TV. Talk with children about what they saw and what the desert was like.
- Preview the selection by reading aloud the title and inviting children to look at the illustrations. Have children name any of the animals they recognize.
- Read aloud the following selection summary.

> Listen <u>to</u> the <u>desert</u>. You will hear the owl go <u>*whoo, whoo, whoo*</u>. You will hear the toad make a <u>plop, plop, plop</u> sound as it moves. You will also hear the snake go <u>*tst-tst-tst*</u> and the dove go c<u>oo coo coo</u>. You will hear the <u>coyote</u> and the <u>fish</u>, and you will even hear <u>mice</u> make a <u>scrrt, scrrt, scrrt</u> sound in the desert.

(Underlined words are key words in the selection.)

- Ask children which of these animals they are most interested in reading about.

OPTION 2

Picture Walk

DISPLAY

desert	to
listen	

Print the key words on the board and read them aloud. Then walk children through the illustrations incorporating these words where possible. As you mention each word, point to it on the board. Here are some suggestions:

Page 89 Read aloud the title and the names of the author and the illustrator. Have children describe what they see in the <u>desert</u> photograph and in the book cover illustration.
Pages 90–91 Ask children what picture clues help them know that this is a picture of a desert. Ask what sounds children think they might hear if they could <u>listen to</u> the desert.
Pages 92–93 Ask children if they have ever heard an owl hoot. Invite volunteers to imitate that sound.
Pages 94–95 Point out the toad on page 95 and ask children how a toad moves. Then ask what sound children think they would hear if they heard a toad hop in the desert.
Pages 96–105 Continue to use the illustrations to discuss the other desert creatures and the sounds they make, bringing out key words as possible.

OPTION 3

Creature Scene

**Selection Master 2
Part 5**

- If you have not done so, preview the selection by reading aloud the title and inviting children to look at the illustrations. Have children name any of the animals they recognize. Explain that the small desert creatures often dig into the ground in order to escape the sun; other creatures use brush, rocks, or trees for shade.
- Have children draw their favorite desert creature in the middle of the master. Tell them to place their creature so that the speech balloon will be near the mouths.
- Suggest that children create a scene that shows their creature living in the desert by drawing cactus plants, sand, bushes, dunes, rocks, water holes, and so on around their creature.
- Tell children to save their work to finish at a later time.

OPTION 1 Read Aloud Pages 90–105 or Have Children Listen to the Audio Tape

Have children follow along in their anthologies as they listen to pages 90–105 of the selection. Encourage children to listen to find out what sounds they might hear in the desert.

Discussion Points
- Ask children what sounds they learned about in this selection so far. Have children make or imitate those sounds and describe the creatures that made them.
- Ask children which of these creatures interested them most and why.
- Discuss children's ideas about what might happen and what they might "hear" in the rest of the selection.

OPTION 2 Guided or Assisted Reading of Pages 90–105

If, while using the guided reading segments that follow, it becomes clear that children are unable to read this selection silently, assist them in reading each segment aloud together. Then use the discussion points to talk about each segment.

Preview to Set a Purpose for Reading
(Predict/Infer Strategy)
- Have children preview the illustrations and make predictions about what creatures they will meet and what sounds they will hear. Write children's predictions on the board.
- If children need help making predictions, model how the illustration on pages 92–93 might lead to the following prediction: On these pages I see an owl sitting in the desert on a cactus. Owls make a hooting sound. So, on these pages, I think I'll hear an owl go *hoot, hoot, hoot.*

> For the first section, children's predictions are necessarily based on their preview of the selection. Before children read each subsequent section, have them think about what they have read and decide if they want to change their original predictions or make new ones. Then have children continue reading to see if their predictions agree with what actually happens in the selection.

Sounds and Creatures of the Desert (Pages 90-97)

Guide the Reading
(Monitor Strategy)
- Remind children that good readers ask themselves if they understand what they are reading. Explain that, when there is something they don't understand, good readers go back and read the words and look at the pictures again to try to clear up any problems.
- Have children read pages 90–97.

Discussion Points
- Discuss the predictions children have made. Talk about which predictions matched what happened in the selection so far and which did not. Then ask children if they want to change or add to their predictions.
- Ask children to name the creatures they read about on these pages and to describe the sound each animal made.
- Ask children which was the most interesting sound they heard in the selection so far. Have volunteers find and read aloud the words that stand for that sound.
- Encourage children to discuss how they went back over parts of the selection that were unclear or confusing.
- Discuss with children any other words or parts of the section that were confusing to them.

More Sounds and Creatures of the Desert (Pages 98-105)

Guide the Reading
- Remind children that good readers look for the most important parts of a selection and retell them in their own words.
- Have children read pages 98–105.

Discussion Points
- Talk with children about which of their predictions match what has happened in the selection so far. Invite children to add to or change their predictions.
- Ask children to name the creatures they read about on these pages and to describe what each animal was doing and the sound the animal made.
- Have volunteers find and read aloud the sentences that tell what the coyote does.
- Ask children what they think are the most important things to remember about the pages they have read in the selection so far. Use the following Think Aloud to model for children how to summarize this information.

> **THINK ALOUD** *I want to summarize what I have read in this selection so far. I'll start by asking myself, "What are the most important parts?" I remember that on each set of pages I found a different animal and its sound. This tells me that the names of the animals and their sounds are the most important parts of the selection. When I look back at the pages again, I see an owl that hoots,* **whoo, whoo, whoo.** *I see a toad that hops,* **plop, plop, plop.**

Encourage children to continue to summarize the selection. Then invite volunteers to go back to the beginning and retell the most important parts in their own words.

- Talk with children about vocabulary or other parts of the selection that were confusing to them.
- Ask children what they think will happen in the rest of the selection. Discuss what other creatures they might "hear" and what sounds they might make.

Reflect on the Purposes for Reading
- Review the predictions on the board. Discuss those that did not match the story and whether that was because they were inappropriate or if they still match the story when children read the remainder of the selection.

Complete Desert Creatures
Selection Master 2
Page 5
- Have children return to the creatures they drew on the Master. Ask if there is anything they would like to add. Give them time to draw more creatures.
- Discuss the sounds these creatures might make. Then read the words along the bottom of the master. Have children decide which ones stand for the sounds made by the creatures in their desert scene. Then have children copy those words into the correct speech balloons.

> **Have children read the rest of the selection cooperatively or have them participate in the reading of this selection with the entire class.**

Use AFTER  Interact *with* Literature

OPTION 1 Develop Critical Thinking: Evaluating

Help children choose a favorite part of this selection.

- Write the following heading on the board: *My Favorite Parts.*
- Review the selection with children. For each pair of pages, ask a volunteer if this was one of his or her favorite parts. If it was, write a brief summary of those pages under the heading. (For example, for pages 92–93, write *The owl hoots whoo, whoo, whoo.*) Continue until all of the volunteer's favorites have been listed.

- Then review the list of favorites and have the volunteer pick his or her most favorite part. Explain to children that making lists and picking most favorites like this is a good way to choose things.
- Continue with other volunteers or let children make their own lists on separate pieces of paper. Help children by pointing out the animal names or sounds to copy onto their lists.

OPTION 2 ## Develop Fluency: Echo Reading

Children who are not familiar with Spanish will benefit from reading pages with you or with someone else who can pronounce the Spanish words. Choose various pages and read each sentence aloud, having children echo your pronunciation and accenting.

Use AFTER **3** Instruct *and* Integrate

OPTION 1 ## Making Generalizations

Page through the selection with children and ask what they can tell about the desert from the words and illustrations. Use the following Think Aloud to model how to use details in the selection to make generalizations about the desert.

> **THINK ALOUD** *What can I tell about the desert from the words and pictures on these pages? I see that there is a lot of sand. I also see that there aren't very many plants. These things tell me that it doesn't rain very much in the desert.*

Ask children how they think these desert creatures feel about rain in the desert. Discuss clues in the words and pictures, along with what children know from real life, that tell them how the animals might feel. (Possible responses: The creatures in the pictures on pages 107 and 110–111 all are smiling. It is raining, and since it doesn't rain much in a desert, these creatures are probably enjoying it. The fish live in water, so they must need rain to fall sometimes.)

OPTION 2 ## Consonant Clusters Review

- Have children turn to page 94 and find the words *plop* and *plap.* Point out the two consonants at the beginning of each word. Remind children that when two consonants are side by side at the beginning of a word, such as *pl* in *plop,* the sounds for the consonants are so close together they almost seem to be one sound.
- Write the clusters *st, dr, tr,* and *cl* on the board and on self-stick notes. Then write *plop* on the board. Ask a volunteer to read *plop* with you. Then let the volunteer experiment with making new words by placing different self-stick notes over the *pl. (stop, drop, clop)* Then let other volunteers experiment in the same way with the words *plop* and *plap.* (*trap, clap*)
- Next, write the clusters *bl, sk, sn, br, dr, gr,* and *tr* on the board and on self-stick notes. Have children make new words by placing different self-stick notes over the *pl* in *plip* and the *z* in *zoom.* (*skip, snip, drip, grip, trip, bloom, broom, groom*).

Get the Giggles

Use BEFORE **Launching the Theme Activities**

Theme Concept **Some stories make us laugh.**

Materials Suggested for the Theme
- Audio Tapes for Get the Giggles
- Selection Masters 3 and 4

OPTION 1 ## Create a Concept Map

Develop a concept map about what makes children laugh. Discuss the items already printed on this map and encourage children to add other items of their own.

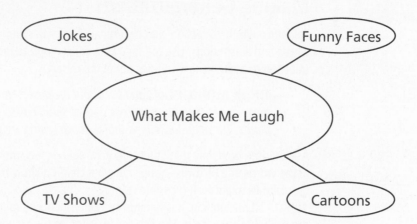

OPTION 2 ## Tell a Tongue Twister

Create some simple tongue twisters together using the beginning letters of children's names. (Examples: Katie's kitten climbed into the kitchen closet. Rachel runs races with red rhinoceroses.) Write the tongue twisters on the board and have children take turns reading them aloud.

On Top of Spaghetti

OPTION 1 Activate Prior Knowledge

- Read aloud the title of the Big Book and the illustrator's name. Explain that this Big Book is a new, funny version of an old song called "On Top of Old Smoky." If possible, sing or play a recording of a verse from "Old Smoky" to familiarize children with the words and melody.
- Display the Big Book cover, pointing out the spaghetti and single meatball. Have children preview the selection, encouraging them to explore the illustrations.
- Ask children whether or not they enjoy eating spaghetti. Allow them to pretend they are eating spaghetti and to imitate themselves doing so.
- Read the following selection summary to children.

> **This selection begins with a mound of <u>spaghetti</u> that is covered with <u>cheese</u> and has a <u>meatball</u> on <u>top</u> of it. <u>When</u> someone sneezes, the meatball rolls off the spaghetti, then off the <u>table,</u> and then onto the <u>floor</u>! From there, the meatball rolls <u>out</u> the <u>door</u>, <u>into</u> the <u>garden</u>, and <u>under</u> a <u>bush</u>.**

(Underlined words are key words in the selection.)

OPTION 2 Picture Walk

DISPLAY

top	when
spaghetti	rolled
meatball	under

Display the Big Book and read aloud the title as well as the name of the illustrator. Tell children that this selection is based on an old song called "On Top of Old Smoky," which is the name of a mountain. Explain that the new words make a funny version about a meatball.

Use the following suggestions to guide children on a picture walk through the selection. Incorporate key words as shown, pointing to each word in the Big Book as it is mentioned.

Pages 2–3 Ask children to describe what is happening in this picture. Ask them if they like cheese on <u>top</u> of <u>spaghetti</u> and what else they like to eat with spaghetti.

Pages 4–5 Display the pages and have children describe what is happening. Ask if they think a <u>meatball</u> could fly off a plate <u>when</u> somebody sneezed. Talk with children about why this could or couldn't happen.

Pages 6–7 Ask children what is happening to the meatball now. Talk about whether or not a meatball could roll off a table and fall onto a floor.

Pages 8–9 Ask children what has happened to the poor meatball now. Then talk about whether a meatball could really roll out a door like this, and why or why not.

Pages 10–11 Talk with children about where the meatball <u>rolled</u> next. Have volunteers point out the garden, the bush, and the meatball <u>under</u> the bush.

Pages 12–13 Have volunteers describe what they see in the illustrations on these pages. Talk with children about what has happened to the meatball. Ask children how the dog seems to feel about the meatball.

OPTION 3 ## Oral Language Development

Write the word *spaghetti* on the board. Then talk with children about spaghetti—how it is cooked; its shape, color, and taste; what children eat on it and with it; and so on. Use children's responses to make a concept web like the one below.

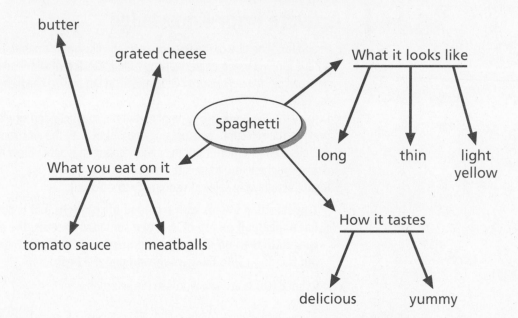

Use BEFORE **2** Interact *with* Literature

OPTION 1 ## Read Aloud for Interest

Pages 2–13 Display the Big Book and read aloud the title and the name of the illustrator. Explain that this book is based on silly verses that go with the music of an old song.

Read aloud pages 2–13. As you read, pause to ask questions such as, What has happened to the meatball now? Where do you think it might go next? Why do you think so? Run your hand under the words as you read and encourage children to chime in.

Ask children what they think might happen to the meatball in the rest of the selection. Talk about where it might go and how it might get there.

OPTION 2 ## Use the Audio Tape

Audio Tape for Get the Giggles: *On Top of Spaghetti*

As you display the illustrations in the Big Book, have children listen to pages 2–13 of the audio tape. Tell children to listen for the different places that the meatball goes.

Discussion Points
• Discuss where the meatball has gone so far. Ask children if they think a meatball could really roll off a table, out a door, into a garden, and under a bush. Talk about why readers might think that this is funny.
• Discuss the rhyming words on the pages. Encourage children to point out each set of rhyming words.
• Ask children what they think will happen to the meatball in the rest of the selection.

Develop Fluency: Partner Reading

Invite children to read the story aloud with partners. Have one child read the right-hand pages while the partner reads the left-hand pages.

OPTION 2 ## Language Experience

Have children suggest more funny places for the meatball to go. As children describe where the meatball is rolling, record their suggestions on chart paper. Have children read aloud what you have written and add illustrations.

OPTION 1 ## Cause and Effect

- Remind children that in real life and in stories, one thing often causes another thing to happen. Mention that good readers look for causes as they read. Reread Big Book pages 12–13 with children and call attention to the illustration. Ask what the girl did with the meatball. (She gave it to the dog.) Then ask why she gave her meatball to the dog. (It was mush.) Help children complete the following sentence:

    The girl gave the dog her meatball because (<u>it was nothing but mush</u>).

- Work with children to complete the following sentences about the selection. For each sentence, discuss with children what happened to the meatball and why it happened.

    The meatball rolled off the spaghetti because (<u>someone sneezed</u>).
    (<u>The meatball grew into a tree</u>) because the dog buried it in the yard.

OPTION 2 ## Digraphs *sh* and *th*

- Reread pages 10–11 with children. Point to the word *bush* and have children listen to the ending sound as you say *bush* several times. Remind children that two letters can stand for one sound. Ask what two letters stand for the ending sound in *bush.*
- Write the following words on the board or on chart paper and read them with children: *fib, put, cap, rug, did, rat, win.* Give each child a self-sticking note on which he or she writes the letters *sh.* Invite volunteers to come to the board, choose a word, place the note over the last letter in the word, and read aloud the new word. (*Fib* becomes *fish;* *sat* becomes *sash;* and so on.)
- Repeat the procedure using the words *lip, red, not, nut,* and *tell.* This time have children place the note over the first letter to make a new word. (*Lip* becomes *ship;* *red* becomes *shed;* and so on.)
- Next, have children listen for the sound of *th* in *with* on page 3 and *the* on page 6. Point out that the letters *th* in these words stand for slightly different sounds.
- Continue as before. Have children place *th* over the last letter in each of these words to make a new word: *bag, win, pad.* (*Bag* becomes *bath,* *win* becomes *with;* and so on.) Repeat the procedure using the words *pen, cat, is, rose, pin,* and *pink,* having children place *th* over the first letter to make a new word. (*Pen* becomes *then;* *cat* becomes *that;* and so on.)

Think About Words Strategy

Point to the word *sneezed* on page 5 of the Big Book. Then model how children could figure out this word if they did not know it.

- **What makes sense**   First I'll read the words that come before this word: *I lost my poor meatball when somebody _____*. This word must tell what somebody did to knock the meatball off the bowl of spaghetti.
- **Sounds for letters**   When I look at the letters I see *s* and *n* at the beginning. These letters stand for the sound I hear at the beginning of *snack* and *snip*. From the sentence on pages 2–3 I also know that the word is supposed to rhyme with *cheese*.
- **Picture clues**   On page 4 I see the meatball falling off the spaghetti. On page 5 I see someone who is either coughing or sneezing. The word *sneeze* begins with *sn* and rhymes with *cheese*. I think the word is *sneezed*. When I read the sentence with the word *sneezed*, I see that *sneezed* makes sense.

Next, point to the word *door* on page 9. Ask volunteers to demonstrate how they would figure out this word. Help and guide children as needed.

> **What makes sense**   The word tells where the meatball rolled.
> **Sounds for letters**   The word begins with the sound for *d*, as in *dog*.
> **Picture clues**   The meatball is rolling through a doorway.

High-Frequency Words

as, be, big, could, tree, under, when, your

- Write the High-Frequency Words on the chalkboard. Then invite children to play a rhyming game. Begin by telling them that you are thinking of a word that rhymes with *see* and names a large plant that has bark, a trunk, and branches. (*tree*) Have children identify the word on the board and find it in the Big Book.
- Continue in the same way with the remaining High-Frequency Words:

> *as:*   rhymes with *has* and is a two-letter word
> *be:*   rhymes with *me* and is a two-letter word
> *big:*   rhymes with *pig* and tells you that something is large
> *could:*   rhymes with *would* and tells if you are able to do something
> *under:*   rhymes with *thunder* and means "below"
> *when:*   rhymes with *pen* and tells about time
> *your:*   rhymes with *door* and tells something about you

The Foot Book

OPTION 1

Activate Prior Knowledge

- Read aloud the title and display the cover illustration. Ask children why the creature in the illustration might be pointing at his foot. Then talk with children about feet—what they look like, what they are used for, what we wear on them, and so on.
- Preview the illustrations on pages 125–143 with children. Ask if they think this selection tells about things that are real or things that are make-believe.
- Read aloud the following selection summary.

> **See all the feet. See <u>left</u> feet and <u>right</u> feet. See <u>morning</u> feet and feet <u>at</u> <u>night</u>. See <u>wet</u> feet and <u>dry</u> feet, feet that are <u>low</u> and feet that are <u>high</u>. See <u>front</u> feet and <u>back feet</u>. See many <u>more</u> kinds of feet.**

(Underlined words are key words in the selection.)

- Invite children to notice feet as they go through school that day. The next day, talk with children about the feet they saw. You may wish to have them suggest candidates for the following: (1) the fastest feet; (2) the most colorful feet; (3) the most amazing feet.

OPTION 2

Picture Walk

Print the key words on the board and read them aloud. Then lead children on a picture walk through the selection, incorporating these words where possible. Point to the words on the board as they are mentioned.

DISPLAY

left	at
foot	night
right	front
feet	back
morning	how

Pages 124–125 Read aloud the title and the name of the author-illustrator. Explain that this is a book about feet. Discuss what the creature on this page is doing with its feet. Ask children which is the creature's <u>left</u> <u>foot</u> and which is its <u>right</u> foot.

Pages 126–127 Discuss what the creature is doing on these pages. Ask children to point out the <u>feet</u> in the <u>morning</u> and the feet <u>at</u> <u>night</u>.

Pages 128–129 Ask children to find the feet on these pages and to describe what they are doing. Ask how the creature might feel about its feet.

Pages 130–131 Have children point out the head and tail of the large creature on these pages. Then ask them to point out its <u>front</u> feet and <u>back</u> feet. Ask what other feet children see on this page and discuss what these feet look like.

Pages 132–133 Ask children to describe the feet on these pages. Then ask children to count <u>how</u> many feet there are on these pages.

Continue with pages 134–143, having children describe the feet they see.

OPTION 3

Opposites

Selection Master 3
Part 5

- Help children identify the different feet at the top of the page. Be sure that children understand which are the big, back, dry, quick, wet, slow, front, and small feet.
- Tell children that many of the feet in *The Foot Book* are opposites. Have children draw lines to match the pictures of feet that are opposites. If necessary, start children off by pointing to the big feet and the small feet and showing how to draw a line connecting them.
- Have children save their work. Explain that they will work on the rest of the page later.

OPTION 1
Read Aloud Pages 124–143 or Have Children Listen to the Audio Tape

Have children follow along in their anthologies as they listen to pages 125–143 of the selection. Suggest that they listen to find out what kinds of feet are in *The Foot Book*.

Discussion Points
- Ask children what kinds of feet were in the selection. As children respond, discuss what the characters did with their feet–where they went, what fun they had, how they acted.
- Ask children if they thought the selection was funny. Have them talk about the parts they thought were especially funny.
- Discuss what children think they will meet in the rest of the selection.

OPTION 2
Guided or Assisted Reading of Pages 124–143

If, while using the guided reading segments that follow, it becomes clear that children are unable to read the selection silently, assist them in reading each segment aloud together. Then use the Discussion Points to talk about each segment.

Preview to Set a Purpose for Reading
(Self-Question Strategy)
- Read aloud the title and the name of the author-illustrator. Then have children preview the illustrations on pages 125–143. As they look at the illustrations, encourage children to think of any questions they might have about the selection. Write these questions on the board.
- If children have trouble thinking of questions, demonstrate how the illustration on page 135 might lead to a question such as, "Why are the feet at the bottom tied with white tape?"
- Have children read pages 125–143 to find answers to their questions.

> For the first section, children's questions are necessarily based on the preview of the selection. Before children read each subsequent section, discuss any answers they found to their questions. Then have them decide if they have additional questions that they want to add to the list and continue reading to find answers to their questions.

The Many, Many Feet We Meet (pages 125–133)

Guide the Reading
- Remind children to use the Think About Words strategy to figure out unfamiliar words.
- Have children read pages 125–133.

Discussion Points
- Discuss the questions children asked and the answers they found in the selection. Then ask if children have new questions they would like to add to the list.
- Ask children to describe the funniest feet they have seen in the selection so far. Have volunteers find and point out those feet and tell what makes those feet so funny.
- Ask children to find the page that tells about times of the day. Have volunteers find and read aloud the words on that page.
- Talk with children about how the Think About Words strategy helped them figure out any words they did not know.
- Ask children if any words or other parts of the selection were confusing to them. Talk with children about those words or parts.

Feet, Feet, and More Feet (pages 134–139)

Guide the Reading
(Monitor Strategy)

- Remind children to ask themselves if they understand what they are reading. If not, they should read the words and look at the pictures again.
- Have children read pages 134–139.

Discussion Points

- Discuss which of children's questions were answered and what new questions could be added to the list.
- Ask children what kinds of feet they read about in this section. Talk with them about which feet were opposites and which feet had rhyming names.
- Ask volunteers to find and read aloud the part that tells how fast some feet go.
- Talk with children about what they did if there was something in this section that they did not understand. Use the following Think Aloud to model the Monitor strategy.

> **THINK ALOUD** *When I read page 136, I was not sure what was happening. I asked myself questions such as, "Who is up, and who is down? Is this the same creature going up and down the stairs, or is it two different creatures?" To answer my questions, I looked back at what came before. On page 127 I saw this same creature four times on the same page. On page 128 this creature had both wet and dry feet. So, I figured out that he was probably on page 136 more than once, too. Now I know that the same creature is running up the stairs and back down again.*

- Talk with children about any vocabulary or other parts of the section that confused them.

More Feet to Meet (pages 140–143)

Guide the Reading

- Remind children to pay careful attention to the illustrations as they read. Explain that this strategy can help readers remember details and figure out new words.
- Have children read pages 140–143.

Discussion Points

- Discuss which of children's questions were answered and which were not. Talk about what new questions could be added to the list.
- Ask children whose feet are being pointed to on page 140. Have them point to the words that help them know this. Ask a volunteer to read those words aloud.
- Have children describe the other feet they read about in this section.
- Talk with children about how paying attention to the illustrations helped them understand what was happening in the selection. Encourage volunteers to share examples.
- Have children point to the main character in the middle of page 143. Discuss the expression on that character's face. Ask children what they think that character is feeling and thinking. Have children discuss the reasons for their answers.
- Talk with children about anything they read that seemed confusing.

Reflect on the Purposes for Reading

Review the questions on the board. Discuss those that have not been answered and whether they might still be answered when they read the rest of the selection.

Complete the Master
Selection Master 3
Part 5

- Have children return to the Meet the Feet master. Ask children if there are any changes they would like to make to the work they have done so far.
- Then, with children, read the words in the two lists on the bottom half of the page. Explain that the words in the first list have opposites in the second list. Give children time to think about the words. Then have children draw lines to match the opposites. Discuss each pair of opposites as children check their work, revising as necessary.

> **Have children read the rest of the selection cooperatively or have them participate in the reading of this selection with the entire class.**

OPTION **1** # Develop Critical Thinking: Solve a Problem

Have children solve the following problem: How many people's feet are there in our class?

- Begin by inviting children to suggest ways to get the total number of feet. Write each suggestion on the board and talk about whether or not the idea will work. (For example, children could count the number of people and then double it. They could count by twos as they point to each person. They could simply count by ones, as each foot is counted. They could count by 2's or add 2 + 2 + 2 . . . on a calculator, and so on.)
- Have children work in small groups. Have each group choose a method of finding the total number of feet. Have groups share their totals and explain their solutions.

OPTION **2** # Develop Fluency: Choral Reading

Have children read each pair of pages chorally, listening especially for words that rhyme. At the end of each choral reading, have a volunteer read aloud any rhyming words.

OPTION **1** # Fantasy and Realism

- Explain that some of the characters and some of the things that happen in this selection could be part of real life. Others are make-believe and could not really happen.
- Have children look at the characters on pages 140–141. Ask which characters seem real and why. Encourage children to describe the details in the illustration that support their answer. (The boy and the girl look like real children; their clothes are like what a real boy and girl would wear.) Then ask children which characters seem make-believe and why. (The character between the boy and girl on page 140 and the character with fuzzy feet on page 141 seem make-believe; their bodies, faces, and actions do not seem like a real creature.)

OPTION **2** # Initial and Final Digraph *ch*

- Read aloud the words on page 145, emphasizing the sound at the beginning of the word *chair*. Write *chair* on the board and underline the letters *ch.* Explain that two letters together can sometimes stand for a single sound. Point to the letters *ch* and have children say the word *chair* with you again.
- Then write the following on the board:

    I see _____.

- Read aloud the incomplete sentence. Ask children to complete the sentence with words that begin with the same sound as *chair*. Write children's suggestions on the board. (If necessary, start children off with words such as *children* and *chalk*.) When each child has suggested at least one word, have children read the words with you. Add the list of *ch* words to the Word Wall.

The Lady with the Alligator Purse

Use BEFORE  Introduce *the* Literature

OPTION 1 Activate Prior Knowledge

- Read aloud the title and the name of the author-illustrator. Display the cover illustration.
- Preview the selection with children, allowing time for them to look at the illustrations. Ask children if they think this selection tells about things that could really happen or about things that are make-believe. Discuss children's reasoning with them.
- Read aloud the following selection summary.

> Miss Lucy <u>had</u> a baby named Tiny Tim. When <u>she</u> put <u>him</u> in the <u>bathtub</u> he <u>drank</u> all the <u>water</u> and <u>ate</u> all the <u>soap</u>. He even tried to eat the bathtub, but it wouldn't fit <u>down</u> <u>his</u> <u>throat</u>! Miss Lucy got worried. She called a <u>doctor</u>, a <u>nurse</u>, and even a <u>lady</u> who had an <u>alligator</u> <u>purse</u>. They rushed to her house. The doctor said the boy had mumps, and the nurse said he had measles. But the lady with the alligator purse said that all this was <u>nonsense</u>.

(Underlined words are key words in the selection.)

Ask children what they think a doctor or nurse might do to help Miss Lucy and Tiny Tim.

OPTION 2 Picture Walk

DISPLAY

Miss Lucy	doctor
Tiny Tim	nurse
she	lady
if	alligator
down	purse

Print the key words on the board and read them aloud. Then lead children on a picture walk through the selection, incorporating these words where possible. Point to those words on the board as they are mentioned. Here are some suggestions.

Pages 162–163   Read aloud the title and the name of the author-illustrator. Explain that this is a book about <u>Miss Lucy</u> and her baby. Have children identify Miss Lucy. Point to the baby and explain that his name is <u>Tiny Tim</u>.

Pages 164–165   Point out Miss Lucy and ask children what they think <u>she</u> is doing. Point out Tiny Tim. Ask children <u>if</u> they think he can swim and why or why not.

Pages 166–167   Ask children where they think the water went and where all the soap bubbles came from.

Pages 168–169   Discuss what Tiny Tim is trying to do now. Ask what is happening to the bathtub and why the tub seems to be pointed <u>down</u> toward Tiny Tim.

Pages 170–171   Ask children why they think Miss Lucy is making phone calls. Tell them that she called three people and have them identify the <u>doctor</u>, the <u>nurse</u>, and the <u>lady</u> with the <u>alligator</u> <u>purse</u>.

Pages 174–175   Tell children that the doctor thinks Tiny Tim has mumps and the nurse thinks he has measles. Discuss with children what measles and mumps are. Then tell children that the lady with the alligator purse says, "<u>Nonsense</u>!" and ask what she means by that.

OPTION 3 Characters

Selection Master 4 Part 5

- Read aloud the names in the boxes on the page and tell children that these are the characters in *The Lady with the Alligator Purse.*
- Have children look at the illustrations on pages 162–175 of the selection and guess which name belongs to each character. To record their guesses, have children draw a picture of the character they think belongs in each box.
- Tell children to save their work to use again later on.

OPTION 1 Read Aloud Pages 162–175 or Have Children Listen to the Audio Tape

Have children follow along in their anthologies as they listen to pages 162–175 of the selection. Suggest that they listen to find out what Tiny Tim did in the bathtub and what happened because of what he did.

Discussion Points
- Ask children what Tiny Tim did in the bathtub and what Miss Lucy did about it.
- Discuss what the doctor, the nurse, and the lady with the alligator purse do and say.
- Ask what children think will happen in the rest of the selection.

OPTION 2 Guided or Assisted Reading of Pages 162–175

If, while using the guided reading segments that follow, it becomes clear that children are unable to read this selection silently, assist them in reading each segment aloud together. Then use the discussion points to talk about each segment.

Preview to Set a Purpose for Reading
(Predict/Infer Strategy)
- Read aloud the title and the name of the author-illustrator. Then have children preview the illustrations on pages 162–175. Ask children what they think will happen in the selection. Write children's predictions on the board so you can come back to them later.
- If children need help making predictions, demonstrate how the illustration on pages 170-171 could lead to the following prediction: The way the woman is making phone calls makes me think that she needs help in a hurry. She calls a doctor and a nurse, as well as a woman who has a purse that looks like an alligator. Therefore, I think that in this selection someone gets sick and the woman calls for help.

> For the first section, children's predictions are necessarily based on the preview of the selection. Before children read each subsequent section, have them think about what they've read and decide if they want to revise their original predictions or make new ones. Then have children continue reading to see if their predictions agree with what happens in the selection.

Tiny Tim in the Tub (pages 163–169)

Guide the Reading
- Remind children to use the Think About Words strategy to help them figure out any words they might not know.
- Have children review the predictions on the board and then read pages 163–169.

Discussion Points
- Discuss the predictions children have made. Talk about which predictions matched what happened in the selection so far and which did not. Then ask children if they want to change or add to their predictions.
- Have a volunteer find and read aloud the words that tell why Miss Lucy put Tiny Tim in the bathtub.
- Ask children if they think it is funny that a baby would drink up all the bath water, eat all the soap, and try to eat the bathtub. Talk with children about whether these are things that could really happen or whether the author put them in just for fun.
- Talk with children about how the Think About Words strategy helped them figure out any words they did not know.
- Ask children if any other parts of this section were confusing. Discuss these with them.

Miss Lucy Calls for Help (pages 170–175)

Guide the Reading
(Summarize Strategy)

- Remind children that, as they read, they should think about which parts of the story are the most important to remember and put those parts in their own words. Explain to children that this will help them remember the story and make it easier to tell it to someone else.
- Have children read pages 170–175.

Discussion Points

- Discuss which of children's predictions match what happened in the selection so far. Ask children if they would like to change any of their predictions or make new ones.
- Ask children who Miss Lucy called for help. Discuss how the doctor and the nurse might be able to help and why the lady with the alligator purse seems an unlikely person to call. Have children point out other things in the text and pictures that they find silly.
- Have volunteers find and read aloud what each of the characters has to say about Tiny Tim. Discuss whether or not each of these comments seems useful or helpful.
- Talk with children about how to summarize what they have read. Then invite volunteers to retell what has happened so far. Use the following Think Aloud to model the process.

> **THINK ALOUD** *I want to summarize what I have read in this selection so far. I ask myself, "What happened at the beginning?" I remember that Miss Lucy put Tiny Tim in the bathtub, and he drank all the water and ate all the soap. Then Miss Lucy called a doctor, a nurse, and a lady with an alligator purse. When these people got to Miss Lucy's house, the doctor said the baby had the mumps, the nurse said he had measles, and the lady with the alligator purse just said, "Nonsense."*

- Talk with children about vocabulary or other parts of the section they found confusing.

Reflect on the Purposes for Reading

Review the predictions on the board. Discuss those that did not match the story and whether that was because they were inappropriate or if they might match the story when students read the remainder of the selection.

Complete the Master
Selection Master 4
Part 5

Have children look at the pictures they drew. Did children correctly guess who each character in the selection was? Talk about the picture clues that helped children identify each character. Then invite children to tell the group which was their favorite character and why.

> **Have children read the rest of the selection cooperatively or have them participate in the reading of this selection with the entire class.**

Use AFTER **2** Interact *with* Literature

OPTION 1 Think About Words Strategy

Read aloud page 165, saying blank for the word *bathtub*. Use the Think Aloud below to model how children can use the Think About Words strategy to figure out this word.

- **What makes sense**   From the other words in the sentence I know that this word names the place where Miss Lucy put the baby to swim.
- **Sounds for letters**   When I look at the word, I see the letter *b* at the beginning. I know this letter stands for the sound I hear at the beginning of the words *baby, be,* and *big.*
- **Picture clues**   Next I look for clues in the illustration. I see a baby swimming around in a large bathtub. The word *bathtub* begins with the sound for *b.* When I try *bathtub* in the sentence, it makes sense. The word is *bathtub.*

Have children tell how they would figure out the word *him* on page 165.

Develop Fluency: Echo Reading

- Read aloud the first line on page 163, having children repeat it after you with the same tone and expression. Then read the remaining words on the page, following the same procedure.
- Continue in the same way through the selection. Gradually increase the number of lines children repeat at a time until children are hearing and reading a whole rhyming pattern.

Use AFTER **3** Instruct *and* Integrate

OPTION **1** ## Sequence

- Write the following sentences on strips of paper.

   Miss Lucy called the doctor, the nurse, and the lady with the alligator purse.
   Tiny Tim drank up all the water and ate up all the soap.
   In came the doctor, the nurse, and the lady with the alligator purse.
   Out went the doctor, the nurse, and the lady with the alligator purse.
   "Pizza!" cried the lady with the alligator purse.
   Miss Lucy put Tiny Tim in the bathtub.

- Read the sentences with children. Then work with them to place the sentences in the same order as the events in the story. Have children review the story pages to make sure the order is correct.

OPTION **2** ## Initial and Final Digraphs Review

- Remind children that two letters together sometimes stand for a single sound. Read aloud pages 164–165. Then write the word *she* on the board, underlining the *sh*. Have children say *she* with you. Ask what letters stand for the /sh/ sound at the beginning of *she*. *(sh)*
- Do the same with pages 170-171 and the ending sound in the word *with*.
- Display page 163. Ask how many children are in the picture. Say *children* and ask what the beginning sound is. Write *children* on the board and ask what letters stand for the beginning sound. *(ch)*
- Continue by naming objects in the illustrations. Discuss the beginning or ending digraph in each name. Use the following illustrations:

   Page 164 <u>sh</u>ower cap
   Page 168 soap di<u>sh</u>
   Page 175 <u>th</u>ermometer
   Page 176 tee<u>th</u>
   Page 180 tra<u>sh</u>; <u>ch</u>eese
   Page 181 <u>ch</u>airs

Invite children to name other objects in the illustrations whose names contain the digraphs *sh, th,* and *ch.* Have children identify the digraph and tell where in each name they hear the sound. Examples include: *splash, sheet, stethoscope, shoes, toothpaste, toothbrush,* and *bath.* Record the name of each object on chart paper, underlining the digraph.

Sharing Time

Use BEFORE Launching the Theme Activities

Theme Concept   **Family and friends help one another and share together.**

Materials Suggested for the Theme
- Audio Tapes for Sharing Time
- Selection Masters 5 and 6

OPTION 1   Lend a Hand, Get a Hand

Use the following to help children recognize how often they lend a hand to others—and how often other people give *them* a hand. On the board, draw two hands several inches apart. On one hand write **Lend a Hand**; on the other, **Get a Hand**. Read the words aloud and discuss what they mean. Then ask children to describe some of the ways in which they "lend a hand" to other people—to friends, family members, classmates, and so on. Discuss children's ideas and write them on the board beneath the **Lend a Hand** heading. Do the same for the ways in which children **Get a Hand** from other people.

OPTION 2   Tell a Group Story

Explain to children that they are each going to tell a part of a long story. You begin the story with one or two sentences. (Example: One day, Billy the Bear walked out of his den to find something to eat. As he was walking, he met a big, furry . . .) Then have a volunteer add a few more sentences to continue the story. Continue until everyone has had an opportunity to contribute. If a tape recorder is available, tape the telling of the story. Children will enjoy listening to themselves afterward.

The Doorbell Rang

OPTION 1 Activate Prior Knowledge

- Ask children if they ever get together with friends at each other's homes. Discuss what they do with their friends when they get together like this. Talk with children about what they and their friends share—food, toys, games, and so on. Then discuss how they go about sharing things with their friends. Ask children how they make sure everyone gets a fair amount or equal number of turns.
- Display the Big Book and read aloud the title and the name of the author-illustrator. Then preview the selection with children, giving them time to look at the illustrations. Ask children if they think this selection tells about things that could happen in real life or things that are make believe.
- Read aloud the following selection summary.

   Sam and Victoria are just about to sit down with a tray of Ma's <u>good</u>, homemade cookies when the doorbell rings and more children come in. <u>Before</u> long, more children ring the doorbell . . . and more and more and more. Each time new people arrive, the children have to figure out how to share the cookies.

- Ask children if they have ever shared cookies or cupcakes with someone and have volunteers explain how they went about sharing.

(Underlined words are key words in the selection.)

OPTION 2 Picture Walk

- Print the key words on the board and read them aloud.
- Display the cover of the Big Book. Read aloud the title and the name of the author-illustrator. Then guide children on a picture walk through the selection using the following suggestions. Incorporate key words where possible, pointing to each word on the board as it is mentioned.

DISPLAY

made	each
from	three
one	two

Page 3 Point to the illustration and tell children that Ma has just <u>made</u> cookies for Victoria and Sam.

Pages 4–5 Ask how many children there are in the picture on these pages (two) and how many cookies there are. (twelve) Discuss how Sam and Victoria can share the cookies. Encourage children to use counters or other manipulatives to figure out that <u>each</u> of them would get six cookies.

Pages 6–7 Explain that the doorbell rang and when Ma opened it she saw two children <u>from</u> next door. She invited them in.

Pages 8–9 Ask how many people are at the table now (four) and how many cookies each child will get. (<u>three</u>) Have volunteers explain how they figured this out. Then call attention to Ma on page 9. Ask children why she might be looking toward the door.

Pages 10–11 Ask what the children at the table are doing and why.

Pages 12–13 Ask how many people are at the table now (six) and how many cookies each child will get. (<u>two</u>) Talk about what children think will happen next.

Pages 14–17 Ask how many children are in the kitchen now (twelve) and how many cookies each child will get. (<u>one</u>)

OPTION 3 Oral Language Development

- Explain that several words in this selection tell what people might do if they were given some cookies.
- Display Big Book page 4. Point to the word *look*. Ask children how they might act when they looked at the cookies. Invite volunteers to pantomime their actions.
- Point out the word *smell* on the same page and have children pantomime how they would act when they smelled the cookies.
- Encourage children to brainstorm other words that could describe how they might use their senses to know about the cookies (taste, feel, hear, and so on). Write children's suggestions on the board and encourage them to pantomime these actions.

Use BEFORE **2** Interact *with* Literature

OPTION 1 Read Aloud for Interest

Pages 3–19

- Display the Big Book. Read aloud the title and the name of the author-illustrator. Talk with children about what usually happens when a doorbell rings at someone's home.
- Read aloud pages 3–19. As you read, pause to ask questions such as *What do you think will happen next? What makes you think this?*
- Run your hand under the words as you read, inviting children to chime in. Ask children what they think will happen next when Ma answers the door.

OPTION 2 Use the Audio Tape

Audio Tape for Sharing Time: *The Doorbell Rang*

Discussion Points

As you display the illustrations in the Big Book, have children listen to pages 3–19 of the audio tape. Tell children to listen to find out what happens each time the doorbell rings.

- Discuss what happens each time the doorbell rings and what the children have to do because of it.
- Ask children if they think the boys and girls in the selection have found a fair way to share the cookies. Have them explain their answers.
- Talk with children about what they think will happen next in the story.

Use AFTER **2** Interact *with* Literature

OPTION 1 Develop Fluency: Echo Reading

Read aloud the first sentence on page 3. Have children repeat the same sentence, echoing your intonation and expression. Continue in the same way, reading one sentence at a time. As children become more and more familiar with the story, read aloud two sentences at a time and have them echo your reading.

OPTION 2 Language Experience

Have children create their own Big Book version of *The Doorbell Rang*. Begin by having children retell the story page by page in their own words. Write the childrens' story on chart paper and let volunteers illustrate the pages. Then have the group read their story, chorally, page by page.

OPTION 1 Compare and Contrast

Have children compare and contrast pages from *The Doorbell Rang*.

- Display the Big Book and read pages 5 and 9 with children. Then ask what is the same about these two pages. (In both pages, Ma is standing in the center of the kitchen with a bucket and mop in her hands; a coffee pot and pan are on the stove; the words say exactly the same thing.) Then ask what is different about the pages. (On page 9 there are muddy footprints on the floor and Ma is cleaning them. Also on page 9 a ball and gym bag are in the corner. None of this is on page 5. Ma is standing in different positions on the two pages.)
- Write children's suggestions on the board. If necessary, prompt them with questions such as, *Is there a person on both pages? What is that person doing on page 5? What is that person doing on page 9? What other things are the same in these two pictures? What other things are different?*
- Continue with pages 13, 17, and 21. Have children identify similarities from scene to scene and guide them in recognizing how each scene changes as more and more children arrive.

OPTION 2 Short *a* and Short *a* Phonogram

- Have children read aloud the second sentence on page 3. Point out the word *and*. Explain that the letter *a* stands for the short *a* vowel sound in *and*.
- Write the word *and* on the board. Ask children to suggest words that rhyme with *and*. (*band, hand, land, sand*) Write children's suggestions on the board and show how all of these words are made by adding a letter to the beginning of *-and*.
- Extend the activity by using the words *that* and *Sam*. Circle the initial consonants in those words and have children make rhyming words by putting other letters in place of the circled consonants. (*that: bat, cat, flat, hat, mat; Sam: clam, ham, jam, ram*)

OPTION 3 Think about Words Strategy

- Point to the word *tray* on page 22 of the Big Book. Model how children could figure out this word if they did not know it.

   What makes sense First I'll read the sentence on page 22. It says: *It was Grandma with an enormous _____ of cookies.* I think the word might be *batch*. "An enormous batch of cookies" makes sense.

   Sounds for letters When I look at the letters I see *tr* at the beginning. I know that the letters *tr* stand for the sounds I hear at the beginning of *tree*. So the word can't be *batch*.

   Picture clues The picture shows Grandma carrying cookies on a tray. Now I see that the word is *tray*. When I reread *It was Grandma with an enormous tray of cookies,* the sentence makes sense.

- Next, point to the word *stared* on page 20 and ask volunteers to explain how they would figure out this word if they did not know it.

> **What makes sense** The word tells what the children did to the cookies on their plates.
>
> **Sounds for letters** At the beginning of the word are the letters *st*, as in *stay* and *stop*.
>
> **Picture clues** Children are looking at the cookies.

OPTION 4 **High-Frequency Words**

before, can, each, from, good, like, made, they

Write the High-Frequency words on index cards or self-sticking notes. Choose eight volunteers and give each child a word. Tell children to listen carefully as you read each word. For each word you read, ask children to raise the corresponding word card. Then have children find their words in the selection and read the sentences in which they appear.

The Little Red Hen

Use BEFORE **1** Introduce *the* Literature

OPTION 1 Activate Prior Knowledge

- Direct children to page 49. Read aloud the title and the name of the author-illustrator, and call attention to the illustration. Explain that the things shown in this illustration are all things people might see in a garden. Have children name the objects. Ask if any of the children have ever grown anything—flowers, vegetables, and so on. Talk with children about what they grew, what they did to help the plants or flowers grow, what tools or plant food they used, and so on.
- Preview the selection with children. Then read aloud the following selection summary.

> Once <u>there</u> <u>were</u> four friends, a pig, a duck, a cat, and a hen. One <u>day</u> the hen found some seeds. She asked <u>who</u> would <u>help</u> her plant the seeds, but each of her friends said, "Not I." So the hen <u>did</u> it by herself. When the seeds grew into stalks of wheat, she asked who would help her cut the stalks. Each friend said, "Not I." So it went. The <u>little</u> red hen's friends would not help her cut the wheat or thresh it or grind it into flour. Each job she did by herself, with no help from her friends.

- Ask children what they eat that is made of flour. Then ask what they think the little red hen will <u>make</u> with the flour.

(Underlined words are key words in the selection.)

OPTION 2 Picture Walk

Print the key words on the board and read them aloud. Then lead children on a picture walk through the selection, discussing what the hen does and what her friends do. Incorporate the key words where possible. Point to the words on the board as they are mentioned.

DISPLAY

there	were
did	help
wheat	stalks

Page 49 Read aloud the title and the name of the author-illustrator. Tell children that this selection is a retelling of a story they may have heard before—the tale of the <u>little</u> red hen.
Pages 50–51 Explain that <u>there</u> <u>were</u> four friends, and have children identify the pig, the duck, the cat, and the hen. Tell children that the hen had three baby chicks.
Pages 52–53 Tell children that the little red hen found some seeds and have children point to the seeds in their anthologies.
Pages 54–55 Explain that the hen asks her friends to <u>help</u> her plant the seeds. Ask children if they think the friends will help and what makes them think so. Have children point out her friends in the illustration.
Page 56 Point to the illustration on page 56 and ask what the hen <u>did</u> next. Then ask children what they see on page 57 (<u>stalks</u> of <u>wheat</u>). Discuss where children think the wheat came from and what will probably happen to it next.
Pages 58–59 Ask children to describe what the little red hen is doing on these pages. Then ask what children think the hen is saying to her friends and what the friends will do.

Continue in the same manner with pages 60–69.

OPTION 3 Picture Sequence

Selection Master 5
Part 5

Tell children that the pictures on this page show the steps used to grow wheat and make flour. Explain that the little red hen does these same things in the story children are about to read. Help children to describe what is happening in each picture and to read the word under the picture.

Then tell children to save their work to use again later on.

② Interact
with
Literature

OPTION 1 Read Aloud Pages 50–69 or Have Children Listen to Those Pages on the Audio Tape

Audio Tape for Sharing Time: *The Little Red Hen*

Have children follow along in their anthologies as they listen to pages 50–69 of the selection. Have them listen to learn what the little red hen found and what she did with what she found.

Discussion Points
• Ask children what the little red hen found and what she did with the seeds she found.
• Discuss the different jobs the hen did and the order in which she did them.
• Ask children if they think the pig, the duck, and the cat were good friends to the little red hen and why or why not.
• Ask children what they think the little red hen will do with the flour and who will help her.

OPTION 2 Guided or Assisted Reading of Pages 50–69

If, while using the guided reading segments that follow, it becomes clear that children are unable to read this selection silently, assist them in reading each segment aloud together. Then use the discussion points to talk about each segment.

Preview to Set a Purpose for Reading
(Predict/Infer Strategy)

Read aloud the title and the name of the author-illustrator. Then have children preview the illustrations on pages 50–69. Ask children what they think will happen in this selection. Write their predictions on the board so you can come back to them later.

If children have trouble making predictions, show how the illustrations on pages 56–57 could lead to the following prediction: *I see the little red hen putting seeds into holes in the ground. On the next page I see large plants. This makes me think that the seeds grew into plants. Therefore, I think that the hen will plant some seeds that will grow into large plants.*

> For the first section, students' predictions are necessarily based on their previews of the selection. Before students read each subsequent section, discuss which of their predictions agreed with what was read and which did not. Have children think about what they've read and decide if they want to revise their original predictions or make new ones.

The Little Red Hen Finds Some Seeds (Pages 50–53)

Guide the Reading
• Remind children to use the Think About Words strategy to figure out unfamiliar words.
• Have children identify the objects in the illustration on pages 52–53 and discuss where this story most likely takes place. (a farm or barnyard) Then have children read pages 50–53.

Discussion Points
• Have volunteers read aloud the part that tells what the little red hen was doing one day.
• Discuss what children think the hen will do with the seeds and why they think as they do.
• Talk with children about how the Think About Words strategy helped them figure out words they did not know. Ask volunteers to give examples of how they used the strategy.

The Little Red Hen Sets to Work (Pages 54–57)

Guide the Reading
• Remind children that if there is anything they don't understand about what they are reading, they should read the words and look at the pictures again.
• Have children read pages 54–57.

Discussion Points
(Monitor Strategy)
• Have a volunteer read aloud what the little red hen asked her friends about the seeds. Then have other volunteers read aloud what each friend said to the hen.

- Ask what the hen said and did when her friends would not help her.
- Talk with children about what they did if anything was confusing or unclear. Use the following Think Aloud to model the strategy.

> **Think Aloud** *When I read page 57, I asked myself, What are these tall orange things? Where did they come from? I wasn't sure, so I went back to page 56. The picture and the words on page 56 told me that the hen was planting seeds. So, when I looked at page 57 again, I realized that these were plants that had grown from the seeds the hen had planted. I read the words on page 57 again and that is what they told me.*

- Talk with children about any words or other parts of the selection that were confusing.

The Little Red Hen Does More Work   (Pages 58–61)

Guide the Reading
- Remind children that, as they read this part of the selection, they should think about what they like or don't like about this part of the selection. Then have children read pages 58–61.

Discussion Points
- Discuss what the hen asked her friends to do and what they said to her.
- Ask children why the hen's friends might not have wanted to help her. Talk about whether or not the friends were right to do as they did.
- Ask children if they have been thinking about whether or not they like this selection. Talk with them about what they like or don't like about the story so far and why.
- Discuss any vocabulary or other parts of the selection that confused children.

From Wheat to Flour   (Pages 62–69)

Guide the Reading
- Tell children to pay close attention to the details in the illustrations so they will understand what is happening in this part of the story. Then have children read pages 62–69.

Discussion Points
- Discuss with children the pattern in this story. Have children point out where on pages 62–65 the hen asks for help, where her friends say they will not help, and where the hen does the work herself. Do the same for pages 66–69.
- Talk with children about how the details in the illustrations helped them understand what the hen did to thresh the wheat and grind it into flour.
- Discuss any parts of the selection that were unclear or confusing to children.
- Ask children what they think will happen in the rest of the selection. Talk with them about what they think the little red hen will do with the flour.

Reflecting on Purposes for Reading
Review the predictions on the board. Discuss those that did not match the story and whether that was because they were inappropriate or if they might still match the story when children read the remainder of the selection.

Complete the Picture Sequence
Have children return to the master. Invite them draw a picture showing what they think the hen will do with the flour and who will help her.

Selection Master 5 Part 5
Have children read the rest of the selection cooperatively or have them participate in the reading of the selection with the entire class.

Use AFTER **2** Interact *with* Literature

OPTION **1** **Think About Words Strategy**

Use the following to model how to figure out the word *meowed* on page 55.

Think Aloud

What makes sense *The first sentence tells me that the pig squealed. The next sentence tells me that the duck quacked. I see the word **cat** in this last sentence, so the word probably tells me what sound the cat made.*

Sounds for letters *The word begins with sound for* **m,** *as in* **me** *and* **my.**
Familiar word parts *I see the letters* **-ed.** *These letters stand for the sound at the end of* **squealed** *and* **quacked.** *The word is probably* **meowed.** *When I try* **meowed** *in the sentence it makes sense.*
Picture clues *The picture shows a pig, a duck, and a cat, all with their mouths open as if they are making sounds.* **Meowed** *names the sound a cat makes.*

- Next, point to the word *eat* on page 74. Have volunteers model how they would figure out this word if they didn't know it. Help and guide children as needed.

OPTION 2 Develop Fluency: Echo Reading

Read aloud the first sentence on page 50–51, having children repeat it after you with the same tone and expression. Read the second sentence on page 51, following the same procedure. Continue through the selection, reading one sentence at a time. However, each time you come to the sentences that tell what the friends say, read all three sentences and have children echo your reading.

Use AFTER  **3** Instruct *and* Integrate

OPTION 1 Story Structure and Summarizing

- Have children name the characters in the story and tell where the story takes place. Record children's responses on the chalkboard.
- Next, help children identify the hen's problems and how she solves each problem. Put the following chart on the board and work with children to complete it.

No one helps plant the seeds.	(The hen plants.)
No one helps cut the wheat.	(The hen cuts.)
No one helps thresh the wheat.	(The hen threshes.)
No one helps grind the wheat into flour.	(The hen grinds.)
No one helps make the bread.	(The hen makes bread.)

- Have children tell in their own words what happens at the end of the story as you record this information. Invite volunteers to use the information on the board to retell the story in their own words.

OPTION 2 Short *e* and Short *e* Phonograms

- Have children read aloud the sentence on pages 50–51. Point to the words *red* and *hen* and tell children that these words have the short *e* vowel sound. Then have children listen for the short *e* sound as you say *let*, *pet*, *when* , *then*, *send*, and *mend*.
- Write the word *red* on the board. Ask children to suggest words that rhyme with red *(bed, Ned, Ted, led)*. Write children's suggestions on the board and show how all of these words are made by adding a different letter at the beginning of -ed. Continue in the same way with the word *hen*.
- Repeat the procedure with the sentence on page 54 and the word *went*.

Flower Garden

OPTION 1

Activate Prior Knowledge

- Have children turn to page 91. Read aloud the title and the names of the author and the illustrator. Explain that in this selection, a girl makes a special kind of garden.
- Ask children about any gardens they have seen. Discuss where these gardens were, what was in them, who took care of them, and what had to be done to make them grow.
- Preview the illustrations with children. Then read aloud the following selection summary.

> **One day, a girl and her father went to the store to get flowers and other things for a garden. The girl took everything home in a cardboard box. Then she and her father set to work. They used papers to protect the floor and a trowel to dig in the soil. Soon, her window box garden was done. It looked great!**

(Underlined words are key words in the selection.)

- Invite children to tell about window box gardens they have seen.

OPTION 2

Picture Walk

DISPLAY

garden	window box
look	great
checkout stand	people

Print the key words on the board and read them aloud. Then lead children on a picture walk through the selection discussing what the girl and her father are doing and where the flowers are in each illustration. Incorporate the key words where possible, pointing to them on the board as they are mentioned. Here are some suggestions:

Page 91 Read aloud the title, *Flower Garden,* and the names of the author and the illustrator. Have children describe what they see in the illustration.

Pages 92–93 Ask children what the girl has in the shopping cart. Talk about the flowers with children. Discuss how they look (pretty, great), what the girl might do with them, and so on.

Pages 94–95 Tell children that the flowers are now at the checkout stand. Have children describe what happens at a checkout stand.

Pages 96–97 Point out the girl and her father and explain that they are walking to the bus. Ask where the flowers are now. Then ask where the girl and her father might be going with the flowers.

Pages 98–99 Ask children if they can see the girl and her father, and discuss how the illustrator shows where they are sitting on the bus. Then have children describe the people on the bus. Ask what these people might be smiling at.

Pages 108–109 Discuss how the window box is being put on the ledge outside the window.

Pages 110–111 Point out the ladybug on the girl's hand. Ask children how it might have gotten there. Be sure children understand that the flowers are still in the window box and that the girl is looking at them from inside her apartment.

OPTION 3

Vocabulary

Selection Master 6
Part 5

- Tell children that in this selection, a girl makes a flower garden in a window box. Explain that the pictures at the top of the page show the kinds of flowers she uses. Read aloud the names of the flowers.
- Have children make predictions about the colors of the flowers in the selection by coloring each flower using any color of crayon or marker they choose.
- Tell children to save their work to use again later on.

OPTION **1**

Read Aloud Pages 92–113 or Have Children Listen to the Audio Tape

Audio Tape for Sharing Time: *Flower Garden*

Have children follow along in their anthologies as they listen to pages 92–113 of the selection. Suggest that they listen to find out what the girl buys in the store and what she does with it.

Discussion Points
- Ask children what the girl bought (flowers) and what she made with the flowers.
- Talk with children about what the characters did to make the garden—fill the window box with soil and planting mix, plant the flowers in a certain order, and put the box on the window ledge.
- Discuss with children why the girl might be making the window box.
- Ask children who else might see the window garden and how they will feel about it.

OPTION **2**

Guided or Assisted Reading of Pages 92–113

If while using the guided reading segments that follow, it becomes clear that children are unable to read this selection silently, assist them in reading each segment aloud together. Then use the discussion points to talk about each segment.

Preview to Set a Purpose for Reading (Self-Question)

Read aloud the title and the names of the author and the illustrator. Then have children preview the selection. As children look at the illustrations, talk with them about the questions that come to mind. Write their questions on the board so you can come back to them later. If children have difficulty thinking of questions, demonstrate how the illustration on pages 102–103 might lead you to ask questions such as *Why is the girl sitting on the floor? Is she tired? Did she fall down?*

> For the first section, children's questions are necessarily based on their previews of the selection. Before children read each subsequent section, discuss any answers they've found to their questions and have children decide if they want to add additional questions to the list. Then have them continue reading to answer their questions.

Getting the Flowers Home (Pages 92–99)

Guide the Reading
- Remind children to use the Think About Words strategy to help them figure out any words they might not know.
- Point to the illustration on pages 96–97 and discuss with children where they think this story takes place. Then have children read pages 92–99.

Discussion Points
- Discuss what has happened in the story so far. (The girl has put the flowers in a shopping cart, gone through the checkout stand, walked to the bus, and ridden on the bus.)
- Ask children how people on the bus acted when they saw the garden in the box. Have children find and read aloud the words that tell them this.
- Ask children to find and read aloud the rhyming words in this section.
- Talk with children about how the Think About Words strategy helped them figure out any words they did not know.

Making the Garden (Pages 100–107)

Guide the Reading
- Remind children that if there is anything they don't understand as they read, they should go back and reread the words and look at the pictures again.
- Have children read pages 100–107.

Discussion Points

- Have children review the words and pictures on pages 104–105 and 106–107. Ask children to describe what the girl and her father did to make the garden shown on page 107. Have children find and read aloud the rhyming words in this section. (*floor/door; thick/fix*) Point out that *thick* and *fix* don't really rhyme but that they sound enough alike to use in a rhyming story like this one.
- Point out the words "Hurry! Hurry!" on page 104. Ask children what the girl and her father are hurrying to do and why they might want to hurry.
- Talk with children about how they went back over any parts of this section that they did not understand. Have volunteers share examples of what they did.

The Garden Finds a Home   (Pages 108–113)

Guide the Reading
(Evaluate Strategy)

- Remind children to think about what they like or don't like about the selection as they are reading it. Then have children read pages 108–113.

Discussion Points

- Have children find and read aloud the rhyming words in this section. (*street/ meet; see/jamboree*)
- Ask children if a window ledge is a good place for a garden. Ask them what parts of the story show this.
- Invite volunteers to tell what they think of this selection so far. Use the following Think Aloud to model the strategy.

> **Think Aloud** *One thing I like about this selection is that it rhymes, like a song or a poem. I also like the pictures because they have lots of color. I think the pictures are interesting because they show things from way down low and way up high.*

Reflecting on Purposes for Reading

Review the questions on the board. Discuss those that have not been answered and whether they might still be answered when children read the remainder of the selection.

Complete the Master

- Have children reread pages 106–107 with you and look again at the picture of the window box garden. Encourage them to compare their predictions about the colors of the flowers with what the girl and her father planted.

**Selection Master 6
Part 5**

Next, invite children to draw and color their own garden in the window box at the bottom of Master 6. When they have finished, have them share their work with the group. As children share, have them name the flowers in their boxes and the colors they used. If they used flowers or colors named on the master, ask children to point to these words as they say them.

> **Have children read the rest of the selection cooperatively or have them participate in the reading of this selection with the entire class.**

Use AFTER  Interact *with* Literature

 Develop Critical Thinking

Choose a Birthday Gift

Tell children to imagine that they are going to give a birthday gift to someone they care about. Select a volunteer and use the following to model the process of choosing a gift.

- Create a concept map like the one below about the person who will get the gift. Begin by listing things the person likes. Then brainstorm things to make or buy that go with what he or she likes.

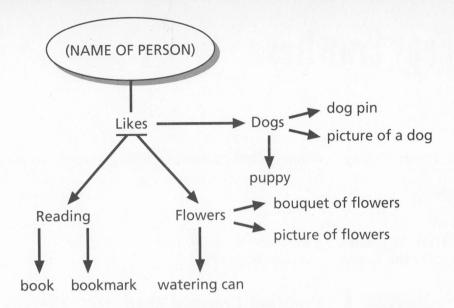

(NAME OF PERSON)

Likes → Dogs → dog pin

Dogs → picture of a dog

Dogs → puppy

Likes → Reading

Likes → Flowers → bouquet of flowers

Flowers → picture of flowers

Reading → book

Reading → bookmark

Flowers → watering can

- Explain that now you have several gifts from which to make a choice. Have children use pictures or written words to create their own concept maps. Invite them to share their maps and to make a final gift choice.

OPTION 2 Develop Fluency: Choral Reading

Read pages 92–95 with children chorally. As you read, emphasize the rhyming words (*great /wait*). Continue with pages 96–99 (*bus/us*), 100–103 (*floor/door*), 104–105 (*thick/mix*), 106–107 (*snow/row*), 108–111 (*street/meet*), 112–113 (*see/jamboree*), 116–119 (*too/you*).

Use AFTER **3** Instruct *and* Integrate

OPTION 1 Developing Comprehension Inferences: Making Predictions

- Remind children that they used clues to figure out many things that the author of this story did not say. Have children turn to pages 94–95. Remind them that they used picture and word clues to figure out that the girl was going to plant a garden. Review those clues with children (the flowers in the picture, the word *garden*, and the fact that in real life people plant flowers in gardens).
- Have children turn to pages 116–117. Review with them what is happening on these pages. Then point out the girl's mother coming through the door. Ask children how they think the mother will feel and what she will do when she sees what has been going on. Ask them what clues in the story help them know that the mother will be surprised and happy.

OPTION 2 Phonics and Spelling: Short *o* and Short *o* Phonograms

Write the following words from the selection on the board: *on, box, stop, mom*. Then have children go on a "word hunt" to find these words in the selection. As they find each word, have them read the sentence in which it appears.

Creepy Crawlies

Use BEFORE Launching the Theme Activities

Theme Concept   **Many creepy crawlies live in the world around us.**

Materials Suggested for the Theme
- Audio Tapes for Creepy Crawlies
- Selection Masters 7 and 8

OPTION 1   Create a Concept Map

Ask children what they think a creepy crawly creature is. Talk with them about insects, small reptiles, and similar creatures. Discuss why people might think of these as creepy crawlies. Create a concept map about the creatures that might be called *creepy crawlies.* Talk with children about types of creatures as well as particular individual creatures. Use the map below as a model to get started. Encourage children to think of as many creepy crawlies as they can.

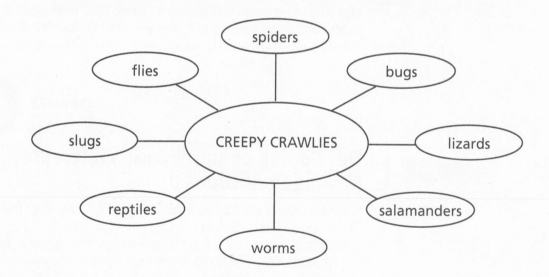

OPTION 2   Make a Creepy Crawly

Have children make up their own creepy crawly creatures. Give each child a piece of construction paper and some crayons and/or markers. Have children draw a creepy crawly they might like to see. Encourage them to be as imaginative as they like. Invite children to share their drawings and describe their creepy crawlies.

The Itsy Bitsy Spider

Use BEFORE  Introduce
the
Literature

OPTION 1 Activate Prior Knowledge

- Read aloud the title and the name of the author-illustrator.
- Talk with children about spiders they have seen. Have them describe the creatures. Then talk about where the spiders live, how they move, what they eat, and so on.
- Ask children if they have ever heard or sung the old rhyme "The Itsy Bitsy Spider," and have children sing or recite it with you. Tell them that this Big Book is a new version of this old rhyme.
- Preview the illustrations in the Big Book with children. Then read aloud the following selection summary.

> The <u>itsy bitsy spider</u> has some interesting adventures. First, she climbs up a <u>waterspout</u>, but she gets <u>washed</u> <u>out</u> of the waterspout in the rain. After the <u>sun</u> dries up the rain, she climbs the waterspout <u>again</u>. Next she gets into the <u>kitchen</u> of the house. She starts to climb the kitchen wall, but a blast of air from a fan makes <u>her</u> fall back to the floor. When the fan is turned <u>off</u>, the spider climbs the wall again. She climbs up a yellow pail, but down she goes again when a mouse <u>flicks</u> her with its <u>tail</u>. No matter how many times she falls, the little spider keeps right on climbing.

(Underlined words are key words in the selection.)

OPTION 2 Picture Walk

- Print the key words on the board and read them aloud.
- Display the cover of the book. Read aloud the title and the name of the author-illustrator. Then use the following suggestions to lead children on a picture walk through the selection. Incorporate key words where possible, pointing to each word on the board as it is mentioned.

DISPLAY

itsy bitsy spider	off
washed out	no
sun	flicked
again	

Pages 4–5 Tell children to find the <u>itsy bitsy spider</u> in the waterspout on page 5. Call attention to the cloudy sky in the illustration and ask children what might happen to the spider when she is in the waterspout.

Pages 6–7 Ask children why the spider now is being <u>washed out</u> of the waterspout.

Pages 8–9 Tell children that now the <u>sun</u> has dried up the rain. Ask what the spider is doing <u>again</u> on page 8. Then point to the illustration on page 9 and tell children that the spider has climbed up a kitchen wall.

Pages 10–11 Ask children what the fan has done to the spider.

Pages 12–13 Explain that now the fan has been turned <u>off</u> and is <u>no</u> longer blowing. Ask what the spider is doing again on page 12. Then point to the illustration on page 13 and ask children what the spider has decided to climb now.

Pages 14–15 Tell children that the mouse has <u>flicked</u> the spider off the pail with its tail. Ask children if they think the spider will climb the pail again, and why or why not.

OPTION 3 Oral Language Development

- Explain that this Big Book contains many words that name things in or around a home.
- Display Big Book pages 4–5. Tell children that this illustration shows the outside of a house. Point out the waterspout and identify it for children. Then ask what else they see. Record children's responses in a concept map. Continue by displaying pages 9–17 and adding children's observatons to the map.

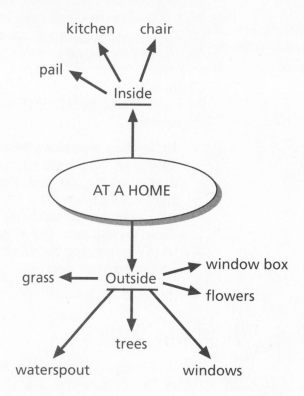

Use BEFORE

② Interact *with* Literature

OPTION 1 Read Aloud for Interest Pages 4–20

Display the Big Book and read aloud the title and name of the author-illustrator. Then read aloud pages 4–20. As you read, pause to ask questions such as, What is the spider doing now? What do you think she will do next? What do you think will happen to her now? How do you know? As you read, run your hand under the words as you read, inviting children to chime in.

Ask children whether they think the spider will try to climb anything else. Talk about what they think might happen if she does try to climb again.

OPTION 2 Use the Audio Tape

Audio Tape for Creepy Crawlies: *The Itsy Bitsy Spider*

As you display the illustrations in the Big Book, have children listen to pages 4–20 of the audio tape. Tell children to listen to find out what happens each time the spider tries to climb something.

Discussion Points
- Discuss what the spider does and what causes each problem that comes up.
- Ask children why the spider keeps climbing different things. Talk with them about what the spider might be looking for or trying to do.
- Talk with children about what they think the spider will try to climb next.

Use AFTER **2** Interact *with* Literature

OPTION 1 ## Develop Fluency: Echo Reading

Reread pages 4–8 with children. Begin by reading the first two lines to the children. Then have them repeat those lines. Do the same with the next two lines. Then read all four lines on page 8 and have children repeat them after you. Continue in this way with the rest of the pages.

OPTION 2 ## Language Experience

Ask children where else the spider might go and what might happen to her there. Write each of the children's ideas on a separate sheet of chart paper. Read them back to children, one at a time. After you read each one, have children tell the story of each new adventure in their own words. Write children's retellings on chart paper. When you have finished, have children read the retellings back to you. Encourage volunteers to draw illustrations for the adventures.

Use AFTER **3** Instruct *and* Integrate

OPTION 1 ## Cause and Effect

- Remind children that a cause is something that makes something else happen. Explain that the cause usually answers the question, "Why did this happen?"
- Make a cause-and-effect chart on the board. Have children fill in the missing parts for each happening.

Cause	What happened?
The sun dried up the rain.	(The spider climbed the waterspout again.)
The fan went off.	(The spider climbed the wall again.)
The spider finished her web.	(The spider rested in the sun.)

OPTION 2 ## Short *i* and Short *i* Phonograms

- Have children read aloud the sentence on page 5. Point out the words *itsy* and *bitsy,* and discuss the vowel sound in the middle of these words. Remind children that these words have the short *i* sound they hear in *sit, spin, ship,* and *spill.*
- Have children search through the selection to find words that have the short *i* sound. Have children read aloud the sentences in which the words appear. *(itsy, bitsy, flicked, his, with, did, in, slipped, rocking, silky)*

Think About Words Strategy

Point to the word *plopped* on page 20 of the Big Book. Model how children could figure out the word if they did not know it.

What makes sense First I'll read the sentence on page 20 of the Big Book. It says, *Down _____ the cat,* and then tells me that the cat went to sleep. From this I know that this word tells me how the cat lay down to sleep.

Sounds for letters When I look at the letters I see *pl* at the beginning of the word. I know that these letters stand for the sound I hear at the beginning of *plant*.

Familiar word parts Now I'll look for word parts that I know. At the end of the word I see the letters *ed*, as in *talked* and *walked*. When I think of words that have these sounds and that tell me how a cat might lay down, I think of *plopped*. It begins and ends with the right sounds, and it has the right meaning.

Picture clues The picture shows the cat sleeping. This helps me be sure that the word is *plopped*. When I read *plopped* in the sentence, it makes sense: *Down plopped the cat.*

Print the word *web* on page 26 and ask volunteers to explain how they would figure out this word if they didn't know it.

What makes sense The word tells what the spider spun.

Sounds for letter At the beginning of the word is the letter *w*, as in *wet* and *we*. At the end is the letter *b,* as in *tub* and *crib*. The word has the short *e* vowel sound, as in *red* and *hen*.

Picture clues a picture of a web

High-Frequency Words

again, no, off, some, sun, try, very

- Write the High-Frequency words. Display and read aloud the pages of the Big Book. Each time you read one of the High-Frequency words, children should raise their hands, point to the word on the board, and read the word aloud.

The Very Hungry Caterpillar

Use BEFORE

1 Introduce *the* Literature

OPTION 1 Activate Prior Knowledge

- Talk with children about butterflies they have seen. Then explain that butterflies begin life as caterpillars. Ask children if they have ever seen a caterpillar. Talk with them about how caterpillars and butterflies are alike and how they are different.
- Read aloud the title and the name of the author-illustrator. Tell children that this is the story of a very, very hungry caterpillar.
- Preview the selection with children. Then, read aloud the following selection summary.

> One morning a tiny, <u>very hungry</u> <u>caterpillar</u> came out of a little egg. As soon as he hatched, the caterpillar started to look for <u>food</u>. Each day the caterpillar <u>ate</u> something different—and more than the day before. On Monday he ate <u>through</u> an apple. On Tuesday he ate through two pears. On Wednesday he had three plums. By Saturday, he was eating everything in sight. He had eaten so much <u>that</u> now he had a <u>stomachache</u>.

- Invite children to tell about times when they have had a stomachache, what caused it, and what it felt like.

(Underlined words are key words in the selection.)

OPTION 2 Picture Walk

DISPLAY
caterpillar
very
hungry
ate
through
stomachache

Print the key words on the board and read them aloud. Then lead children on a picture walk through the selection, incorporating these words where possible. Point to each word on the board as it is mentioned.

Cover Display the cover and read aloud the title and the name of the author-illustrator.
Pages 140–141 Have children locate the little egg. Ask what they think might be inside the egg.
Pages 142–143 Tell children that one Sunday morning a caterpillar hatched from the egg. Ask children to describe the <u>caterpillar</u>. Explain that the tiny caterpillar was <u>very</u> <u>hungry</u>.
Pages 144–145 Ask children what food they see on page 144, and explain that on Monday the caterpillar <u>ate through</u> one apple. Tell children that the next page shows what the caterpillar ate on Tuesday. Have children count how many pears he ate through. (two)
Pages 146–149 Continue in the same way, guiding children to see that the story follows the order of the days of the week and counting order.
Pages 150–153 Ask children what the caterpillar ate on these pages. Then ask how children think he feels (He had a <u>stomachache</u>), and why they think this.

OPTION 3 Calendar

Selection Master 7
Part 5

- Have children identify the foods shown on the master and read the names of those foods aloud with you. Explain that these are some of the foods the caterpillar in this Big Book eats during the first week of his life.
- Point to the calendar grid and read aloud the names of the days of the week.
- Ask children what kind of food they think the caterpillar will eat on Monday. Tell children to cut out that food and tape or paste it under the box for Monday. Continue in the same way with the other days, Tuesday through Friday.
- Save children's work, as well as the remainder of the master, to use again later on.

Use BEFORE 2 — Interact *with* Literature

OPTION 1 — Read Aloud Pages 140–153 or Have Children Listen to the Audio Tape

Audio Tape for Creepy Crawlies: *The Very Hungry Caterpillar*

Discussion Points

- Have children follow along in their anthologies as they listen to pages 140–153 of the selection. Tell them to listen to learn what the very hungry caterpillar found to eat.
- Ask children what the caterpillar found to eat. Write the foods on the board as children name them. Then discuss the order in which he ate these things.
- Ask children if they think a real caterpillar would eat all of these different things. Have children explain their answers.
- Ask children what they think the caterpillar will eat next.

OPTION 2 — Guided or Assisted Reading of Pages 140–153

If, while using the guided reading segments that follow, it becomes clear that children are unable to read this selection silently, assist them in reading each segment aloud together. Then use the discussion points to talk about each segment.

Preview to Set a Purpose for Reading
(Self-Question Strategy)

- Have children read aloud the title and the name of the author-illustrator. Then as children look at the illustrations, encourage them to think of any questions they might have about the selection. Write these questions on the board so you can come back to them later. If children have difficulty thinking of questions, demonstrate how the illustration on pages 146–147 might lead to questions such as *What are these three purple things? Why are there four strawberries on this page? Is the caterpillar eating these things?*

For the first section, students' questions are necessarily based on their preview of the selection. Before students read each subsequent section, discuss any answers they've found to their questions and have students decide if they want to add additional questions to the list. Then have them continue reading to answer their questions.

The Caterpillar is Born (pages 140–143)

Guide the Reading

- Remind children that if there is anything they don't understand as they read, they should go back and read the words and look at the pictures again.
- Have children read pages 140–143.

Discussion Points

- Ask children how the caterpillar felt when he came out of the egg.
- Have children find and read aloud the sentence that tells what the caterpillar did as soon as he came out of the egg.
- Talk with children about how they went back over any parts of the selection they did not understand. Have volunteers discuss examples of what they did.

The Caterpillar Starts to Eat (pages 144–147)

Guide the Reading

- Preview the section and have volunteers identify each type of fruit eaten by the caterpillar.
- Tell children to pay close attention to the illustrations as they read pages 144–147.

Discussion Points

- Have children tell what the caterpillar ate on each day from Monday through Thursday.
- Have volunteers explain how the illustrations helped them know what the caterpillar ate.
- Have children read aloud the phrases that are repeated again and again.
- Ask children if there are any words or other parts of this section that they find confusing. Talk with children about those things.

The Caterpillar Eats Some More   (pages 148–149)

Guide the Reading
(Summarize Strategy)

- Remind children that, as they read, they should think about which parts of the story are the most important ones; then they should put those parts in their own words. Explain that doing this will help them understand and remember the story.
- Have volunteers identify the kind of fruit eaten by the caterpillar on pages 148–149.
- Review the pattern in the story. Remind children that on Monday the caterpillar ate through one apple; on Tuesday, he ate through two pears; and so on.
- Have children read pages 148–149.

Discussion Points

- Ask children what the caterpillar ate on Friday. Then, have children find and read aloud the words that tell how the caterpillar felt after he finished eating on Friday.
- Have children tell in their own words the most important parts of the story so far. Use the following Think Aloud to model the strategy.

> **THINK ALOUD** *When I think of this story, these are the most important parts: A caterpillar was born and was very hungry right away. On Monday he ate one apple; on Tuesday, two pears; on Wednesday, three plums; on Thursday, four strawberries; and on Friday, five oranges. From this I notice that the story follows the order of the days of the week. I also notice that it follows counting order, from one to five.*

The Caterpillar Really Eats   (pages 150–153)

Guide the Reading

- Remind children that, as they read, they should think about what they like or do not like about the selection so far.
- Have volunteers name the foods the caterpillar ate through on pages 150–153.
- Have children read pages 150–153.

Discussion Points

- Ask children what the caterpillar ate on Saturday and how this was different from what he ate on the other days.
- Ask children if they thought about what they liked or didn't like about this selection so far. Have volunteers discuss what they did or didn't like and explain their thinking.
- Talk with children about anything they have read so far that is confusing.
- Ask children what they think the caterpillar will do in the rest of this section.

Reflecting on Purposes for Reading

Review the questions on the board. Discuss those that have not been answered and whether they might still be answered when children read the remainder of the selection.

Complete the Calendar
Selection Master 7
Part 5

- Work with children to compare what they predicted for the caterpillar's food with what the caterpillar actually ate in the selection each day. Each time their prediction matches the selection, have them put a check in the space below the food.
- Next, review pages 150–153 with children, and have them draw and label their favorite food from among the ten foods the caterpillar ate on Saturday.

> **Have children read the rest of the selection cooperatively or have them participate in the reading of this selection with the entire class.**

OPTION 1 Think About Words Strategy

- Use the following to model how to figure out the word *small* on page 158.

Think Aloud

What makes sense When I read the sentence: *He built a ___ house, called a cocoon, around himself,* I know that the word tells about the caterpillar's house.

Sounds for letters The word begins with *sm* as in *smart*. It ends with *ll* as in *tell*. I think the word is *small*. *Small* has the sounds for *sm* at the beginning and the sound for *ll* at the end. It also tells how big a caterpillar's house is. When I try *small* in the sentence, it makes sense: *He built a small house, called a cocoon, around himself.*

Picture clues I can see the cocoon on pages 158–159. I've seen these things in real life before, and I know that they are small. This helps me be sure that the word is *small*.

OPTION 2 Develop Fluency: Choral Reading

Read pages 144–149 chorally with children. As you read, emphasize the repeated words, *But he was still hungry*.

OPTION 1 Sequence

- Remind children that the things that happened in *The Very Hungry Caterpillar* happened in a particular order. Explain that some things happened at the beginning of the story, others happened in the middle, and others happened at the end.
- List the following story events on the board. As you read each event, have children decide whether it happened in the beginning, the middle, or the end of the selection.

  The caterpillar becomes a butterfly.
  The caterpillar eats five oranges.
  The caterpillar comes out of the egg.
  The caterpillar eats a leaf.
  The caterpillar makes a cocoon.

OPTION 2 Short *u* and Short *u* Phonogram

- Have children follow along as you read aloud the sentence on page 142 of *The Very Hungry Caterpillar.* Then say the words *Sunday*, *sun*, and *hungry*, emphasizing the short *u* vowel sound in each word. Remind children that this is the same short *u* vowel sound they hear in the words *cup*, *fun*, *tub*, and *tug*.
- Write the word *tub* on the board and read it aloud. Then have children read it with you. Erase the *t* and ask volunteers to come to the board and make rhyming words by adding different consonants at the beginning of the word (*cub*, *rub*, *stub*, *club*). List the words children make on chart paper.
- Continue in the same way with the words *duck* (*cluck*, *luck*, *stuck*, *truck*); *puff* (*cuff*, *fluff*, *muff*, *stuff*); *hum* (*drum*, *chum*, *gum*, *plum*).
- Have children read the words in the lists. Have volunteers use the words in oral sentences.

A Color of His Own

Use BEFORE  Introduce *the* Literature

 ## Activate Prior Knowledge

- Display the cover and explain that this creature is a chameleon. Explain that African chameleons can change color to match green or brown leaves; American chameleons change colors when something changes around them or when they want to communicate. Have children share what they know about chameleons.
- Preview the selection with children. As they look at the illustrations, discuss whether this selection is about things that happen in real life or about things that are make-believe. Then read aloud the following selection summary.

> **Most animals have a <u>color</u> of their <u>own</u>. But <u>chameleons</u> <u>change</u> color. One day a chameleon decided he wanted a color of his own. So he tried to remain on a leaf. That, he believed, would keep him green forever. When autumn came, the leaf turned yellow, and so did the chameleon. Then the leaf turned red and so did the chameleon. By winter, both the leaf and the chameleon had been blown to the ground, and soon the chameleon was black in the long winter night. When spring came, he walked onto the green grass. There he met another chameleon. He asked, "Won't we ever have a color of our own?"**

(Underlined words are key words in the selection.)

Picture Walk

DISPLAY

own	chameleons
color	thought

- Display the cover and ask children what creature they see in the illustration. Explain that some chameleons change color to match the greens and browns of leaves, while some change color when something around them changes or when they want to communicate.
- Print the key words on the board and read them aloud. Then lead children through the selection, incorporating these words. Point to each word on the board as it is mentioned.

Pages 174–177 Have children name each animal and its color. Explain that each of these animals has its <u>own</u> <u>color</u>.

Pages 178–179 Point to the creatures on these pages and remind children that <u>chameleons</u> change their color. Ask children what colors these chameleons are.

Pages 180–183 Tell children that some chameleons change their color to match what they are near. Point to the chameleon in each illustration. Ask children what color the chameleon is, and why. Explain that a real chameleon could not change to all of these colors and it could not change its color to match a tiger's stripes.

Pages 186–187 Tell children that one day the chameleon <u>thought</u> he would stay green forever if he climbed onto a leaf. Point to the illustration on page 187 and ask if the chameleon was right. Ask children what they think has happened.

- Continue in the same way with pages 188–193. Then ask children what they think might happen after the chameleon meets another creature just like him.

 ## Sentences

Selection Master 8
Part 5

- Remind children that some chameleons change colors to match things around them. Point out the drawings of chameleons in boxes 1, 2, and 3.
- Read the words in box 1 with children. Have them complete the drawing and color it to match the words.
- Continue in the same way with boxes 2 and 3. Tell children to save their work to use again.

OPTION 1 # Read Aloud Pages 174–193 or Have Children Listen to the Audio Tape

Audio Tape for Creepy Crawlies: *A Color of His Own*

Have children follow along in their anthologies as they listen to pages 174–193 of the selection. Suggest that they listen to find out why the chameleon wants a color of his own and what he does to get it.

Discussion Points
- Ask children how the chameleon feels about not having a color of his own.
- Ask how the chameleon tried to get a color of his own. Discuss whether or not his plan has worked so far, and why or why not.
- Ask children what they think will happen now that the chameleon has met someone else like himself.

OPTION 2 # Guided or Assisted Reading of Pages 174–193

If, while you are using the guided reading segments that follow, it becomes clear that children are unable to read this selection silently, assist them in reading each segment aloud together. Then use the discussion points to talk about each segment.

Preview to Set a Purpose for Reading
(Predict/Infer Strategy)
- Read aloud the title and name of the author-illustrator. Then have children preview the illustrations. Ask children what they think will happen in this selection. Write children's predictions on the board so you can come back to them later.
- If children have trouble making predictions, show how the illustrations on pages 188–189 could lead to the following prediction: *On these pages I see the chameleon standing on a leaf and turning red. Then I see the leaves and the chameleon falling through the air. Leaves turn red and fall from the trees in autumn. So I think the chameleon will be on the leaf in autumn, until the leaf falls from the tree.*

> **For the first section, students' predictions are necessarily based on their previews of the selection. Before students read each subsequent section, discuss which of their predictions agreed with what was read and which did not. Have students think about what they've read and decide if they want to revise their original predictions or make new ones.**

Creatures and Their Colors (Pages 174–179)

Guide the Reading
- Remind children to use the Think About Words strategy to help them figure out any words they might not know. Then have children read pages 174–179.

Discussion Points
- Ask children how chameleons are different from the other animals they have read about so far. Have children find and read aloud the words that tell them this. Explain that although chameleons can change colors, they cannot change to the bright colors shown on these pages. Tell children that the author put this in just for fun.
- Talk with children about how the Think About Words strategy helped them figure out words they did not know.

The Chameleon Wants His Own Color (Pages 180–185)

Guide the Reading
(Evaluate Strategy)
- Remind children to think about what they like or don't like about the selection as they are reading it. Then, have children read pages 180–185.

Discussion Points
- Have children find and read aloud the part that explains when the chameleon has stripes. Ask children if they think chameleons really could change to tiger stripes. Be sure children understand that although chameleons can change colors, they cannot change patterns to match animals like tigers. Explain that this is something else the author put in just for fun.
- Ask children why the chameleon decided to stay on a leaf and if this was a good idea.
- Ask children what time of year it probably was when the chameleon climbed onto the green leaf and how they know this.
- Have volunteers discuss what they did or didn't like about the story, and have them explain their thinking. Use the following Think Aloud to model the strategy.

> **THINK ALOUD** *As I was reading, I asked myself, "What do I like about this story?" I like the chameleon because of all the colors it can be. Another question I asked myself was, "How is this story like other stories I've read?" It is like* **The Very Hungry Caterpillar** *because both stories are about small creatures. Both stories have many different, bright colors in the illustrations. I like these stories because I like the little creatures and I like the illustrations.*

- Talk with children about vocabulary or other parts of the selection that were unclear.

The Chameleon Tries Even Harder (Pages 186–189)

Guide the Reading
- Remind children that if there is something they don't understand, they should go back and read the words and look at the pictures again.
- Point to the word *autumn* on page 187. Remind children that the leaves on many kinds of trees change color in autumn, or fall. Then have children read pages 186–189.

Discussion Points
- Ask children how they think the chameleon felt when he started to turn yellow and red.
- Have children read aloud the words that tell what the winter winds did to the chameleon.
- Discuss how children went back over parts of this section that were unclear or confusing. Then discuss any questions or problems children still have with this part of the selection.

The Chameleon Finds a Friend (Pages 190–193)

Guide the Reading
- Remind children that, as they read, they should think about which parts of the story are the most important ones; then they should put those parts in their own words.
- Have children read pages 190–193.

Discussion Points
- Have volunteers find and read aloud what the chameleon said to his new friend.
- Ask children whether or not the chameleon has managed to do anything to solve his problem. Have children suggest ways in which he might solve it.
- Have children tell in their own words the most important parts of the story so far. If children have difficulty summarizing, have them go back to the beginning of the story and page through it, discussing the problem the chameleon has and the most important events.
- Ask children what they think will happen in the rest of the selection. Discuss whether they think the chameleon will get a color of his own.

Reflecting on Purposes for Reading
Review the predictions on the board. Discuss those that did not match the story and whether that was because they were inappropriate or if they might still match the story when children read the remainder of the selection.

Complete the Master
- Have children return to the master. Ask if there are any changes or additions they'd like to make to what they have done for boxes 1–3.

Selection Master 8
Part 5
- Then ask children to think about what the two chameleons might look like in the rest of the selection. Have children color the chameleons to show their predictions.

> **Have children read the rest of the selection cooperatively or have them participate in the reading of this selection with the entire class.**

OPTION 1 ## Critical Thinking: Make a Decision

Use the following to help children find a way to choose their favorite color chameleon.

- Have children go through the selection page by page and identify all the different colors of the chameleon. Then ask children how they might keep track of all these colors. Children may suggest drawing a chameleon in each color, making crayon marks in each color, writing the color names, and so on.
- Discuss children's ideas. Then have the group choose one idea and use it to record the possible color choices.
- Have a volunteer choose the chameleon color(s) on the chart paper he or she likes best. If the volunteer picks more than one color, make a new list of just these new choices. Then ask the volunteer to select his or her favorite(s) from among these favorites. Keep going in this same way until the choice has been narrowed to a single color.
- Explain that narrowing choices in this way is a good way to pick a favorite. Continue with other volunteers or have children work independently to choose their favorite colors.

OPTION 2 ## Develop Fluency: Partner Reading

Divide the group into pairs. Have one child read aloud the left-hand pages while the other reads the right-hand pages. Encourage children to keep the pauses between pages as brief as possible when they change readers.

OPTION 1 ## Fantasy/Realism

- Read aloud pages 192–193. Ask children if what happens on these pages could really happen or if it is make-believe, and how they know.
- Have children page through the selection, looking for things that could happen in real life and things that could only be make-believe. (Possible responses: Real—An elephant is gray. Leaves change color in autumn. A chameleon is green on a green leaf. Make-Believe—A chameleon is striped. A chameleon talks. Mushrooms are red with white polka-dots.)

OPTION 2 ## Double Final Consonants

- Remind children that sometimes two letters at the end of a word stand for one sound. Point out the word *will* on page 185 of *A Color of His Own.* Ask children what letters they see at the end of the word (*ll*) and what sound those letters stand for (/l/).
- Next, remind children that when a word ends with a double consonant, the vowel sound is often short. Ask what vowel sound children hear in *will* (the short *i* sound).
- Have children go through the story looking for words that end in double final consonants (page 177: *all*; page 185: *shall, will*; page 192: *grass*; page 195: *will, still*). Have children read each word aloud and discuss the vowel sound in the word.

Unexpected Guests

Use BEFORE Launching the Theme Activities

Theme Concept | Animals can show up in unexpected places.

Materials Suggested for the Theme
- Audio Tapes for Unexpected Guests
- Selection Masters 9 and 10

OPTION 1 When Have You Been Surprised?

Start a discussion with children about unexpected guests. Ask if anyone or anything has ever come to their homes (or classrooms) unexpectedly. Record children's experiences on chart paper. When finished, read the chart aloud as a group. (Examples: I was surprised when... my neighbor came to visit, a mouse was in the house, the principal came into the classroom.)

OPTION 2 What Guests Would You Like to See?

Ask children to think of some guests whom they wish could visit their classrooms unexpectedly. Write the list on the board or on chart paper. Read the list together when finished.

Guests We Would Like to See

Mickey Mouse
My grandmother
Michael Jordan
Our principal
Red Riding Hood

EEK! There's a Mouse in the House

Use BEFORE

OPTION 1 Activate Prior Knowledge

- Ask children if a fly, bee, mouse, or other creature has ever come into their home for a "visit." Talk with children about what kind of creature it was, what it did, and what people did about it.
- Preview the selection by reading aloud the title and having children look at the illustrations.
- Read aloud the following selection summary.

> When a <u>mouse</u> gets into a little girl's <u>house</u>, she calls, "<u>Send in</u> the cat to chase that rat." But the cat knocks over a lamp, so the girl calls, "Send in the dog." The dog is supposed to <u>catch</u> the cat, but instead, the dog breaks a dish. And now the cat <u>is after</u> the fish. As the girl calls more animals into the house, the animals cause more trouble. Will any of them get the mouse out of the house?

(Underlined words are key words in the selection.)

- Ask children what kind of trouble they think these animals might get into inside a house.

OPTION 2 Picture Walk

DISPLAY

mouse	catch
house	hog
send in	

Display the cover of the Big Book. Read aloud the title and the name of the author-illustrator. Then lead children on a picture walk through the Big Book. Incorporate key words as shown, pointing to each word in the Big Book as it is mentioned.

Pages 2–3 Explain that the girl has just seen the <u>mouse</u> in her <u>house</u>. Have children name everything they see in the illustration. Then ask what they think the girl will do about the mouse.

Pages 4–5 Tell children that the girl called, *Send in the cat to chase that rat.* Ask what the cat is doing. Then ask what other animal children see and where they see it (a dog, outside the window).

Pages 6–7 Explain that now the girl has a dog to <u>catch</u> the cat, but that the dog has broken a dish. Ask children what the cat and the mouse are doing. Then ask what other animal children see and where they see it (a pig, in a picture on the wall).

Pages 8–9 Ask children what animal has come into the house (a pig). Explain that *hog* is another name for a pig. Ask children what the hog is doing. (eating cake). Then ask what the dog, the cat, and the mouse are doing. Ask what animal children think will show up next and how they know.

Continue in the same way with pages 10–17, having children identify the new animal to come into the house and what it is doing. Then have them describe what all the other animals are doing and predict which animal will enter next.

OPTION 3 Oral Language Development

Display Big Book pages 2–3. Point to the mouse in the illustration and to the word *mouse* on page 2. Then have children tell you what they know about mice–what mice look like, where they live, what they eat, and so on. As children respond, record their ideas in a concept map such as the one here.

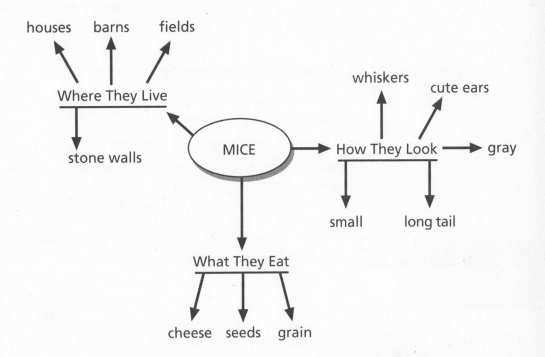

Use BEFORE

2 Interact *with* Literature

OPTION 1 Read Aloud for Interest

- Display the Big Book and read aloud the title and the name of the author-illustrator. Talk with children about what they would do if they suddenly found a mouse in their home.
- Read aloud pages 2–17. As you read, pause to ask questions such as *What animal has come into the house now? What are the other animals doing? What do you think will happen next?*
- Run your hand under the words as you read, inviting children to chime in.
- When you have finished, ask what animal children think will come into the house next and whether or not that animal will get the mouse out of the house.

OPTION 2 Use the Audio Tape

Audio Tape for Unexpected Guests: *EEK! There's a Mouse in the House*

As you display the illustrations in the Big Book, have children listen to pages 2–17 of the audio tape. Tell children to listen to find out what happens each time the girl calls in a new animal.

Discussion Points
- Discuss the girl's problem and why things keeps getting worse and worse in the house.
- Ask children how they could tell ahead of time what animal was coming into the house.
- Talk with children about what animal will come into the house next and what it might do there.

Use AFTER **2** Interact *with* Literature

OPTION 1 Develop Fluency: Echo Reading

Reread pages 2–9 with children. Read the first two lines to the children. Have them repeat the same lines, echoing your intonation and expression. Continue in the same way, reading one entire rhyming segment at a time and having children echo your reading.

OPTION 2 Language Experience

Have children create their own story about a mouse who comes into their classroom.
• Write the following on the board:

> EEK! There's a mouse in the classroom.

• Have children suggest sentences that tell something that happens when the mouse comes to the classroom.
• Write children's responses on the board. Have children practice reading aloud the completed sentences.
• If children seem interested, have them select one sentence to illustrate. Have them write the sentence under their picture.

Use AFTER **3** Instruct *and* Integrate

OPTION 1 Noting Details

• Remind children that noticing details can make a story more interesting and fun to read.
• Display the cover of the Big Book and have children find the cheese in the illustration. Point out that the girl is having a cheese sandwich and that she looks very surprised to see the mouse at the table.
• Ask children what they think the mouse wants. (the cheese) Then as you display the pages of the Big Book, have children find the cheese and tell what is happening to it.

OPTION 2 Long *a* CVC*e*

• Display pages 8–9 of the Big Book. Point to the word *cake* and read it aloud with children. Ask children what vowel sound they hear in the word *cake* (the long *a* sound). Point to the letters that correspond to the consonant-vowel-consonant-*e* pattern in the word and explain that words with this pattern often have a long vowel sound.
• Write the words below on the board. Have children read each word aloud with you and identify the vowel sound. If the word has the long *a* vowel sound, have volunteers point to the letters that correspond to the consonant-vowel-consonant-*e* pattern in the word.

rake	mask
mane	cap
cape	can
cane	plate

• Have children draw pictures illustrating the long *a* words.

OPTION 3 **Think About Words Strategy**

Point to the word *tangled* on page 12 of the Big Book. Model how children could figure out this word if they did not know it.

- **What makes sense** First I'll read the other words in the sentence: *The sheep is _____ in yarn.* From this I know that the word tells what happened to the sheep with the yarn. I think the word might be *wrapped. Wrapped in yarn* makes sense.
- **Sounds for letters** When I look at the word I see the letter *t. T* stands for the sound at the beginning of *take* and *to.* Now I know that the word can't be *wrapped.*
- **Picture clues** The picture shows the sheep with yarn all around it. I know that *tangled* is another word for *wrapped* or *caught. Tangled* begins with the same sound as *take* and *to.* So now I think the word is *tangled.* When I read the sentence, *tangled* makes sense: *The sheep is tangled in yarn.*

Next, point to the word *marched* on page 20. Have volunteers model how they would figure out this word if they didn't know it. Help and guide children as needed.
- **What makes sense** how the cat and cow moved as they went out of the house
- **Sounds for letters** begins with *m* as in *mine* and *my*
- **Picture clues** cow and cat moving together, like marchers in a parade

OPTION 4 **High-Frequency Words**

door, has, rain, stop, them

Pose word riddles to children. Display Big Book pages 18–19 and tell children to guess the word you have in mind. Explain that the word names what you walk through when you go into a house. When children identify the word *door,* have a volunteer find it on the page and read the sentence in which it appears. Continue with these words and clues:

Pages 6–7, has (sometimes means "owns something")
Pages 20–21, ran (means "moved quickly")
Pages 10–11, stop (means "to quit doing something")
Pages 16–17, them (names other people or animals)

There's an Alligator Under My Bed

Use BEFORE 1 Introduce *the* Literature

OPTION 1

Activate Prior Knowledge

- Preview the selection by reading aloud the title and having children look at the illustrations.
- Read aloud the following selection summary.

> Once there was a boy who had an <u>alligator</u> living under his bed. When it was time to go to <u>sleep</u>, the boy had to be careful because the alligator was always there. His parents <u>never</u> <u>saw</u> the alligator. Even so, the boy <u>just</u> knew it was there. One night, the boy decided to do something about the alligator. He got some alligator <u>bait</u> from the kitchen and put it around the house. Then he watched as the alligator came out.

(Underlined words are key words in the selection.)

Discuss whether this selection is about things that are real or things that are make believe.

OPTION 2

Picture Walk

DISPLAY

alligator	sleep
hid	never saw
just	bait

Print the key words on the board and read them aloud. Then lead children on a picture walk through the selection, incorporating these words where possible. Point to the words on the board as they are mentioned.

Pages 48–49 Tell children that this is a selection about how a boy got rid of an <u>alligator</u> that lived under his bed. Talk with children about why they might not be able to see the alligator in the illustration.

Pages 50–51 Explain that whenever the boy was ready to go to <u>sleep</u>, he had to very careful. Point to the board and have children explain why it is there.

Pages 52–53 Ask children if they think an alligator really <u>hid</u> under the boy's bed the way the picture shows.

Pages 54–57 Explain that whenever the boy called for his mom and dad, they <u>never</u> <u>saw</u> the alligator. Ask children why they might not have seen it. Then explain that the boy decided he <u>just</u> had to do something about the alligator.

Pages 58–65 Tell children that the boy decided to use food as <u>bait</u> to get the alligator out from under his bed. Explain that the boy got the food from the kitchen and started making a trail of bait by putting some of the food in the garage. Have children look at the illustrations on these pages and describe where the trail of bait goes. Be sure children understand that the boy made a trail from the garage, down the hall, up the stairs, and back to his bedroom. Then ask children what the boy's plan was for solving his problem.

OPTION 3

Diagram

Selection Master 9
Part 5

- Explain that in this selection a boy got rid of an alligator that lived under his bed by using food as bait.
- Have children look at the illustrations on pages 58–65. Tell children that the boy got the food from the kitchen and made a trail of bait from the garage back up to his bedroom.
- Help children name each room or area of the house shown on the master. Then have children use the illustrations in the selection to help them draw a line through the house to show the trail of bait the boy made.
- Tell children to save their work to use again later on.

OPTION 1

Read Aloud Pages 48–67 or Have Children Listen to the Audio Tape

Audio Tape for Unexpected Guests: *There's an Alligator Under My Bed*

Have children follow along in their anthologies as they listen to pages 48–67 of the selection. Suggest that they listen to find out how the boy in this selection planned to get rid of an alligator that lived under his bed.

Discussion Points
- Ask children how the boy seemed to feel about the alligator.
- Discuss the boy's plan for getting rid of the alligator. Ask children whether they think this plan will work, and why or why not.
- Ask children what they think the alligator will do now and what will happen.

OPTION 2

Guided or Assisted Reading of Pages 48–67

If, while using the guided reading segments that follow, it becomes clear that children are unable to read this selection silently, assist them by reading each segment aloud together. Then use the discussion points to talk about each segment.

Preview to Set a Purpose for Reading
(Predict/Infer Strategy)

Read aloud the title and the name of the author-illustrator. Then have children preview the illustrations. Ask children what they think will happen in this selection. Write their predictions on the board so you can come back to them later. If children have trouble making predictions, show how the illustrations on page 65 could lead to the following prediction: *On this page I see the alligator coming out from under the bed to eat the food the boy has put on the floor. This makes me think that the alligator will follow the food all the way out of the house and into the garage.*

> For the first section, children's predictions are necessarily based on their previews of the selection. Before children read each subsequent section, discuss which of their predictions agreed with what was read and which did not. Have children think about what they have read and decide if they want to revise their original predictions or make new ones.

The Alligator Under the Bed (Pages 48–57)

Guided Reading
- Remind children to use the Think About Words strategy to help them figure out any words they might not know. Then have children read pages 48–57.

Discussion Points
- Have children find and read aloud the words that tell what the alligator did whenever the boy looked for him. Discuss what the author meant by the words *he hid . . . or something.* Guide children to see that the boy was probably not sure why he couldn't see the alligator when he looked for it.
- Ask children if they think there really is an alligator under the boy's bed. Have children explain their reasoning. Ask what details in the selection might give someone the idea that the alligator is real and what details might make someone think that the alligator is only in the boy's imagination.
- Ask children why they think the boy finally decides to do something about the alligator.
- Talk with children about how they used the Think About Words strategy to figure out any words they did not know. Have volunteers model the strategy for the other children.
- Talk with children about vocabulary or other parts of the selection that may have been unclear to them.

Using the Bait (Pages 58–64)

Guided Reading
- Remind children that good readers stop and ask themselves questions to make sure they understand what they are reading. If they don't understand something, they go back to read the words and look at the illustrations again.
- Have children read pages 58–64.

Discussion Points
- Talk with them about what his plan is and whether it seems like a good idea or not.
- Ask children what kind of bait the boy put in the hall. Have children find and read aloud the part that tells about this.
- Talk with children about how they went back over anything that was confusing to them.
- Discuss anything the children still find unclear or confusing in this part of the selection.

The Alligator Comes Out (Pages 65–67)

Guided Reading
(Evaluate Strategy)
- Remind children that, as they read, they should think about what they like or don't like about a selection. Have children read pages 65–67.

Discussion Points
- Ask children where the boy hid when the alligator came out of his room. Have them find and read aloud the words that tell about this.
- Ask children if they think the boy's plan is working, and have them explain their thinking.
- Talk with children about what they like or don't like about the selection so far. Use the following Think Aloud to model the strategy.

> **Think Aloud** *As I was reading I thought about how I feel about this selection. I am enjoying reading it because I like the boy's plan. I think he was brave and smart to think of making a trail of bait to lead the alligator out to the garage. I like that the plan is working and I want to keep reading to find out how the selection ends.*

- Talk about anything children found confusing or unclear.
- Ask children if they think the boy will finally be rid of the alligator and why they think so.

Reflect on the Purposes for Reading
Review the predictions on the board. Discuss those that did not match the story and whether that was because they were inappropriate or if they might still match the story when children read the remainder of the selection.

Complete the Master
- Have children return to Selection Master 9. Give them time to look over their work. Ask them if they would like to make any changes now that they have read part of the selection.
- Have children mark where they think the alligator will go next.

> **Have children read the rest of the selection cooperatively or have them participate in the reading of this selection with the entire class.**

Use AFTER **2** Interact *with* Literature

OPTION **1** **Think About Words Strategy**

Use the following to model how to figure out the word *sandwich* on page 61.

- **What makes sense** First I'll read the sentence: *I put a peanut butter ___, some fruit, and the last piece of pie in the garage.* I can tell that this word names a food that the boy got from the refrigerator. It is a food made with peanut butter.
- **Sounds for letters** I see the letter *s* at the beginning of the word. This tells me that the word begins with the same sound as *said* and *see*.
- **Picture clues** Now I'll look for clues in the picture. On the floor of the garage I see two slices of bread with some brownish stuff between them. That looks like a peanut butter sandwich. So now I know that the word is *sandwich*.

Next, point to the word *slammed* on page 72. Have volunteers model how they would figure out this word if they didn't know it. Help and guide children as needed.

- **What makes sense** tells what the boy did with the door
- **Sounds for letters** begins with *sl* as in *sled* and *slip*
- **Familiar word parts** ending *-ed*
- **Picture clues** the door is shut

Develop Fluency: Echo Reading

Read the sentence on page 49 aloud, emphasizing slightly the phrase *used to be*. Have children echo your expression and intonation as they read the sentence aloud. Continue with the following pages, having children echo the particular features indicated.

Page 53—pause indicated by points of ellipsis
Page 54—emphasis on the phrase *I just had to do something*
Page 65—emphasis on the phrase *Sure enough*
Page 72—tone indicating triumph
Page 73—tone in the phrase *There wasn't even any mess to clean up,* indicating that the boy is pleased with himself
Page 75—emphasis on the word *trouble*

Use AFTER

Story Structure and Summarizing

Remind children that knowing the important parts of a story can help readers remember it and retell it to someone else. Then help children identify the most important parts of *There's an Alligator Under My Bed.*

- Have children name the characters in the story and tell where the story takes place. Record children's responses on the chalkboard.
- Next, help children identify the boy's problem and the steps he takes to solve it. Record these responses on the chalkboard.
- Finally, have children tell in their own words what happens at the end of the story as you record this information.

Invite volunteers to use the information on the board to retell the story in their own words.

Long *i* CVC*e*

- Display pages 50–51 of the selection. Point to the word *time* and read it aloud with children. Ask children what vowel sound they hear in the word *time* (long *i*). Point to the letters that make up the consonant-vowel-consonant-*e* pattern in the word. Tell children that words with this pattern often have a long vowel sound.
- Write the words below on the board.

    bike   trick   hill   dime   side   lip   nine   size

  Have children read each word aloud with you and identify the vowel sound. If the word has the long *i* vowel sound, have volunteers point to the letters that correspond to the consonant-vowel-consonant-*e* pattern in the word.

- Finally, have children find another long *i* word that has the CVC*e* pattern on page 59. *(like)*

If You Give a Moose a Muffin

Use BEFORE **1** Introduce *the* Literature

 Activate Prior Knowledge

- Display the cover and read aloud the title and the names of the author and the illustrator.
- Ask children what they see on the cover illustration. Point out the muffins and tell children that this is a funny story about some of the silly things that might happen if a boy gave a muffin to a moose. Have children brainstorm a list of all the funny things that might happen if *they* gave a moose a muffin.
- Then read aloud the following selection summary.

> If a boy gave a <u>moose</u> a <u>muffin</u>, the moose might want <u>blackberry</u> <u>jam</u> for his muffin. Then the moose might want more muffins. This might cause the boy to have to go to the store to buy muffin <u>mix</u>. Then the moose might want to go with the boy. Because it's chilly <u>outside</u>, the moose might <u>ask</u> to borrow a sweater. These are just *some* of the things that might happen if a boy gave a moose a muffin.

(Underlined words are key words in the selection.)

OPTION 2 **Picture Walk**

DISPLAY

moose	*jam*
muffin	*mix*
blackberry	

Display key selection words. Then guide children on a picture walk through the selection, incorporating key selection words when possible. Point to the words as they are mentioned.

Pages 86–87 Point to the illustration and ask children what the boy is doing. Ask what they think the <u>moose</u> might do with the <u>muffin</u>.

Page 88 Ask how the boy looks when he sees the moose coming inside. Have children offer their ideas about why the moose might come inside the house.

Page 89 Explain that the boy is looking in the refrigerator for some <u>blackberry</u> <u>jam</u> to go with the moose's muffin.

Pages 90–91 Point out the sequence of the three illustrations on these pages. Ask children what they think is happening.

Pages 92–93 Explain that the moose has eaten all the muffins and still wants more. Tell children that the boy will have to go to the store for more muffin <u>mix</u>. Ask children how the muffin mix will help.

Continue this kind of discussion to guide children through the rest of the selection.

 Graphic Organizer

**Selection Master 10
Part 5**

Help children identify each picture under the words <u>What the Moose Asked For</u>. (socks, cardboard and paint, sheet) Tell children that the moose used each of these items to make something. Have them guess what the moose made. Tell children they will write what the moose made with each item after they read the selection.

Direct children's attention to the words and page numbers. Tell children that these are words they will read in the selection. Read the words together. Then have children turn to page 87 and find the picture of the muffin. Ask them to use the picture to describe how a muffin looks. Continue in the same way with other words.

Read Aloud Pages 86–108 or Have Children Listen to the Audio Tape

Audio Tape for Unexpected Guests: *If You Give a Moose a Muffin*

Have children follow along in their anthologies as they listen to pages 86–108 of the selection. Suggest that they listen to learn what might happen if a boy gives a moose a muffin.

Discussion Points
- Ask what happened when the boy gave the moose a muffin.
- Discuss the different things the boy had to get for the moose. Talk about what the moose did with each thing.
- Ask if the boy seemed to be having a good time with the moose. Have them point out details that support their ideas.
- Ask children what they think the moose will want next.

Guided or Assisted Reading of Pages 86–108

If, while using the guided reading segments that follow, it becomes clear that children are unable to read this selection silently, assist them in reading each segment aloud together. Then use the discussion points to talk about each segment.

Preview to Set a Purpose for Reading
(Self-Question Strategy)

Have children preview the selection. As children look at the illustrations, talk with them about questions that come to mind. Write their questions on the board. If children have difficulty thinking of questions, demonstrate how the illustration on pages 98–99 might cause them to ask questions such as, *What is the moose doing with puppets? Why are boy and moose hurrying around? Why do they have pieces of cardboard and boxes of paint?* Have children read pages 86–108 to find answers to their questions.

> For the first section, children's questions are necessarily based on their previews of the selection. Before children read each subsequent section, discuss any answers they found to their questions and have children decide if they want to add additional questions to the list. Then have them continue reading to answer their questions.

The Moose and the Muffin   (Pages 86–94)

Guide the Reading
- Briefly discuss the Think About Words strategy with children. Remind them to use the strategy to figure out words they do not know.
- Have children read pages 86–94.

Discussion Points
- Ask what is the first thing that might happen if you give a moose a muffin.
- Have children read aloud the sentences on pages 90–91 that tell what the moose will do when he eats the muffin.
- Ask why the moose will ask to borrow a sweater.
- Discuss what will happen when he puts on the sweater.
- Have the children who used the Think About Words strategy demonstrate what they did. If children are still confused about anything in this section, discuss and clarify as neccessary.

The Moose and the Puppet Show (Pages 95–102)

Guide the Reading
- Remind children that, as they read, they should ask themselves questions to make sure they understand what they are reading. Point out that if something is confusing to them they should reread that part and look again at the pictures to try to clear up their confusion.
- Have children read pages 95–102.

Discussion Points
- Have a child read aloud the sentence on page 95 that tells what the button will make the moose think about.
- Discuss what the moose will do when he remembers the puppets his grandmother used to make.
- Ask children why the moose will want to have a puppet show.
- Have children describe how the boy and the moose will make scenery for the puppet show.
- Ask if anyone was confused about something in this section. Have them share what they did to clear up the confusion.

The Moose and the Sheet (Pages 103–108)

Guide the Reading
(Summarize Strategy)
- Remind children that stopping from time to time to summarize what they are reading will help them remember a selection and makes it easier for them to talk about it with someone else.
- Have children read pages 103–108.

Discussion Points
- Ask why the moose will ask for a sheet.
- Discuss why he'll ask for soap to wash the sheet.
- Have a volunteer find and read aloud the sentence on page 107 that tells what the moose will probably want to do with the wet shirt.
- Ask volunteers to demonstrate how they would retell what they have read so far. If necessary, use the Think Aloud below to demonstrate how the important parts of this selection could be retold.

    Think Aloud *When I think about this selection, these are the most important things I remember: If you give a moose a muffin, the moose will want jam, more muffins, a sweater, a needle and thread, some old socks, some cardboard and paints, and a shirt. I could summarize this by saying, "If you give a moose a muffin, he will want lots of other things."*

- Discuss any vocabulary or events that children found confusing.
- Ask children what they think the moose will do next.

Reflect on the Purposes for Reading
Review the predictions on the board. Discuss those that did not match the story and whether that was because they were inappropriate or if they might still match the story when children read the remainder of the selection.

Complete the Master
Have children return to the master. Discuss with them what the moose made with each of the items he asked for. Ask children to find those words on the page and write them on the correct lines.

> Have children read the rest of the selection cooperatively or have them participate in the reading of this selection with the entire class.

OPTION 1   Develop Critical Thinking: Create a Story

Help children develop a story for their own tale about what would happen if they gave a cow a cookie. Ask children to think of the first thing that might happen. Then help them think what that event might cause to happen next. Continue helping children identify how each new event leads to another. Record children's ideas on the board. After children have identified several events in their story, have them reread the story together.

OPTION 2   Develop Fluency: Partner Reading

Have partners read pages 87–95, with one child reading the left-hand pages and the other, the right.

OPTION 1   Inferences: Making Predictions

- Remind children that they used clues to figure out many things that the author of this selection did not say. Remind children that, as they read, they probably asked themselves questions such as, What kind of trouble will the moose cause next? I think he will see something else that he will want. What could it be?
- Have children turn to pages 112–114. Review what happens on these pages. Then point out the boy's mother coming through the door. Ask children how they think she will feel and what she will do when she sees what has been going on. Have them give reasons for their responses.

OPTION 2   Long *o* and Long *u:*   CV, CVCe

Write the following words on the board: *so, home, use.* Have children locate these words on pages 89 and 106, and take turns reading aloud the sentences that the words appear in. Point out the CV and CVCe pattern in the words. Remind children that words with these patterns often have a long vowel sound. Have children suggest other words that fit this pattern. Write children's suggestions on the board and work with them to find the vowels and consonants in the words. Remind children that words with these patterns often have a long vowel sound.

Big and Little

Use BEFORE **Launching the Theme Activities**

Theme Concept **Size can affect how we do things.**

Materials Suggested for the Theme
- Audio Tapes for Big and Little
- Selection Masters 11 and 12

OPTION 1 What is Big? What is Little?

Discuss the words *big* and *little* with children. What things can they think of that are big? What things can they think of that are little? Write each word children think of on an index card. Then make sentence strips like the ones below. Ask volunteers to choose a card and insert it into an appropriate sentence strip. Help children read the completed sentence aloud.

A _____ is big.
A _____ is little.

OPTION 2 How Else Can You Say Big?

Explain to children that two words can sometimes mean the same thing (for example, *sleepy* and *tired* or *happy* and *glad*). Since the new theme is called *Big and Little,* have children brainstorm as many words as they can that mean *big* and *little.* Record the words on a chart like the one below.

Big	Little
huge	small
enormous	teeny
large	tiny
gigantic	eency
tall	weency

If the Dinosaurs Came Back

Use BEFORE  **1** Introduce *the* Literature

OPTION 1 ## Activate Prior Knowledge

- Read aloud the title and the name of the author-illustrator. Discuss with children what they know about dinosaurs: What are they? How do they look? How long ago did they live? How do children know about dinosaurs? Make sure that children understand that dinosaurs lived on the earth long before people did and that dinosaurs have not lived on the earth for a very long time.
- Print the words *Helpful, Fun,* and *Scary* on the board. Read the words. Ask if children think it would be helpful, fun, or scary if the dinosaurs came back. Have children explain why they think as they do.
- Next have a volunteer name one thing that might happen if the dinosaurs came back. Have the group decide whether this is something helpful, something fun, or something scary, and place a check under the corresponding word on the board. Continue until all children have contributed an idea. Count up the checks to see if, as a group, children think having the dinosaurs back would be helpful, fun, or scary.
- Have children preview the illustrations and determine whether this selection tells about helpful, fun, or scary things that happen when the dinosaurs come back. Have children give examples that support their opinions. Then read aloud the following selection summary.

> **If the <u>dinosaurs came back</u>, they could be a big help to <u>people</u>. They could <u>carry</u> people from place to place. They could help people <u>build</u> things. They could help people have fun. They would even make great pets for people who <u>love</u> dinosaurs.**

(Underlined words are key words in the selection.)

 ## Picture Walk

DISPLAY
dinosaurs _____
back _____
work _____
people _____

Display the Big Book and read aloud the title and the name of the author-illustrator. Use suggestions such as those shown below to guide children on a picture walk through the selection. Incorporate key words, pointing to each word in the Big Book as it is mentioned.

Cover Point out the dinosaurs in the illustration as well as the tall buildings and buses and cars. Ask children why this is a strange illustration. Make sure students understand that the last dinosaur left the earth long before there were any people, cars, or buses.

Page 7 Point out the boy in the illustration. Tell children that this boy has a dream about <u>dinosaurs</u>. He dreams that the dinosaurs come <u>back</u> to earth. The selection tells what happens when the dinosaurs come back.

Pages 8–9 Point out the people seated on top of the dinosaur and explain to children that these people are on their way to <u>work</u>. Ask children if they think a dinosaur, a bus, or a car would be better for taking <u>people</u> to work and why.

Pages 10–11 Discuss what the dinosaurs on these pages are doing. Ask how grass usually gets cut and how painters usually reach the tall places on a house. Ask children why dinosaurs would be particularly helpful for these jobs.

Continue guiding children through pages 12–22, discussing what the dinosaurs are doing and why the dinosaur is so well suited for each job.

OPTION 3 Oral Language Development

Tell children that this selection contains several words that name jobs. Display Big Book page 11 and ask what the man in this picture is called. Write the words *house painter* on the board. Follow the same procedure with the following words:

> *Page 13: farmer*
> *Page 14: lumberjack*
> *Page 16: firefighters*
> *Page 24: librarian*
> *Page 25: dentist*

Briefly discuss with children what they know about each job listed on the board. Then whisper the name of one of the jobs to each child. Have children demonstrate through actions and words how they would perform each job. Have the other children identify the job that is being demonstrated.

Use BEFORE **2** Interact *with* Literature

OPTION 1 Read Aloud for Interest

Read aloud the title and the name of the author-illustrator. Discuss the cover illustration with children. Invite children to follow along as you read aloud pages 6–22. Discuss which of the things the dinosaurs did that children think would be the most helpful or the most fun and why.

Tell children that the rest of the selection tells what is the very best thing about the dinosaurs coming back to earth. Have students predict what the very best thing might be.

OPTION 2 Use the Audio Tape

Audio Tape for Big and Little: *If the Dinosaurs Came Back*

Have children listen to pages 6–22 as you display the pages of the Big Book. Tell children to listen to find out what jobs usually done by people are done by dinosaurs. Tell children to pay attention to the pictures to see how the dinosaurs do these jobs.

Discussion Points
- Ask children what a farmer would use to plow his fields. Then ask how the dinosaur plowed the field.
- Ask what a lumberjack would use to cut down a tree, and how the dinosaurs cut down the trees.
- Discuss how the dinosaurs in this selection helped people have fun.

Use AFTER **2** Interact *with* Literature

OPTION 1 Develop Fluency: Assisted/Choral Reading

Reread the selection with children. Remind them that the words *When the dinosaurs came back . . .* appear several times. Invite children to read aloud these words as a group. Then assign each child one or more pages of the story to read aloud with you. Base the assistance you provide to each child on the amount of support needed.

OPTION 2 Language Experience

Have children create their own story about what would happen if the dinosaurs came to their classroom.

Write the words *If dinosaurs came to our classroom, they* _____. on the board. Then have children take turns finishing the sentence with something that might happen if dinosaurs came to the classroom. Write children's responses on the board. Have children practice reading aloud the completed sentences.

If children seem interested, have them select one sentence to illustrate. Have them write the sentence under their picture.

Use AFTER **3** Instruct *and* Integrate

OPTION 1 Making Generalizations

Making Generalizations

Tell children that they can use the pictures of the dinosaurs in this story to figure out things about other dinosaurs. Print the following sentences on the board, underlining as shown:

<u>Most</u> dinosaurs have _____.
<u>Most</u> dinosaurs have long _____.
<u>Some</u> dinosaurs have _____.
<u>Some</u> dinosaurs have long _____.

Point out the underlined word *most* in the first sentence. Have children look through the illustrations and ask what the pictures show them that most dinosaurs have. Follow the same procedure for the other sentences. After the sentences have been completed, have children explain how the pictures show what these statements say.

OPTION 2 Long *e: e, ee*

Print the words below on the board.

h<u>e</u>   f<u>ee</u>d   s<u>ee</u>s

Point out the underlined letter(s) in each word. Then pronounce each word, emphasizing the long *e* sound in each word. Tell children that the letters *e* and *ee* in these words stand for the long *e* sound.

Direct children's attention to page 10 of the selection. Ask them to find a word on this page that rhymes with *he*. Print *we* on the board under *he*. Then ask children to think of another word that rhymes with *we* and *he*. (*be, she, me*) Write that word on the board and have children read the list of rhyming words.

Ask children to find a word on page 10 that rhymes with *feed*. Print the word *need* on the board under *feed*. Then ask children to think of another word that rhymes with *feed* and *need*. (*seed, weed*) Write children's responses on the board and have children read aloud the list of rhyming words.

Direct children's attention to page 14. Ask them to find a word on the page that rhymes with *sees*. Print the word *trees* under *sees*. Ask children to think of another word that rhymes with *trees* and *sees*. (*bees*) Write that word on the board and have children read aloud the list of rhyming words.

OPTION 3

Think About Words Strategy

Print the word *beach* on the board, then direct children to the sentence on page 19. Model for children what you would do if you didn't know this word.

What makes sense First, I'll read the rest of the sentence. From the other words in the sentence, I can tell that this word names a place where swimmers go.

Sounds for Letters I know the sound for *b* is the sound I hear at the beginning of *bed* and I know the sound for *ch* is the sound I hear at the end of the word *teach*. I see the letters *ea* and I know that these letters stand for the long *e* sound as in the word *read*.

Picture Clues In the picture I see the ocean and I see the sand beside the ocean. I know that the land beside the ocean is called the *beach*. That must be the word. I'll read the sentence again and see if the word *beach* makes sense. Yes, it does. The word is *beach*.

Have children take turns demonstrating how they would use the Think About Words strategy to figure out the following words:

> Page 11: ladders
> Page 12: robbers

Provide clarification and feedback as necessary.

OPTION 4

High-Frequency Words

DISPLAY

about

build

read

work

always

new

take

Print each High-Frequency word on a card. Give each child a card and ask children to find the words on their cards in the selection. Have children write the sentence in which their word appears on a piece of paper. Ask children to exchange their sentence with a classmate. Have children take turns reading aloud the sentence they are given.

George Shrinks

Use BEFORE

Introduce
the
Literature

OPTION 1 Activate Prior Knowledge

- Ask if anyone has ever had clothing shrink in the washer or dryer. Have volunteers describe what happened. Then read aloud the title of the story and the name of the author-illustrator. Explain that George wakes up one morning to find he has shrunk. He is now very small.
- Read aloud the following selection summary.

> While George was asleep, he <u>dreamt</u> that he was very, very <u>small</u>. He woke up to find that it was true. Before he got out of bed, he saw a note from his <u>parents</u>. The note told him all the things his parents wanted him to do while they were gone. Each of these things became an adventure because of George's new size. George sat on a faucet while brushing his teeth. He took his bath while riding in a toy boat. He washed the dishes by skiing down plates on a sponge. George even got a ride on his little brother's back. But there were dangers too. As George tried out the things he can do now that he is small, he frightened the family cat.

(Underlined words are key words in the selection.)

- Encourage children to share times when they have felt very small. What did they like about the experience? What did they dislike about feeling small?

OPTION 2 Picture Walk

DISPLAY

dreamt

small

parents

Write the key words on the board and read them aloud. Then guide children through the illustrations, discussing what children think is happening in each one. Incorporate the key words into the discussion, pointing to each word on the board as it is mentioned.

Page 129 Tell children that the boy holding the teddy bear is George. Ask children to describe him. Explain that George <u>dreamt</u> that he was <u>small.</u> To find out what happens when he wakes up, have children look for George and his stuffed bear on the pages that follow.
Pages 130–131 Ask children what seems to have happened to George and how they can tell this. Then point out the sheet of paper on George's night table. Explain that it is a note from George's <u>parents</u>. It lists the things his mother and father want him to do while they are gone.
Pages 132–133 Ask children what George is doing on page 132 and what problem he has doing it. Then ask why George might be staying close to the wall in the picture on page 133.
Pages 134–145 For each illustration, have volunteers tell what George is doing and how he does it now that he is very small. Ask children if they think George is having fun being small, and have them use the illustrations to explain their answers.

OPTION 3 Predictions

**Selection Master 11
Part 5**

- Ask children what the word *shrink* means. Write their ideas on the board.
- Have children name chores they do at home. Ask how they might do these things if they were to shrink to a very small size.
- Tell children that even though George has shrunk to a very small size he has chores to do. Have children follow along as you read the list of George's chores on Master 11. Have children choose two of his chores and predict how a small George might do them. Have children write one chore in each box and draw a picture of how George will do that chore.
- Save children's work to return to later on.

OPTION 1

Read Aloud Pages 129–147 or Have Children Listen to the Audio Tape

Audio Tape for Big and Little: *George Shrinks*

As children listen to the selection, have them follow along in their anthologies. Suggest they listen to find out what George does when he wakes up and finds that he is very small.

Discussion Points
- Have children name the things George does and describe how he does each thing.
- Discuss how George seemed to feel about being very small.
- Discuss how children think George's little brother feels about the change in George, and how they think the family's cat feels about the change.

OPTION 2

Guided or Assisted Reading of Pages 129–147

If, while using the guided reading segments that follow, it becomes clear that children are unable to read this selection silently, assist them by reading each segment aloud together. Then use the discussion points to talk about each segment.

Preview to Set a Purpose for Reading
(Self-Question Strategy)
- Have children preview the selection by reading the title and looking at the illustrations. Ask them to think of questions about the story. Write their questions on the board.
- If children have difficulty thinking of questions, model how the illustration on page 130 might lead to such questions as *Why is George so very small? Why is George's teddy bear so much bigger than he is? What is in the note on his night table?*

> For the first section, children's predictions are necessarily based on their previews of the selection. Before students read each subsequent section, discuss which of their predictions agreed with what was read and which did not. Have students think about what they've read and decide if they want to revise their original predictions or make new ones.

George Finds He Has Shrunk (Pages 129–135)

Guide the Reading
(Monitor Strategy)
- Remind children that good readers check to see if they understand the story as they read. If they are confused, reread or read ahead and use the illustrations for clues. Suggest that children look carefully at the pictures if they are confused by anything in this story.
- Have children read pages 129–135.

Discussion Points
- Ask children to find and read aloud the words on page 129 that tell what George dreamt and what he found out when he woke up.
- Have children explain what was in the note that George's parents left him. Have them use the pictures to describe how George does each of the things his parents ask him to do.
- Ask children if anything they read was confusing. Ask volunteers to show how they cleared up their confusion. If necessary, model the Monitor strategy using the Think Aloud below.

> **Think Aloud** *I was confused when I read page 131. I saw quotation marks but I did not know who was talking. When I reread pages 130 and 131, I found that George's parents left him a note and that the quotation marks tell what the note says.*

George Begins His Day (Pages 136–139)

Guide the Reading
- Tell children to look carefully at the illustrations as they read this section because the pictures tell what really happens when George tries to do what his parents ask.
- Remind children to use the Think About Words strategy to help them figure out unfamiliar words. Suggest questions they can ask themselves when they come to a word they don't know: What makes sense? What are the beginning sounds? What word parts do I know? What clues can I find by looking at the pictures?
- Have children read pages 136–139.

Discussion Points
- Have children describe how George cleans his room and then goes to get his little brother.
- Discuss with children how they think George's little brother feels about the change. What is he thinking as he watches his big brother relax on a spoon as he eats his breakfast?
- Have children read aloud the words that tell what George's parents told him to eat. Then have children describe George's breakfast and decide if it was the kind of breakfast his parents told him to have.
- Have a volunteer use the illustration on page 139 to explain how George washed the dishes.
- Have volunteers explain how they used the Think About Words strategy to figure out unfamiliar words.
- Encourage children to share anything in the story that is still confusing to them. Clarify and discuss as needed.

George Does His Chores (Pages 140–143)

Guide the Reading
- Tell children to continue to pay attention to the way George does things so they can summarize what has happened in the story so far. Then have children read pages 140–143.

Discussion Points
- Discuss how George takes out the garbage and who helps him.
- Ask children to describe the way the cat seems to feel about George. Encourage volunteers to use the illustrations on pages 141 and 143 to support their answers.
- Ask children how being small seems to turn watering plants and feeding fish into adventures. Have children count the toads George sees as he waters the plants. Discuss whether he would see the toads if he were larger.
- Have volunteers take turns summarizing what has happened in the story so far.

George Checks the Mail and Gets Fresh Air   (Pages 144–147)

Guide the Reading
- Encourage children to think about how they feel about George as they read the next section. Does he seem real? Why or why not? Would children do things differently if they shrunk as George did? What things would they like to do the same way?
- Have children read pages 144–147.

Discussion Points
- Ask children to use the picture on page 144 to tell what George finds in the mail.
- Have volunteers describe how George decides to get fresh air.
- Ask children who is watching George as he plays outside. Have children decide what the two characters are thinking as they watch him and why.
- Discuss what children think of George and of the way he does things. Do they like him? Why or why not? Would they like to do what he does? Would they do anything differently?
- Ask children what new questions they have as they watch George fly back into the house. Tell children they will find the answers when they read the rest of the story.

Reflect on the Purposes for Reading
Review the predictions on the board. Discuss those that did not match the story and whether that was because they were inappropriate or if they might still match the story when children read the remainder of the selection.

Complete the Master
Have children return to their pictures and compare their predictions with what George did in the story. Discuss parts of the story that surprised children.

OPTION 1 Develop Critical Thinking: Application

- Have children think of other adventures a very small George might have. For example, ask them to imagine what might happen if George were to shrink on a school day. Have children begin by listing the things they do at school. Write their ideas on the board. Then ask them to think about how a tiny George would do each of these activities.
- Ask each child to choose one activity from the list and draw a picture showing how a tiny George would do it. Ask children to write or dictate captions for their pictures. Encourage them to share their work with the group.
- Have the group organize the pictures into a book and choose an appropriate title for it.

OPTION 2 Develop Fluency: Choral Reading

Have children reread the selection chorally in small groups. Demonstrate for them how to keep the pauses between pages to a minimum and then have the groups practice this, rereading the entire selection several times.

OPTION 1 Compare and Contrast

Tell children that noticing how things are alike or different can help them understand and enjoy what they read. Have children compare the picture on page 129 with the one on page 130. Begin by writing the following on the board. Then ask children to fill in the details.

How the Pictures Are Alike
Both show ___(George in bed)___.
Both show ___(his teddy bear)___.

How the Pictures Are Different
In one, George is big and in the other he is ___(small)___.
In one, the bear is smaller than George and in the other it is _(larger than George)_.

Follow a similar procedure with the picture on page 151 and the one on page 153.

OPTION 2 Vowel Pairs: *ea, oa, ow*

Print the word *eat* on the board and have children read it with you. Ask what vowel sound children hear in the word *eat.* (long e) Underline the vowel pair *ea* and remind children that *ea* can stand for the long e sound.

Next print the words *boat* and *grow* on the board. Read aloud each word and ask children what vowel sound they hear (long o). Have volunteers underline the letters that stand for the long o sound in each word.

Display the following sentences and read them aloud. Call attention to each underlined word. Have volunteers identify the vowel sound and tell what letters stand for that sound.

After George shrinks, he <u>grows</u> again.
When George shrinks, he can sail in a toy <u>boat</u>.
When George shrinks, he can use a spoon for a <u>seat</u>.

The Tug of War

Use BEFORE **1** Introduce *the* Literature

OPTION 1 Activate Prior Knowledge

- Read aloud the title and the names of the author and the illustrator. Encourage children to share any experiences they have had playing tug of war.
- Tell children that this story is a play. Discuss with them how reading a play is different from reading a story. Use page 172 to point out how the names of the characters tell who is speaking. Then point to the word *shouting* and explain that this is a direction. It tells the reader how to read the words the character says. Call attention also to the sign at the top of the page. Read it aloud and explain that this information tells the reader that the scene, or setting, has changed and what the new setting is.

> **Tapidou is tired of being teased by Elephant and Hippo. They make fun of him because he is a possum and so much smaller than they are. So Tapidou tells them that even though he is small, he is really very strong. But Elephant and Hippo just laugh at him. One day Tapidou decides to teach Elephant and Hippo a lesson. He asks each of them to have a tug of war with him. Can Tapidou really win and prove himself stronger than the mighty Elephant and Hippo?**

(Underlined words are key words in the story.)

- Have children share what they know about possums (or opossums), hippos, and elephants.

OPTION 2 Picture Walk

DISPLAY
possum
mighty
tug of war

Write the key words on the board and read them aloud. Then guide children through the illustrations, discussing what they think might be happening in each one. Whenever possible, incorporate the key words into the discussion, pointing to each word on the board as it is mentioned.

Page 169 Point out the little possum, Tapidou, next to the mighty elephant and hippo. Ask which animal children think would be the mightiest, or strongest, and which would be the weakest.
Pages 174–175 Explain that Tapidou has just told Elephant and Hippo that he is the strongest of the three. Ask children what they think Elephant and Hippo are doing or saying about that.
Pages 176–177 Ask children what they think is happening in this picture. Will Tapidou really have a tug of war with Elephant?
Pages 178–179 Ask children what they think is happening now. Who do they think will win the tug of war?

OPTION 3 Problem-Solution Chart

Selection Master 12
Part 5

- Tell children that in this story Tapidou, a possum, has a problem. The elephant and hippo make fun of him because he is so small.
- Read aloud the problem and discuss it with children.
- Discuss with children ways Tapidou might be able to solve his problem. Have them draw or write their ideas in the left-hand box.
- Tell children that after the reading they will write what Tapidou does in the story in the box at the right.

OPTION 1 Read Aloud Pages 167–183 or Have Students Listen to the Audio Tape

Audio Tape for Big and Little: *The Tug of War*

As children listen to the selection, have them follow along in their anthologies. Suggest they listen to find out who has a tug of war and why.

Discussion Points
- Discuss who the three animals are in the story.
- Ask children to describe the problem Tapidou is having.
- Have children explain what Tapidou does to try to make Elephant and Hippo think that he is the strongest one of them all.

OPTION 2 Guided or Assisted Reading of Pages 167–183

If, while using the guided reading segments that follow, it becomes clear that children are unable to read this selection silently, assist them by reading each segment aloud together. Then use the discussion points to talk about each segment.

Preview to Set a Purpose for Reading
(Predict/Infer Strategy)
- Have children preview the selection by reading the title and looking at the illustrations. Ask them to make predictions about who will have a tug of war, why they will have a tug of war, and who will win. Record children's predictions on the board.
- If children have difficulty thinking of predictions, model how the illustration on pages 176–177 might lead to predictions such as *I think the little possum will have a tug of war with the elephant. I think the elephant will win because he is bigger.*

> For the first section, students' predictions are necessarily based on their previews of the selection. Before students read each subsequent section, discuss which of their predictions agreed with what was read and which did not. Have students think about what they've read and decide if they want to revise their original predictions or make new ones.

Tapidou and Elephant (Pages 167–171)

Guide the Reading
- Remind children to ask themselves if they are understanding what they are reading. Suggest that children reread if they are confused by anything they read in this section.
- Read aloud the scene description at the top of page 168. Explain to children that Liberia is a country in Africa. Then have children follow along as you read page 168 aloud. Explain that in Liberia the storyteller begins by saying "Once upon a time," and the people in the audience shout, "Time!" That means they are ready to listen.
- Have children read pages 167–171 to see if their predictions match the reading.

Discussion Points
- Have children describe the big problem Tapidou has with Elephant and Hippo. Have them point to words or pictures that support their answers.
- Ask children what Tapidou says after Elephant nearly steps on him. Why does Elephant laugh when Tapidou says he's the strongest one of all?
- Ask if children were confused by what they read. Have volunteers describe what they did to help themselves understand the story better. Find out if the play format is causing children problems and clarify as needed.
- Clarify and discuss anything in the story that is still confusing to children.

Tapidou and Hippo (Pages 172–175)

Guide the Reading
- Remind children to summarize characters and events as they read this part of the story to keep track of what they are reading. Then have children read pages 172–175.

Discussion Points
- Ask children to describe what happens to Tapidou as he is walking by the river. Have them find words and pictures that support their answers.
- Read aloud page 173. Encourage children to tell whether they think Tapidou really is strong. Ask them why they think he keeps saying he is strong to Elephant and Hippo.
- Ask what Tapidou decides to do to stop Elephant and Hippo from teasing him. Discuss with children what kind of a trick Tapidou could play.
- Have children work together to summarize what has happened so far. Encourage them to name all three characters, and to explain the problem Tapidou has and what he plans to do.
- Discuss questions children have about any words or events in this section.

Tapidou Plans a Trick (Pages 176–179)

Guide the Reading
- Remind children to use the Think About Words strategy to figure out any unfamiliar words.
- Have children read pages 176–179.

Discussion Points
- Ask what Tapidou says he will do to prove he is the strongest.
- Ask children what they thought when they read that Tapidou was also asking Hippo to have a tug of war with him. Find out if children have guessed what trick Tapidou will play during the tug of war. Ask them to predict what will happen next in the story.
- Ask if anyone used the Think About Words strategy to figure out unfamiliar words in this section. If so, have volunteers explain what they did.

The Tug of War (Pages 180–183)

Guide the Reading
(Evaluate Strategy)
- Tell children that in this section they will see the trick Tapidou plays on his friends. Suggest that children ask themselves what they think about this trick.
- Have children read pages 180–183.

Discussion Points
- Ask children to tell who is really having a tug of war. Have them point to words or pictures that show they understand Elephant is having a tug of war with Hippo and that Tapidou is not having a tug of war with anyone.
- Have children read aloud what Elephant says on page 182 and what Hippo says on page 183. Ask why Elephant and Hippo are changing their minds about how strong Tapidou is.
- Ask children whether they think Tapidou's plan is a good one and why or why not. Use the following Think Aloud to model the evaluate strategy.

> **Think Aloud** *When I saw the picture on pages 182 and 183, I understood what Tapidou's trick was. I think it is a good trick and very funny because Elephant and Hippo are pulling against each other, but they think they are pulling against Tapidou. I hope they don't find out that Tapidou is hiding in the bushes.*

- Ask children to predict how this tug of war will end.
- Ask if there are any remaining questions children would like to discuss.

Reflect on the Purposes for Reading
Review the predictions on the board. Discuss those that did not match the story and whether that was because they were inappropriate or if they might still match the story when children read the remainder of the selection.

Complete the Problem-Solution Chart
Have children return to the Problem-Solution Chart to fill in the right box. Discuss Tapidou's trick and help students record a brief description of it in the box.

> **Have children read the rest of the selection cooperatively or have them participate in the reading of this selection with the entire class.**

OPTION 1 Think About Words

Read aloud the first two lines on page 177, saying *blank* for *vine.* Use the suggestions below to model how children can use the Think About Words strategy to figure out this word.
What makes sense I know that the word names something Tapidou is showing Elephant.
Sounds for letters I see that the word begins with the sound for *v.* I see that it has the CVC*e* pattern, so the vowel sound is probably the long *i* sound. I also know that this story follows a pattern of rhyming word. This word rhymes with *mine.* I think the word is *vine.* **Picture clues** The picture shows a long part of a plant that has leaves on it. It looks like a vine. When I reread these lines, *vine* makes sense. Now I know the word is *vine.*

OPTION 2 Develop Fluency: Partner Reading

Assign the parts of Hippo and Tapidou to partners and have each pair do a dramatic reading of page 173. Remind children to use the speaker name to tell which of them should speak, but to read only the dialogue.

OPTION 1 Cause and Effect

- Ask children why Tapidou decided to play a trick on Elephant and Hippo. Explain that the teasing caused Tapidou to decide to play a trick.
- Write the following sentences on the board:

    Cause: *Elephant and Hippo teased Tapidou.*
    Effect: *Tapidou decided to play a trick on Elephant and Hippo.*

- Explain to children that they can identify which sentence is the cause by using the word *because.* Demonstrate, using the following examples:

    1. *Elephant and Hippo teased Tapidou because Tapidou decided to play a trick on Elephant and Hippo.*
    2. *Tapidou decided to play a trick on Elephant and Hippo because Elephant and Hippo teased Tapidou.*

- Ask children which example is correct. Circle the word *because* in the second example and underline the words that follow it. Tell children that the part that follows *because* is the cause. The part that comes before *because* is the effect.
- Help children identify which of the following sentences is the cause and which is the effect:

    Hippo and Elephant pulled all day.
    Hippo and Elephant got tired.

Then help them restate the cause and effect in one sentence using the word because.

OPTION 2 Vowel Pairs: *ai, ay*

- List the following story words on the board: *rain, day, play.*
- Have children read the words. Discuss the sound that the vowel pairs *ai* and *ay* stand for in the words. Help children notice that the vowel pairs sound the same—all have the long *a* sound. Repeat the words slowly with children, if necessary.

Family Treasures

Use BEFORE Launching the Theme Activities

Theme Concept | Happiness can come from being part of a family.

Materials Suggested for the Theme
- Audio Tapes for Family Treasures
- Selection Masters 13 and 14

OPTION 1 What Special Things Do You Do with Your Family?

Start a discussion with children about the things that families like to do together. Ask children what they like to do with their families. Write their answers on the board or on chart paper. Read the list together when finished.

OPTION 2 Draw a Family Portrait

Provide large paper and crayons for children to draw portraits of their families. Have children label their family members. Ask for volunteers to share their pictures with the group, naming the different family members.

A Mother for Choco

OPTION 1

Activate Prior Knowledge

- Talk with children about ways they are like other members of their families (or like their friends). Encourage them to think about a range of similarities, such as liking the same foods, liking the same activities, wearing similar clothes, or looking alike.
- Tell children that this Big Book is about a little bird named Choco who sets off on a journey to find his mother whom he believes will look just like him.
- Display the Big Book and read aloud the title and the name of the author-illustrator. Then read aloud the following summary:

> **<u>Choco</u> is a <u>little</u> <u>bird</u> who lives <u>all</u> <u>alone</u>. He wishes that he had a <u>mother.</u> So he sets <u>off</u> to <u>find</u> one. On his way, he meets several animals. Could one of them be his mother? They all tell Choco they <u>couldn't</u> possibly be his mother because they don't look like him. Choco becomes very sad. But then he meets Mrs. Bear. She definitely doesn't look like him, but could she help him anyway? Read the story to find out.**

(Underlined words are key words in the selection.)

OPTION 2

Picture Walk

DISPLAY

Choco	mother
set off	first
just	like
next	

Print the key words on the board and read them aloud. Then display the cover of the Big Book. Read aloud the title and name of the author-illustrator. Guide children on a picture walk through the selection using the following suggestions. Incorporate key words where possible, pointing to each word in the Big Book as it is mentioned.

Page 3 Tell children that <u>Choco</u> is a little bird who has just decided that he wants to find a <u>mother</u>. He is about to <u>set off</u> to find her.

Pages 4–5 Explain that <u>first</u>, Choco meets Mrs. Giraffe. He thinks she might be his mother because she is yellow <u>just</u> <u>like</u> him. But she says no, she doesn't have wings like Choco. How could she possibly be his mother?

Pages 6–7 Tell children that <u>next</u>, Choco meets Mrs. Penguin. Ask children why Choco thinks she might be his mother. (because she has wings just like him) Then explain that she says she is not his mother because she doesn't have big, round cheeks like Choco.

Pages 8–9 Ask children who Choco meets next. Ask why he thinks she might be his mother. (because she has big, round cheeks just like him) Then ask what children think Mrs. Walrus might say.

Pages 10–13 Explain that Choco is now sad because he can't find a mother who looks like him. Ask children who they think he will neet next. (Mrs. Bear)

Pages 14–21 Have children describe what is happening in the illustrations on these pages. Discuss how Choco's feelings seem to change and ask children why they think he looks happy now.

OPTION 3   Oral Language Development

- Help children practice oral language by asking them to describe Choco and all the different animals Choco meets. Encourage children to use as many descriptive words as possible. Study the illustrations and then model the procedure by describing Choco: *Choco is a little yellow bird. He has big yellow cheeks and a big black beak. He has two feet with black and yellow stripes. Each foot has four toes.*
- When children have finished describing the animals, ask for volunteers to pantomime each animal.

Use BEFORE  Interact *with* Literature

OPTION 1   Read Aloud for Interest

Pages 3–21

- Display the Big Book. Read aloud the title and the name of the author-illustrator. Ask children what they think Choco is leaning on. Tell children that by the end of the story, they will have figured it out.
- Read aloud pages 3–21. As you read, pause to ask questions such as *What do you think will happen next? What makes you think that?*

OPTION 2   Use the Audio Tape

Audio Tape for Family Treasures: *A Mother for Choco*

Have children listen to pages 3–21 of the story while you display the Big Book. Ask children to listen to find out if Choco finds his mother.

Discussion Points

- What do you think Choco's mother is going to look like?
- What kind of animal do you think Choco's mother will be?
- Do you think that Choco's mother has to look like Choco?

Use AFTER  Interact *with* Literature

OPTION 1   Develop Fluency: Partner Reading

Have partners read the story together while alternating pages.

OPTION 2   Language Experience

Work together with children to create a summary of the story. Ask children to tell you what happened in the beginning, middle, and end of the story. Record the summary on the board or on chart paper. Help children read the summary aloud when finished. You may wish to refer to this summary in the Comprehension activity later in the lesson.

OPTION 1 **Story Structure and Summarizing**

- Review with children that most stories revolve around a main character's problem. Explain that the main character usually finds a solution to the problem. (If available, refer to the story summary written earlier in the Language Experience activity. If not, help children briefly summarize *A Mother for Choco*.)
- Help children discover the story elements (*where, main character, problem,* and *solution*) for *A Mother for Choco*. Record the information on a chart like the one below.
- Then help children discover the story elements from other familiar Big Books, stories, or fairy tales children know. Appropriate Big Books from previous themes include *There's an Alligator Under My Bed, George Shrinks,* and *The Doorbell Rang.* Record the information and read the chart together when finished.

	A Mother for Choco	*There's an Alligator Under My Bed*
Where	outside	house
Main Character(s)	Choco	boy
Problem	Choco wanted a mother.	The boy was afraid of the alligator.
Solution	Mrs. Bear became his mother.	He locked the alligator in the garage.

OPTION 2 **Sounds for *y***

- Start by telling children that you have created a list of some special words from *A Mother for Choco*. Point out that all the words in the list have *y* at the end. Write the list on the board: *sorry, cry, mommy, very, funny, why, Hippy, Ally, Piggy, happy*.
- Read the list aloud several times, asking children to listen carefully to the vowel sounds at the ends of the words.
- Ask children what they notice about the vowel sounds. Lead them to discover that the *y* sometimes stands for the long vowel *i* sound and sometimes stands for the long vowel *e* sound.
- Write all the story words ending with *y* on index cards. Use additional words if you wish. Turn the cards face down. Have children pick up the cards one at a time and sort them into two groups—words with long vowel *e* sound and long vowel *i* sound.

Think About Words Strategy

- Point to the word *apples* on page 13 of the Big Book. Model how children could figure out this word if they did not know it.

  What makes sense First I'll read the sentence on page 13. It says: *When Choco saw Mrs. Bear picking _____, he knew she couldn't be his mother.* I wonder if the word is *cherries.* It makes sense.

  Sounds for letters When I look at the letters I see *a* at the beginning. I know that the letter *a* can stand for the sound I hear at the beginning of alligator. So the word can't be *cherries.*

  Picture clues The picture shows Mrs. Bear picking something red from a tree. What other red things could she pick from a tree? How about apples? When I reread *When Choco saw Mrs. Bear picking apples, he knew she couldn't be his mother,* the sentence makes sense.

- Next, point to the word *dance* on page 21 and ask volunteers to explain how they would figure out this word if they did not know it.

  What makes sense The word describes something Choco wishes his mother would do with him.

  Sounds for letters At the beginning of the word is the letter *d,* as in *dig.* In the middle of the word is the letter *n,* as in *no.*

  Picture clues Mrs. Bear and Choco look like they are singing and dancing.

High-Frequency Words

children, first, gave, lived, next, together, would

Place self-sticking notes over the following words in the Big Book: *lived* (page 3); *first* (page 5); *next* (page 6); *would* (pages 15, 17, 18, 21, 24); *gave* (pages 18, 32); *children* (pages 26, 29, 32). Then write each word on an index card and give one or two cards to each child. Reread the selection to children, pausing as you come to each covered word. Ask children which word belongs in the sentence. Have the child with that word card uncover the word and check to see that the word matches the card.

Something from Nothing

Use BEFORE  Introduce *the* Literature

OPTION 1 ## Activate Prior Knowledge

- Read title and the name of the author-illustrator aloud. Display the cover illustration.
- Discuss with children whether they think it's possible to make something from nothing. Ask them what they think that means.
- Read aloud the following selection summary.

> **When Joseph is born, his grandfather makes him a beautiful blanket. Joseph loves his blanket. But as he gets older, so does his blanket. One day his mother tells him it is time to <u>throw</u> it away. Joseph wants to keep his blanket, so he asks his grandfather to fix it. After cutting and sewing, Grandfather <u>turns</u> the blanket into a jacket for Joseph. When Joseph outgrows his jacket, his mother wants him to throw it away. And so it continues. As Joseph keeps growing, his grandfather keeps turning the <u>material</u> from the blanket into different things for Joseph. But with each change, the blanket gets smaller. What will happen when there is nothing left?**

(Underlined words are key words in the selection.)

- Encourage children to share stories about a favorite toy or blanket that they remember (or may still have) and explain why they like it.

OPTION 2 ## Picture Walk

Print the key words on the board and read them aloud. Guide children through the illustrations, discussing what Grandfather makes for Joseph out of the same cloth. Whenever possible, incorporate the key words into the discussion, pointing to each word on the board as it is mentioned. Here are some suggestions:

DISPLAY
needle
material
throw

Page 41 Point out the scissors and thread in the illustration and ask children what they are used for. Discuss with children other things that are needed to sew, such as a <u>needle</u> and some <u>material</u>.

Page 43 Point out the pins on the table and the scraps of cloth on the floor. Ask children what Grandfather is doing here. Explain that he is making a blanket for his grandson, Joseph.

Page 45 Ask children to describe the blanket now. Explain that Joseph's mother wants him to throw it out. Ask children if they think Joseph will be willing to give up his blanket.

Page 46 Ask children what they think Joseph is doing and what his Grandfather will do for him.

Pages 48–49 Ask children what has happened to the blanket on page 48 and how they can tell. Then ask why the jacket seems small on Joseph on page 29. What do children think Joseph's mother will say to him next? What will Joseph want his grandfather to do?

OPTION 3 ## Graphic Organizer

Selection Master 13
Part 5

- Tell children that in this story, a little boy named Joseph has a blanket he loves very much. As the boy grows, the blanket goes through many changes. Read aloud the items in the boxes of the Graphic Organizer. Discuss how a blanket could be made into a jacket, and how a jacket could be made into a vest. Then tell children that as Joseph grows, the vest gets old and worn. Brainstorm with children ideas of what the vest could become.
- Tell children they will return to this master after reading to fill in the rest of the boxes.

Read Aloud Pages 41–61 or Have Children Listen to the Audio Tape

Audio Tape for Family Treasures: *Something from Nothing*

As children listen to the selection, have them follow along in their anthologies. Suggest they listen to find out the different things the blanket is turned into as Joseph grows.

Discussion Points
- Ask children to name the things Grandfather makes out of the blanket material. Write their suggestions on the board. Then help children number the items in story order.
- Ask children how they think Joseph feels about his grandfather, and how Grandfather feels about Joseph. What makes them think that?

OPTION 2

Guided or Assisted Reading of Pages 41–61

If, while using the guided reading segments that follow, it becomes clear that children are unable to read this selection silently, assist them in reading each segment aloud together. Then use the discussion points to talk about each segment.

Preview to Set a Purpose for Reading
(Self-Question)
- Have children preview the selection by reading the title and looking at the illustrations. Ask them to think of questions about the story. Write their questions on the board.
- If children have difficulty thinking of questions, model how the illustration on page 45 might lead to questions about why the little boy and his mother look unhappy. Possible questions include *What has happened to the blanket? Does the mother want the little boy to quit carrying around the blanket? Will the little boy lose the blanket?*

> For the first section, children's questions are necessarily based on their previews of the selection. Before children read each subsequent section, discuss any answers they've found to their questions and have children decide if they want to add additional questions to the list. Then have children continue reading to answer their questions.

Joseph's Grandfather Makes a Wonderful Blanket (Pages 41–45)

Guide the Reading
- Remind children to check to see that they understand what they are reading. Suggest that they use the illustrations for clues if they are confused by anything in this section.

Discussion Points
- Ask children what Joseph's grandfather makes for him. Have volunteers find and read aloud words or describe pictures that support their answers.
- Ask children how old they think Joseph is and to explain how they know.
- Have children who were confused by anything in the story describe what they did to help themselves understand the story better.

Joseph Asks His Grandfather to Fix the Blanket (Pages 46–49)

Guide the Reading
- Point out the words *needle* and *material* on page 47. Explain that people sew pieces of material together using a needle and thread. Then remind children to use the Think About Words strategy to figure out any other words that are unfamiliar to them.
- Have children read pages 46–49.

Discussion Points
- Have children explain what Grandfather did to Joseph's blanket.
- Ask children how they think Joseph felt about his new jacket. Have them point to words or pictures that support their answers.
- Discuss with children what happens as Joseph gets older. What does his mother want to do with the jacket? What do children think will happen next?
- Ask a volunteer who used the Think About Words strategy to figure out an unfamiliar word to explain what they did.
- Discuss questions children still have about any words or events in this section.

Grandfather Makes a Vest for Joseph (Pages 50–53)

Guide the Reading
(Summarize)
- Remind children that good readers stop from time to time to summarize what they have read so far. Tell children to pay attention to the illustrations to help them remember the important events in this section.
- Have children read pages 50–53.

Discussion Points
- Have children read aloud the words on page 53 that tell why Joseph's mother wants him to throw out the vest.
- Ask children if they think Joseph will go to his grandfather for help again. What do they think Grandfather will be able to make this time?
- Discuss the pattern in the story and have children use the repeated sentences to summarize what has happened so far. Use the Think Aloud below to model the strategy.

> **THINK ALOUD** *From what I have read so far, I see a pattern. Grandfather keeps making things from the blanket material each time it wears out or Joseph outgrows it. So all I have to do is remember what Grandfather makes each time. I can summarize the story by saying: Joseph's grandfather made him a blanket. When the blanket got old, Joseph's mother wanted him to throw it out, but Joseph asked Grandfather to fix it. Grandfather made a jacket for Joseph out of the blanket. When Joseph outgrew the jacket, his mother wanted him to throw it out, but Joseph asked Grandfather to fix it again. This time Grandfather made a vest, but when it got worn out, Joseph's mother wanted him to throw it out.*

Joseph's Blanket Changes Again (Pages 54–61)

Guide the Reading
- Remind children to continue to use the story pattern to keep track of events.
- Have children read pages 54–61.

Discussion Points
- Have children tell what Grandfather made out of Joseph's vest.
- Ask children how old they think Joseph is now. Use the illustrations to point out that as this story has gone on, Joseph has started school and his parents have had another baby.
- Have children read aloud the words on page 57 that describe what happens to Joseph's tie.
- Ask children what Joseph does with the handkerchief Grandfather makes out of the tie.
- Encourage children to predict what Grandfather will make out of the handkerchief. Tell them that they will find out when they finish reading the story.
- Discuss questions children have about words or events in the story.

Reflect on the Purposes for Reading
Review the questions on the board. Discuss those that have not been answered and whether they might still be answered when children read the remainder of the selection.

Complete the Master
Help children work together to come to an agreement on the order of events, encouraging them to refer to the illustrations in the selection, if necessary. Then have children fill in the rest of the boxes. In the last box, children can write their prediction about what happens next. Have children retell sections of the story in turn, using their masters for reference.

> **Have children read the rest of the selection cooperatively or have them participate in the reading of this selection with the entire class.**

OPTION 1 Think About Words

- Read the second sentence on page 45, saying *blank* for the word *frazzled*. Model how children can use the Think About Words strategy to figure out this word.

  What makes sense From the rest of the sentence, I know that the word tells something about how terrible the blanket looks. It could mean something like *ragged* or *ripped*.

  Sounds for letters I see that the word starts with the sounds for *fr*, has the sound for *z* in the middle, and ends with *-ed* . I think the word is: *fraz-zled*.

  Picture clues When I check the picture for help, I can see that the blanket does looks ragged. *Frazzled* means something like *ragged* or *ripped,* so the word is probably *frazzled*.

OPTION 2 Develop Fluency: Partner Reading

Model reading aloud pages 43–48, giving expression to the dialogue. Then have partners alternate reading each page until each child has had a chance to read two or three times.

OPTION 1 Sequence

- Remind children that a story has a beginning, a middle, and an end and that things happen in each part. Have volunteers tell what happened in the beginning of the story and write their answers on the board. Follow a similar procedure for the middle and end of the story.
- Review the events on the board with children and help them understand that the events should be in an order that make sense. Encourage them to reorder any events that don't make sense or did not happen in that order. Also, point out any order words that children use, such as *first, next*, and *then*.
- Ask volunteers to retell the story using the events on the board.

OPTION 2 Vowel Pairs: *oo, ew, ue, ou*

- List the following vowel pairs on the board:

  oo   ew   ue   ou

- Write words with the vowel pairs *oo, ew, ue,* and *ou* on index cards. Have children work together sorting the words cards by vowel pairs. Ask children to read their words cards as you write them on the board under the correct vowel pair.
- Finally, have children find and read aloud words in *Something from Nothing* that have these vowel pairs.

Use BEFORE ① Introduce *the* Literature

OPTION 1 — Activate Prior Knowledge

- Read aloud the title and the name of the author-illustrator. Display the cover illustration. Ask children what they think the title means.
- Read aloud the following summary.

  Being the youngest of three sisters can be a lot of fun. There is always something to do together–walk to school, play hopscotch, go to the bakery, or ride in a taxi or a subway. And there's plenty of <u>company</u>. But being the youngest is hard when older sisters think you are too young to go with them and leave you behind in the <u>apartment</u> with <u>Mama</u> and <u>Daddy</u>. There's nothing fun about that. Or is there?

(Underlined words are key words in the selection.)

- Encourage children to tell what they like to do with their brothers, sisters, or friends.
- Ask children what activities they like to do on their own.

OPTION 2 — Picture Walk

DISPLAY

Mama

Daddy

apartment

company

Print the key words on the board and read them aloud. Guide children through the illustrations, discussing what the girls are doing in each one. Whenever possible, incorporate the key words into the discussion, pointing to each word as it occurs. Here are some suggestions:

Page 84 Explain that the girls are playing hopscotch on the sidewalk outside their <u>apartment</u> building. Ask children what they like to do when they play outside their home.

Page 90 Ask children what the girls are doing in this picture. Point out the girls' mother and father and explain that the girls call their mother <u>Mama</u> and their father <u>Daddy</u>.

Page 98 Ask children what they think is happening in this picture and how they think the youngest sister feels.

Page 101 Point out that the youngest sister is all alone now. She has no one to keep her <u>company</u>. Ask children how they think she feels about playing alone with her doll. How can they tell?

OPTION 3 — Activity Chart

Selection Master 14
Part 5

- Tell children that in this story, three sisters do many things together.
- Brainstorm with children activities that are fun to do with other people. List the ideas on the board. Help children draw or write the activities they each like to do in the top box in the second column.
- Tell children to think about things they like to do alone. Have children draw or write their own favorite activities in the bottom section of the second column.
- Read aloud and discuss the activities the sisters like to do together and alone. Tell children they will return to the Activity Chart after reading to fill in more activities for the sisters.

OPTION 1

Read Aloud Pages 80–101 or Have Children Listen to the Audio Tape

Audio Tape for Family Treasures: *One of Three*

As children listen to the selection, have them follow along in their anthologies. Suggest they listen to find out about the different things the three sisters do together.

Discussion Points
- Discuss who the three girls are and which one is telling the story.
- Ask children to name some of the things the girls do together.
- Ask how the youngest sister feels when the older two don't want her along.

OPTION 2

Guided or Assisted Reading of Pages 80–101

If, while using the guided reading segments that follow, it becomes clear that children are unable to read this selection silently, assist them in reading each segment aloud together. Then use the discussion points to talk about each segment.

Preview to Set a Purpose for Reading
(Predict/Infer)
- Have children preview the selection by reading the title and looking at the illustrations. Ask them to make predictions about what the girls do in the story. Write their predictions on the board.
- If children have difficulty thinking of predictions, model how the illustration on pages 86–87 might lead to predictions about what the girls are doing. Possible predictions might be: *I think the girls will buy something at the bakery. I think they're waiting to buy cookies.*

> For the first section, children's predictions are necessarily based on their previews of the selection. Before children read each subsequent section, discuss which of their predictions agreed with what was read and which did not. Have children think about what they've read and decide if they want to revise their original predictions or make new ones.

Three Sisters   (Pages 80–85)

Guide the Reading
- Tell students that in this section they will read about many things the three sisters did together. Remind students that as they read, it is helpful to stop and summarize what they've read. Keeping what happens clear will help them understand the story better as they read on.

Discussion Points
- Have a volunteer read the title aloud. Ask children what the "three" are and which sister is the "one." Help them understand that the youngest sister is telling the story.
- Ask children to name some of the activities the girls do together. Have volunteers look for words or pictures that tell what they do.
- Read aloud page 85. Ask children to describe where the three sisters live.
- Have children work together to summarize what has happened so far. Point out that the youngest sister's name is not given in the story. For convenience, you might suggest that children just call her "Sister."

People the Sisters Know   (Pages 86–91)

Guide the Reading
- Remind children that good readers check to see that they understand a story as they read. Suggest that children use the illustrations for clues if they are confused by anything they read in this section.
- Have children read pages 86–91.

Discussion Points

- Have children turn to pages 86–87. Ask them who the man in the picture is. Ask children whether they think the girls will visit other members of their community in this story and why.
- Read aloud pages 88 and 91. Have children name other people in the sisters' family.
- Have children who were confused by anything in the story tell what confused them and what they did to help themselves understand the story better.

Going Places   (Pages 92–97)

Guide the Reading
(Think About Words Strategy)

- Remind children to use the Think About Words strategy to figure out any unfamiliar words.
- Have children read pages 92–97.

Discussion Points

- Have children describe some of the things the girls do in this section. Ask children how they think the youngest girl likes having two older sisters. Have volunteers find words or pictures that show how she feels.
- Have volunteers who used the Think About Words strategy explain what they did. Use the Think Aloud below to model how to figure out the word *daisy*.

> **THINK ALOUD** *From the sentences around this word, I know the girls are at a flower shop, so I think that the store owner probably gives them a flower. This word could be a kind of flower. If I check the picture, I see that the man does give them flowers. So the word must name a flower. The word starts with **d** and ends with a sound for **y**. **Daisy** is a name for a flower. **Daisy** has the right sounds, so the word must be **daisy**.*

- Encourage children to share anything in the story that is confusing to them. Clarify as needed.

Left Alone   (Pages 98–101)

Guide the Reading

- Explain to children that in this section, there is a big change in the story. Advise children to look carefully at the pictures as they read this section. They pictures will tell them even more than the words.
- Have children read pages 98–101.

Discussion Points

- Ask children to explain the big change that happens in this section. Have volunteers point out words or pictures that show what is different.
- Discuss with children why Eva and Nikki sometimes want to go somewhere without their younger sister. Ask children to talk about whether they think the older girls are being nice to their youngest by not letting her go with them.
- Have children describe what the youngest sister does on her own and how she is feeling.
- Encourage children to predict what will happen next in the story. Tell them they will find out when they finish reading the story.
- Ask if there are any remaining questions children have about words or events in the story that they would like to discuss.

Reflect on the Purposes for Reading

Review the predictions on the board. Discuss those that did not match the story and whether that was because they were inappropriate or if they might still match the story when children read the remainder of the selection.

Complete the Activity Chart

Have children return to the Activity Chart to fill in activities that the girls do together. Encourage children to page through the illustrations as a reminder of the things the girls do. Have individuals share with the rest of the group one thing that the girls do that they also like to do. If someone doesn't like anything they do, have that child share an activity from his or her chart that he or she does enjoy.

> Have children read the rest of the selection cooperatively or have them participate in the reading of this selection with the entire class.

OPTION 1 Develop Critical Thinking: Personal Opinion

- Remind children how unhappy the youngest sister was when her two older sisters didn't want her to go with them.
- Review with children some of the things the youngest sister did at home with her parents and list them on the board. Ask children whether they think the youngest sister had fun with her parents.
- Encourage children to imagine what it would have been like for the youngest sister if she had gone with Eva and Nikki. Ask questions to help them think about what might have happened, such as: *Where do you think Eva and Nikki might have gone? Would the youngest sister have enjoyed going there? How might Eva and Nikki have treated their youngest sister if they didn't really want her along?* List children's ideas on the board.
- Ask children if they were the youngest sister, what they would rather do—go with their sisters or stay home with their parents. Encourage them to give reasons for their answers.

OPTION 2 Develop Fluency: Echo Reading

Read aloud page 85, stopping after *2, eyes, cans,* and *time* so that children can repeat each phrase after you. Read along with children, if necessary.

OPTION 1 Inferences: Drawing Conclusions

- Explain that readers can sometimes find out things in a story even if the author doesn't actually come right out and say them.
- Have children turn to page 101 and describe how the youngest sister feels. Read aloud page 100. Point out that there are no words that tell how she feels.
- Ask children how they knew how the youngest sister felt. Help them understand that they used clues from the pictures and drew upon their own experiences to guess how she felt.
- Ask children where the sisters live and how they know. Help children understand that while the author actually says that the sisters live in an apartment, children can tell they live in a city from clues in the pictures (page 80) and in the text (riding the subway, page 93).

OPTION 2 Base Words with Endings: *-s, -ing, -ed, -er, -est, -y, -ly, -ful*

- Write the following word endings on the board: *-s, -er, -est, -ly.* Remind children that these are endings that can be added to words.
- Write the following words on the board:

     girls   older   youngest   sadly

- Challenge children to identify the base word and endings in the words.
- Have children take turns using the words in sentences about the story, such as:

    There are three <u>girls</u>. The <u>youngest</u> is telling the story. Sometimes she can't go with her <u>older</u> sisters. So she <u>sadly</u> plays with her doll.

Theme: Something Fishy

Use *BEFORE* Launching the Theme Activities

Theme Concept | **There are many very interesting fish.**

Materials Suggested for the Theme
- Audio Tapes for Something Fishy
- Selection Masters 15 and 16

OPTION 1 What Is Special about Fish?

Start a discussion with children about fish. What are some different kinds of fish? Where do fish live? What do fish look like? How do fish move? Make a chart with children called, *What We Know About Fish*. Read the chart together when finished.

What We Know About Fish

Fish live in the water.

Fish sometimes eat other fish.

Goldfish are orange.

You can catch fish from a lake.

OPTION 2 Make an Underwater Mural

In preparation for an underwater mural, brainstorm with children a list of things that could be in an underwater scene. (water, fish, seaweed, rocks, buried treasure) Provide construction paper, crayons, scissors, and paste for children to make fish and other objects. When all the objects are made, paste them on a large piece of blue construction paper. Encourage children to label the objects they made.

OPTION 1

Activate Prior Knowledge

- Talk with children about fish they have seen at home, at school, in a lake or river, at the beach, or in aquariums. Have them describe these fish–what they look and sound like, where they live, how they move, what they eat, and so on.
- Tell children that this selection gives many facts about fish that live in the ocean. Give children an example of a fact about fish, such as "The stingray has a stinger on its tail." Then ask volunteers for other facts they know about fish, reminding children that facts are pieces of information that are true.
- Read aloud the following selection summary.

> **So many fish! This selection tells about some wonderful creatures that live in the ocean. Many fish seem to look and act the same way until you learn more about them. They have different ways of catching their <u>prey</u>, or food, and different ways of staying safe and protecting themselves. Did you know that the stripes on a zebrafish can change color, or that a parrotfish has a <u>beak</u>? A flounder even has both its eyes on the <u>same</u> side of its head! Some fish have <u>snouts</u>, and others can make noises like a pig. <u>Which</u> fish might have very sharp teeth–a toadfish or a sawfish? Read *Fishy Facts* and find out!**

(Underlined words are key words in the selection.)

- Ask children what questions they have about the selection. Record the questions on the board and refer back to them after the story is read. Also ask children what other fish they think they might find out about as they read.

OPTION 2

Picture Walk

Display the cover of the Big Book and read aloud the title and the name of the author-illustrator. Explain that this selection is full of facts about fish. Guide children through the illustrations on pages 2–23, using the suggestions below to incorporate key words. Point to each word as it is discussed.

DISPLAY

toothed	prey
snout	electricity
beak	lantern
same	

Pages 2–3 Have children tell why *zebrafish* is a good name for this fish.

Pages 4–5 Ask what tool this fish's long, <u>toothed</u> <u>snout</u> looks like and why.

Pages 6–7 Ask children in what ways this parrotfish looks like a parrot. If necessary, point out how its mouth looks like a <u>beak</u>.

Pages 10–11 Discuss children's ideas about why the flounder's eyes are on the <u>same</u> side of its head.

Pages 12–13 Ask children what they think the jagged white lines show about the electric eel. Tell them that the eel makes <u>electricity</u> to stun its <u>prey</u> before it eats it.

Pages 20–21 Point out the two spots at either end of this fish. Ask which children think is the eye and why.

Pages 22–23 Discuss what might be special about the <u>lantern</u> fish. Point out its bright white spots that look a little like light bulbs.

OPTION 3 Oral Language Development

Read aloud page 18 of the selection. Ask children what two words tell what the shark does *(swims, chases)*. Have children pantomime these action words. Then tell children that you are going to read aloud some other action words from the selection. After discussing the meaning of each word, ask volunteers to demonstrate each action. Suggested words include *cuts up, grow, bite, grunts, kiss, rises, swallow, stings.* After children have demonstrated the words, ask them to use the words in oral sentences.

Use BEFORE  **2** Interact *with* Literature

OPTION 1 Read Aloud for Interest

Display the cover and read aloud the title. Remind children that a fact is a piece of information that is true. Ask children what facts they think they might learn about fish from this selection. Then read aloud pages 2–23 of the story, displaying the Big Book for children as you read. Pause as you read to allow children to look at the illustrations and talk briefly about the text.

When you have finished reading, ask children which fish is their favorite so far, and why. What other kinds of fish do they think they might read about?

OPTION 2 Use the Audio Tape

Audio Tape for Something Fishy: *Fishy Facts*

Have children listen to pages 2–23 of the story while you display the Big Book for them. Suggest they listen to find out what makes each kind of fish special and different from the others.

Discussion Points
- Have volunteers choose a fish and describe what is special about it. Encourage children to look at both the text and the illustrations as they describe their choices.
- Ask children which fishy fact they found the most interesting and why.
- Discuss other facts children have learned about fish so far.

Use AFTER  **2** Interact *with* Literature

OPTION 1 Develop Fluency: Partner Reading

Assign pairs of children to read aloud two or four pages of the selection. As one child reads aloud, ask the other child to pantomime what the text says about the fish. Partners can then switch roles and either read about a new fish or the same fish, depending on whether they are reading two or four pages. Encourage partners to practice their pages together before they read aloud to the group.

OPTION 2 Language Experience

Ask children to evaluate *Fishy Facts* by discussing questions such as the following: Were the facts interesting and exciting? What did I like and not like about the text and the illustrations? Record children's responses on chart paper, helping them to organize what they think into a short paragraph or two. Then ask children to read aloud their evaluation as a group.

OPTION **1** ## Text Organization and Summarizing

Read aloud pages 12–13 of the selection. Remind children that the topic of a paragraph is what it is mostly about. Ask children to name the topic of the two pages they just heard you read (the electric eel). Write that topic on a strip of paper for children.

Next, write the following sentences on strips of paper:

> The electric eel moves many ways.
> The electric eel moves up or down.
> An eel can move forward or backward.

(The first sentence is the main idea; the others are supporting details.) Shuffle the strips, including the topic strip, and give them to the group. Guide children to arrange the strips with the topic first, the main idea next, and the supporting details last. Remind children that knowing the topic and main idea of a paragraph can help them summarize and remember what they have learned.

As children work together to arrange the strips, have them describe how they can tell the main idea from the supporting details. If children have difficulty identifying the main idea, have them reread each sentence strip and ask them, "Does this sentence tell the most important information about the electric eel?" Provide guidance and clarification as necessary. Then ask children to summarize pages 12–13 in their own words.

OPTION **2** ## Base Words and Endings: *-es, -ies*

Read aloud pages 2–3 of the selection. Then write the following sentences on the board:

> It is fun to read fact ____ about fish.
> A zebrafish change ____ color to hide.
> A zebrafish match ____ the color of its surroundings.

Ask children to write each of the letters *i, e,* and *s* on a separate self-sticking note. Have volunteers fill in the blanks on the board with the correct letter or letters. Remind children that some base words need an *-es* instead of an *-s* ending to make them easier to say. Point out how the ending sound of *match* changes when *-es* is added.

Next, read aloud the first sentence on page 14. Write the following sentence on the board:

> The <u>body</u> of small fishes fit in the goosefish's mouth.

Ask a volunteer to add an ending to the underlined word, using the self-stick notes. Remind children that when a base word ends with a consonant followed by the letter *y,* the *y* must be changed to an *i* before adding *-es.*

Then write the following words on separate strips of paper, leaving room for endings to be added: *dish, bay, baby, gas, funny, fix, brother, batch, stripe, snout, hiss, six.* Ask children to use their self-stick notes to add the ending *-s, -es,* or *-ies* to each word. Have them use the new words in sentences.

Think About Words Strategy

Place a self-stick note over the word *kiss* on page 17. Read the page aloud to children, saying *blank* for the covered word. Then uncover the word and model how children could figure it out, using the Think About Words strategy.

- **What makes sense** As I read the sentence again, I find out that the word means something that happens when the fish put their mouths together. Maybe the word is *talk* or *kiss.*
- **Sounds for letters** I see that the word starts with the sound for *k* as in *kitten.* So the word can't be *talk.* I wonder if the word is *kiss.*
- **Picture clues** The picture shows the fish with their mouths together. They could be kissing, or looking like they're kissing, as they do this. When I reread the sentence, the word *kiss* makes sense.

Have children use the strategy to figure out the following words. Possible clues are given.

sharp (page 5)
context: describes the cutting edges of the sawfish's snout
sounds for letters: begins with sound for *sh;* ends with the sound for *p*
picture clues: teeth on the snout look pointy

quickly (page 18)
context: describes how the shark swims
sounds for letters/word parts: begins with the sound for *qu;* has word part *-ick* and ending *-ly*
picture clues: shark chases smaller fish; needs to move fast to catch them

High-Frequency Words

Place self-stick notes over the following words in the Big Book: *which* (pages 6 and 13); *same* (page 10); *hard, tell* (page 20); *air* (page 26); *only* (page 29); *until* (page 30). Then write each word on an index card and give one or two cards to each child. Reread the selection to children, pausing as you come to each covered word. Ask children which word belongs in the sentence. Have the child with that word card uncover the word and check to see that the word matches the card. After you have finished reading the selection, ask children to use each word in a sentence.

Enzo the Wonderfish

OPTION 1 Activate Prior Knowledge

- Read aloud the title and the name of the author-illustrator on page 126. Ask children who they think Enzo is on the title page. Why do children think Enzo is called a wonderfish?
- Talk with children about fish. What kinds of fish have they seen? What might it be like to have a pet fish? Then preview the illustrations on pages 126–156. Ask children to predict what might happen in the story. Be sure to ask for reasons to support their predictions.
- Read aloud the following summary.

   A little girl wants a pet. She asks her mom and dad many times for different pets— a horse, a dog, a cat, a bird. But her parents always say no. Finally, for her birthday she gets a goldfish named Enzo. The girl gets a library book about pet tricks. She tries to teach Enzo to <u>perform</u> many great <u>feats</u>. When Enzo jumps from his bowl into a teacup, it looks as though Enzo is dead. Did Enzo really learn a trick? Will he be all right?

(Underlined words are key words in the story.)

- Encourage children to share what they know about animals that do tricks. Ask children if they think fish can learn tricks. Why or why not?

OPTION 2 Picture Walk

DISPLAY
perform
feats

Print the key words on the board and read them aloud. Then lead children on a picture walk through the selection, incorporating these words where possible. Point to the words on the board as they are mentioned. Here are some suggestions:

- **Pages 126–127** Read aloud the title. Tell children that the girl wanted a pet, so her parents gave her Enzo for her birthday. Have children find Enzo on page 126 and tell what kind of pet Enzo is. Have them guess what other pets the girl may have wanted, based on the picture on page 127.
- **Pages 130–133** Explain to children that the girl asked her parents for many different pets before they gave her Enzo. Have children look for the different types of animals the girl asked for. Ask why they think her parents might have said no to each of these pets.
- **Pages 139–141, 144** Tell children that the girl wants to teach Enzo to do tricks, or to <u>perform</u> great <u>feats</u>. Ask children how the girl tries to teach Enzo to perform tricks (pages 139, 144). Have children tell what kind of feats the girl tries to teach her pet (pages 140–141, 144). Ask children if they think a fish can learn to perform these feats, and why or why not.

OPTION 3 Concept Map

**Selection Master 15
Part 5**

- Explain to children that in this selection, they will read about a girl who wanted a pet. Her parents say no to most of the pets the girl asks for because of the different things that each pet needs.
- Read aloud the heading and the examples on the Concept Map. Explain that these are examples of things that this pet needs—what an owner needs to do for a horse. Encourage children to think of another pet and the things the pet owner has to do for that animal. Help children record their ideas on the Concept Map.
- Have volunteers share their concept maps with the group. Then explain that after reading, children return to the master.

OPTION 1 Read Aloud Pages 126–152 or Have Children Listen to the Audio Tape

Audio Tape for Something Fishy: *Enzo the Wonderfish*

Have children follow along in their anthologies as they listen to find out about the different pets the girl wants and what she does to teach tricks to her pet.

Discussion Points
- What kind of pets the girl asks for
- Why her parents say no
- What kind of pet the girl gets and the tricks she tries to teach him

OPTION 2 Guided or Assisted Reading of Pages 126–152

If, while you are using the guided reading segments that follow, it becomes clear that children are unable to read this selection silently, assist them in reading each segment aloud together. Then use the discussion points to talk about each segment.

Preview to Set a Purpose for Reading
(Predict-Infer Strategy)

Read the title of the selection aloud. Then have children preview the illustrations and make predictions about what kind of pets the girl asks for, what kind of pet she gets, and what tricks she tries to teach her pet. Write children's predictions on the board. If children have difficulty thinking of predictions, model how the illustrations on pages 130–131 and 134 might trigger predictions, such as page 130, *I think the girl wants a horse or a dog;* page 134, *It looks like the girl gets a fish for a pet.*

> For the first section, children's predictions are necessarily based on their preview of the selection. Before children read each subsequent section, discuss which of their predictions agreed with what was read and which did not. Have children think about what they've read and decide if they want to revise their original predictions or make new ones.

The Girl Asks Her Parents for a Pet (Pages 126–134)

Guide the Reading
(Think About Words Strategy)

- In this section, children may encounter unfamiliar words. Remind children to use the Think About Words strategy if they come across words they don't know. Review the steps they should follow when using the strategy: think about what makes sense, use sounds for letters, look for familiar word parts, and look for picture clues.

Discussion Points

- Ask children why the girl wanted a pet. Have them read the words on page 127 that tell this.
- The girl says sometimes she "was cuddled" by her older brother and sister. What might this have to do with why she wants a pet?
- Have children tell what kinds of pets the girl asked for and what excuses the girl's parents gave for not getting each of those pets.
- Ask children who used the Think About Words strategy to demonstrate what they did. If necessary, model using the strategy with the word *prodded* on page 128.

    THINK ALOUD *I'm not sure what this word is, but if I read the entire sentence, I see that it has something to do with **poked**. The word begins with the sounds for **pr** and has the ending **-ed**. From the picture, I can see the girl's brother and sister are tickling and sticking her with their fingers. I think the word must be another word that means "poked" or "stuck." I think the word is **prodded**. That fits when I try it in the sentence, too.*

- Discuss any words or information children still don't understand.

The Girl Gets a Fish and Tries to Teach Him Tricks   (Pages 134–144)

Guide the Reading
- Explain that this section tells about the different tricks the girl tries to teach Enzo. Suggest that children summarize this section after reading it so they can keep track of the kinds of tricks the girl tries to teach her pet.
- Have children read pages 134–144.

Discussion Points
- Ask children how the girl feels about getting a pet fish and how they can tell this.
- Have children read aloud the sentences that tell about the girl's nicknames for Enzo.
- Discuss with children what the girl does to help herself teach Enzo tricks. Ask children whether or not they think a fish can learn tricks, and why.
- Help children to summarize this section. Encourage volunteers to tell what kinds of tricks the girl tried to teach Enzo. Then guide children to tell in one or two sentences what the section is about. Write the summary sentences on the board.
- Clarify any points that still confuse children.

Enzo Is Missing   (Pages 145–152)

Guide the Reading
- In this section, which describes how the girl finds Enzo floating in her tea cup, children may not understand why a child is drinking tea. Explain that the author is from Australia, and in Australia, as in England, many people—including children—drink tea every day.
- Children may also be confused about how someone could lose a fish. Remind children that whenever they are unsure of something they read, they can read the words again, look at the pictures, or ask others what is happening.
- Have children read pages 145–152.

Discussion Points
- Ask children why they think the girl doesn't want Enzo to be "like some *ordinary* fish."
- Encourage children to tell whether or not they think a fish can live in tea. Have volunteers tell how tea is different from water.
- Ask children if they were confused by something they read and, if so, what they did to help themselves understand. Then discuss any vocabulary or parts of this section that are still confusing to them.
- Encourage children to predict what they think will happen to Enzo next.

Reflect on the Purposes for Reading
Review the predictions on the board. Discuss those that did not match the story and whether that was because they were inappropriate or if they might still match the story when children read the remainder of the selection.

Complete the Concept Map
Discuss children's concept map. Ask children if they want to make changes or add information they learned as they read the selection.

> **Have children read the rest of the selection cooperatively or have them participate in the reading of this selection with the entire class.**

Use AFTER **2** Interact *with* Literature

OPTION 1

Develop Critical Thinking: Making Judgments

Remind children that the girl's father said that "a fish is just as good as any other pet." Show children how to decide whether or not they think this is true. First have them identify reasons why they think this statement is true, then reasons why they think it is not true. List their responses on the board. Help children use the completed lists to decide whether they agree or disagree with the father's statement.

OPTION 2 **Develop Fluency: Partner Reading**

Have partners read pages 148–152 aloud to each other. Encourage children to show the girl's concern as they read. As one partner reads, the other should listen and help out when necessary.

Use AFTER **3** Instruct *and* Integrate

OPTION 1 **Inferences: Making Predictions**

- Remind children that readers use clues from what they know and what they read to make predictions about what will happen in a story. This keeps the story interesting and makes the reader want to keep reading.
- Have a volunteer read page 150 aloud. Ask children what prediction the girl makes about where Enzo went. ("Enzo must have leapt.") Have them tell what clue the girl used. ("The library book was open to the page on leaping.")
- Then read pages 151–153 aloud. Ask partners to find clues in the text and to use what they know to make a prediction about what might have happened to Enzo if he'd stayed in the teacup. Have partners share their predictions and reasoning with the group.

OPTION 2 **Contractions; Base Words and Endings: *-ed, -ing, -er, -est***

- Remind children that contractions are single words made up of two words. Then, display the following words and contractions and discuss how each contraction was formed.

could not	couldn't
did not	didn't
was not	wasn't

- Direct children to the following pages, and tell them to find the contractions: page 133*(couldn't)*; page 136*(didn't)*; page 149*(wasn't)*.

- Next display the following and remind children that adding an ending to a base word sometimes means the spelling changes.

prod	-ed	prodded
snicker	-ing	snickering
sad	-er	sadder
little	-est	littlest

Discuss how the ending was added to each base word, pointing out any spelling changes.

- Have children look on the following pages for words with one of the displayed endings. Help children identify each base word, and explain how each ending was added.

page 132	(scratched, sneaked, telling, snickering)
page 141	(retrieving, decided, easier)
page 144	(showed, sitting, swimming, showing)
page 296	(poked, prodded, tickled, teased, cuddled, littlest)

Pages 169–189 of
Swimmy

Use BEFORE **1** Introduce *the* Literature

OPTION 1 — Activate Prior Knowledge

- Read aloud the title and the name of the author-illustrator on page 169.
- Ask children what they can predict about the story based on the cover illustration.
- Then preview the illustrations on pages 169–197 with children. Ask children who Swimmy is and why they think he has that name.
- Ask children to predict what they think might happen in the story. Be sure to ask for reasons to support their predictions. (You may wish to recall other fish stories the children have read so far.)
- Read aloud the following summary.

   Swimmy lives with his big family until, one day, a big tuna fish eats all his brothers and sisters. Swimmy swims alone in the sea, where he sees many animals—wonderful <u>creatures</u> Swimmy thinks are real <u>marvels</u>. Finally, Swimmy meets a <u>school</u> of little fish who are hiding from big fish, and Swimmy has an idea. What could Swimmy's idea be?

(Underlined words are key words in the story.)

- Discuss with children what they know about sea life. Encourage volunteers to tell about how fish they have seen, in aquariums or in nature films, swim in schools.

OPTION 2 — Picture Walk

DISPLAY
school of fish
creatures
marvel

Print the key words on the board and read them aloud. Then lead children on a picture walk through the selection, incorporating these words where possible. Point to the words on the board as they are mentioned. Here are some suggestions:

- **Page 169** Read aloud the title. Ask children who Swimmy is and why they think he has that name.
- **Pages 170–171, 172–173** Explain to children that Swimmy lived with his brothers and sisters. Like Swimmy's family, little fish often swim in groups or <u>schools</u> (pages 170–171). Ask children why little fish might want to swim in schools (pages 172–173). Explain that the big tuna fish ate Swimmy's brothers and sisters. Swimmy was very sad.
- **Pages 176–187** Tell children that Swimmy is all alone on a journey through the sea. Even though he is scared and lonely, Swimmy sees many different animals, or <u>creatures</u>, while on his journey. Swimmy thinks these creatures are so wonderful that he calls them <u>marvels</u>. Ask children if they can name some of these creatures. Have them tell what kind of creature they would call a *marvel,* and why.

OPTION 3 — Comparison Chart

Selection Master 16 Part 5

- Explain to children that in this selection, they will read about a fish named Swimmy who decides to swim in a school, or group, with other fish so they will all be safer.
- Read aloud the heading and examples on the Comparison Chart. Help children think of other examples of how fish in schools and children in groups are alike and how they are different. Have children write these examples on their charts.
- Explain that after reading, children will know more about schools of fish and will be able to add more examples to their charts.

OPTION 1

Read Aloud Pages 169–189 or Have Children Listen to the Audio Tape

Audio Tape for Something Fishy: *Swimmy*

As children listen to the selection, have them follow along in their anthologies. Suggest that they listen to find out who Swimmy is and what kinds of creatures he meets on his journey.

Discussion Points
- Who Swimmy is
- Why he is alone
- What kinds of creatures he meets

OPTION 2

Guided or Assisted Reading of Pages 169–189

If, while you are using the guided reading segments that follow, it becomes clear that children are unable to read this selection silently, assist them in reading each segment aloud together. Then use the discussion points to talk about each segment.

Preview to Set a Purpose for Reading
(Self-Question Strategy)

Read aloud the selection title. As children preview the illustrations, encourage them to think of questions prompted by what they see. Write their questions on the board. If children need help thinking of questions, model how the illustrations on pages 172–173 might raise questions, such as *Is the big fish eating the little fish? Does the little black fish get away?*

> For the first section, children's questions are necessarily based on their preview of the selection. Before children read each subsequent section, discuss any answers they've found to their questions and have children decide if they want to add additional questions to the list. Then have them continue reading to answer their questions.

A Big Tuna Fish Eats Swimmy's Family (Pages 169–173)

Guide the Reading
- This section includes several words which may be unfamiliar to children. Remind children to use the Think About Words strategy if they come across words they don't know.

Discussion Points
- Ask children why Swimmy got away from the big fish and the little red fish didn't.
- Have children read aloud the sentence on page 173 that tells what the tuna fish was like.
- Ask children if they came across any words they didn't know and, if so, to demonstrate what they did.
- Clarify any points that are still confusing for children.

Swimmy Sees Many Creatures (Pages 174–187)

Guide the Reading
(Summarize Strategy)
- Print the words *medusa* and *sea anemones* on the board. Pronounce the words and explain that these are the names of two fish in this section. Direct children to the illustrations showing these fish on pages 177 and 187.
- Since this section introduces many sea animals, suggest that children summarize so they can keep track of the different creatures Swimmy meets on his journey.
- Have children read pages 174–187.

Discussion Points	• Ask children to read aloud the sentence that tells how Swimmy felt as he set out on his journey.
	• Have children discuss how Swimmy feels about the creatures he sees.
	• Ask children why Swimmy might describe the lobster's walk as a "water-moving machine."
	• Discuss with children how they think a fish "pulled by an invisible thread" would swim. Have volunteers demonstrate.
	• Encourage children to tell what animals or things the eel (pages 184–185) and sea anemones (pages 186–187) remind them of, and why.
	• Help children to summarize this section. Use the Think Aloud below to model the strategy.

> **THINK ALOUD** *Swimmy meets a lot of sea creatures and plants. If I make a list, that would help me keep track of them—medusa, lobster, fish, seaweed, eel, and sea anemones. I can summarize this section like this:* **Swimmy sees a medusa, a lobster, some fish, seaweed, an eel, and sea anemones as he swims alone in the sea.**

• Ask children if there are any words or information they still don't understand and would like to discuss.

Swimmy Meets a School of Little Fish (Page 188–189)

Guide the Reading	• In this section, children may be confused when Swimmy encounters another school of fish that look just like his family that was eaten. Remind children that whenever they are unsure of something they read, they can read the words again, look at the pictures, or ask others what is happening.
	• Have children read pages 188–189.
Discussion Points	• Ask children how they think Swimmy felt when he found another school of fish that looked just like his brothers and sisters.
	• Read page 188 aloud. Ask children to tell if they think the little red fish were smart to hide, and why. Then have children preview the illustrations on pages 190–197. Encourage children to predict what plan Swimmy thinks of to help the little red fish.
	• Ask children if they were confused by anything they read and, if so, to tell what they did to help themselves understand.
	• Discuss any vocabulary or parts of this section that are still confusing to children.
Reflect on the Purposes for Reading	Review the questions on the board. Discuss those that were not answered and whether they might still be answered when children read the remainder of the selection.
Complete the Concept Map	Have children return to their Comparison Chart. Discuss any additional information they learned about schools of fish as they read the selection, and any additional ideas they have about groups of children. Help them record the information on the chart.

> **Have children read the rest of the selection cooperatively or have them participate in the reading of this selection with the entire class.**

Use AFTER **2** Interact *with* Literature

OPTION 1 **Think About Words Strategy**

• Use the Think Aloud below to model how to figure out the word *swaying on page 186.*

What makes sense From what the other words in the sentence say, I know that this word has something to do with palm trees in the wind. I know the wind would move the leaves of a palm tree.

Sounds for letters The word begins with the sounds for *s* and *w*. It has the letters *ay*, which stand for the long *a* sound as in *day*. When I put *sw* and *ay* together, I get the word sway.

Familiar word parts The word ends with *-ing* as in *playing*. I think the word is *swaying*.

Picture clues I see creatures that look like palm trees in the water. The water would make the creatures move or sway. When I read the sentence with the word *swaying,* it makes sense.

OPTION 2

Develop Fluency: Group Reading

Have children read page 188 aloud. Assign children the roles of the narrator and Swimmy, and have the rest of the group be the school of fish. Point to children when it's their turn to read. Encourage children to show in their voices Swimmy's happiness and the fright of the other fish.

Use AFTER **3** Instruct *and* Integrate

OPTION 1

Fantasy and Realism

• Display the following sentences:

1. A tuna fish swallows the little red fish. (pages 172–173)
2. The fish are pulled by an invisible thread. (pages 180–181)
3. The rocks are made of sugar candy. (page 182–183)
4. Fish swim in schools. (pages 192–193)
5. A little fish makes a plan to scare the big fish. (pages 196–197)

• Have children turn to the pages indicated. Read each displayed sentence aloud. Ask if the statement tells about something that could happen in real life or about something make-believe, and why. Write *real* or *make-believe* next to each sentence.

OPTION 2

r-Controlled Vowels: *ar, or*

• Display and read aloud the following words:

d<u>ar</u>k   sh<u>ar</u>k   m<u>or</u>e   f<u>or</u>med

Explain that the letters *ar* often stand for the vowel sound heard in *dark* and *shark*, and the letters *or* often stand for the vowel sound in *more* and *formed*.

• Have children return to the story to find words that contain the letters *ar* and *or* and that stand for the vowel sounds in *dark* and *horn*. (page 170, *corner*; page 176, *marvel*; page 183, *forest*; page 188, *dark*)

Wake Up!

By Mindy Menschell

High-Frequency Words:	*all, I, jump, run, the, time, up*
Phonics/Decoding	Initial Consonants: *b, g, k, m, t, v, z*

Preview and Predict

- Display *Wake Up!* and have the title read aloud. Read the names of the author and illustrator. Briefly discuss the front and back cover illustrations. Ask children what they think this story will be about.
- **Picture Walk**   Ask what children do when they wake up in the morning. Then page through the book and discuss the illustrations, incorporating story vocabulary as you do so. For example: Ask what time the clock shows on page 1; discuss how the speech balloons show who is speaking; explain who the turtle is, reading the word *coach* on his jacket and explaining what a coach does; ask what the turtle wants the rabbit to do on pages 1 and 2 (*wake up, sip*) and what the rabbit does on pages 3 to 7 (*zip up, run, jump*).

Read and Discuss

- Tell children you will read the story aloud together. Ask children what they notice about the first line of the story. (It is also the title.) Read page 1 with children. Help children notice the pattern by having them find the words *wake up* in the speech balloon for the rabbit.
- If children read *sip* for *zip* on page 3, say: This word looks like *sip* and has the same ending sounds, but the first letter is different. What letter does it begin with? What word begins with the sound for *z* and ends with the sounds for *sip*? That's right, *zip*. Does *zip* make sense in the sentence?
- If children read *hop* for *jump* on page 6, say: *Hop* makes sense, but this word begins with the letter *j*. What word begins with *j* as in *jam* and names something else that rabbits do? Yes, *jump*. Does *jump* make sense in the sentence?
- Ask what three words end each of the rabbit's sentences. (*all the time*) Have volunteers find and read aloud all the sentences that include these words.
- Ask what the letter *z* stands for in a speech balloon. (the sound for sleeping or snoring)

Responding

Invite children to suggest why the rabbit was so tired and couldn't really "wake up." Ask what the rabbit might do next time so that he will be ready to run another morning.

Additional Support

If the children's responses indicate that they had difficulty decoding or reading high-frequency words, use the following lesson:

Phonics/Decoding (Initial Consonants) and High-Frequency Words for Lesson 1, page 203

Rereading for Fluency

Have students reread the story aloud at least three times. Suggest that they each reread the story to themselves, to a partner, and to an older reader—you, a volunteer, an older student, or a classroom aide.

The Hen Sat

By Kathryn Lewis

> **High-Frequency Words:** *and, cat, dog, fast, one, three, two, went*
>
> **Phonics/Decoding** Initial Consonants: *c, d, l, n, p, t, y*

Preview and Predict

- Display *The Hen Sat* and have the title read aloud. Read the names of the author and illustrator. Briefly discuss the front and back cover illustrations. Ask children what they think this story will be about.
- **Picture Walk** Ask what children know about hens. Page through the book and discuss the illustrations, incorporating story vocabulary as you do so. For example: Specify *one rat, two cats, three dogs* to describe the animals, and point to the words; show by sweeping your hand how they went fast; note that one more animal is in each picture; together count the animals, pointing to the words—*one, two, three.* Ask what the hen did on each page.

Read and Discuss

- Tell children you will read the story aloud together. Note that there are no words on page 1, and have them tell what the picture shows. Turn to page 2. Point out that in this book, two pages side by side show one picture and one sentence that goes across both pages. Read the sentence with children. Continue through the story.
- If children read *ran* for *went* on page 3, say: *Ran* makes sense, but look at the beginning of this word. What letter does it begin with? What word begins with the sound for *w* as in *worm* and would make sense if you said you saw something go?
- If children read *kittens* for *cats* on page 4, say: *Kittens* makes sense with the picture. But look at this word. (Point to *cats*.) What letter does it begin with? Yes, *c* can have the sound you hear at the beginning of *kittens*, but the word *kittens* has too many sounds to be this short word. What word begins with *c* as in *can* and names grownup kittens. Yes, *cats*.
- Ask what two words are repeated several times in the story. (*went, fast*) Have volunteers find and read aloud all the sentences that include these words.
- Ask: Who will find and read the sentence that tells what the hen did?

Responding

Discuss with children why the hen didn't get up. Ask what they think the hen might have done if she had not been sitting on the eggs and why.

> **Additional Support**
>
> If the children's responses indicate that they had difficulty decoding or reading high-frequency words, use the following lesson:
>
> **Phonics/Decoding (Initial Consonants) and High-Frequency Words for Lesson 1, page 204**

Rereading for Fluency

Have children reread the story aloud at least three times. Suggest that they each reread the story to themselves, to a partner, and to an older reader—you, a volunteer, an older student, or a classroom aide.

Snuffy, Fluffy and the Mice
By Philemon Sturges

High-Frequency Words: *a, baby, have, my, our, see, we, with*

Phonics/Decoding   Initial Consonants: *f, h, l, s, w, qu*

Preview and Predict

- Display *Snuffy, Fluffy and the Mice* and have the title read aloud. Read the names of the author and illustrator. Briefly discuss the front and back cover illustrations. Ask children what they think this story will be about.
- **Picture Walk**   Display page 1 and read the pictured sign aloud. Ask children to share what they know about pet shows. Then page through the book and discuss the illustrations, incorporating story vocabulary as you do so. For example: On pages 1, 3, and 5, describe the pictures by saying, "these children have a baby dog, . . . have a baby cat, and . . . have three baby mice; name the dog on page 2, Snuffy, and the cat on page 4.

Read and Discuss

- Tell children you will read the story aloud together. Read page 1 with children and continue through the story. Point out the rhyming words on pages 2 and 4 and on pages 6 and 8.
- If children read *flower* for *rose* on page 4, say: *Flower* makes sense with the picture. But this word begins with the letter *r* and should rhyme with *nose*. What word begins with the sound for *r*, rhymes with *nose*, and names a flower? Yes, the word is *rose*.
- If children read *mouse* for *mice* on page 5, say: *Mouse* doesn't make sense; it names only one pet. How many pets are in the cage? Yes, *three*. What word begins with *m* and names more than one mouse? Does *mice* make sense?
- Have volunteers find and read aloud the sentences on pages 4 and 6. Ask what words in these sentences tell that these pets belong to someone (*my, our*).
- Ask children which story sentences are questions and how they know. Have volunteers find and read aloud the questions.
- Ask: Why do you think the mice all jump when Fluffy runs? Why does Snuffy jump up?

Responding

Discuss with children which pet in the story they would like to have and why. Have children tell something new about their pet by completing this sentence frame: *I see a* _____ *with a* _____.

Additional Support

If the children's responses indicate that they had difficulty decoding or reading high-frequency words, use the following lesson:

Phonics/Decoding (Initial Consonants) and High-Frequency Words for Lesson 1, page 204

Rereading for Fluency

Have children reread the story aloud at least three times. Suggest that they each reread the story to themselves, to a partner, and to an older reader—you, a volunteer, an older student, or a classroom aide.

Jump, Jill, Jump

By Kay Winters

> **High-Frequency Words:** *but, for, is, it, not, will, you*
>
> **Phonics/Decoding** Final Consonants: *f, l, r, s, t*

Preview and Predict

- Display *Jump, Jill, Jump* and have the title read aloud. Read the names of the author and illustrator. Briefly discuss the front and back cover illustration. Ask children what they think this story will be about.
- **Picture Walk**   You may wish to invite volunteers to show how to jump rope; first singly, then with rope turners. Then page through the book and discuss the illustrations, making sure to introduce the characters by name. Incorporate story vocabulary as you do so. For example: Ask who is jumping, is not jumping, and will jump next; together count how many children are jumping on each page and point to the words *one*, *two*. For each picture, ask what baby Jill is doing.

Read and Discuss

- Tell children you will read the story aloud together. Read page 1 with children. Have them identify Kit, Bill, and baby Jill in the illustration. Point out the end of line rhymes—*Bill, Jill*. Then read the sentences on page 2 with children. Continue through the story.
- If children read *Kit* for *Bill* on page 3, say: *Kit* makes sense, but look at this word. (Point to *Bill*.) What letter does it begin with? end with? Yes, it begins with *b* and ends with *l*. What name in this story begins with the sound for *b* and ends with the sounds for *l*? Yes, the name is *Bill*.
- If children read *see* for *sit* on page 8, say: *See* makes sense and begins with the letter *s*, but this word ends with the letter *t*. What word begins with *s*, ends with *t*, and tells what everyone is doing on the bench? Yes, *sit*. Does *sit* match the letters you see in this word?
- Ask what phrase is repeated several times in the story, with different names in it. (*Jump, _____, jump.*) Have volunteers find and read aloud the repeated sentences.

Responding

Discuss with children why baby Jill will not jump with Bill and Kit. Ask what they think might happen if Jill tried to do it.

> **Additional Support**
>
> If the children's responses indicate that they had difficulty decoding or reading high-frequency words, use the following lesson:
>
> **Phonics/Decoding (Final Consonants) and High-Frequency Words for Lesson 2, page 204**

Rereading for Fluency

Have children reread the story aloud at least three times. Suggest that they each reread the story to themselves, to a partner, and to an older reader—you, a volunteer, an older student, or a classroom aide.

Me Too!

By Maryann Dobeck

> **High-Frequency Words:** *am, came, he, me, said, too*
>
> **Phonics/Decoding** Final Consonants: *b, k, g, m*

Preview and Predict

- Display *Me Too!* and have the title read aloud. Read the names of the author and illustrator. Briefly discuss the front and back cover illustrations. Ask children what they think this story will be about.
- **Picture Walk**   Have volunteers tell about races they have run. Then page through the book and discuss the illustrations, incorporating story vocabulary as you do so. For example: Talk about who came for the race on page 1; on pages 3 and 7, ask children to find the words that are the same as the story title, *me too*. For each picture, ask who is winning the race.

Read and Discuss

- Tell children you will read the story aloud together. Read page 1 with children and have them identify Pam and Sam in the picture. Then turn to page 2. Read the sentences with children and continue through the story.
- If children read *Pam* for *Sam* on page 3, say: *Pam* has the same end sounds as this word, but the first letter is different. What name begins with the sound for *s* and ends with the same sounds as *Pam*. Yes, *Sam*. Does *Sam* make sense in the sentence?
- If children read *tall* for *big* on page 4, say: *Tall* makes sense, but look at this word. (Point to *big*.) Think of a word that can mean "tall"—one that begins with the sound *b* has in *ball* and ends like *pig*. Yes, the word is *big*.
- Ask children to find and read the words with special type on pages 4, 6, and 8. Have volunteers read the sentences, emphasizing these words. Ask how putting the words in special type helped children understand the story better.
- Ask: How did Sam win the race?

Responding

Discuss with children why Pam thought she would win the race. Ask if they, too, thought Pam would win because she was fast *and* big. Discuss the lesson the story teaches.

> **Additional Support**
>
> If the children's responses indicate that they had difficulty decoding or reading high-frequency words, use the following lesson:
>
> **Phonics/Decoding (Final Consonants) and High-Frequency Words for Lesson 2, page 205**

Rereading for Fluency

Have children reread the story aloud at least three times. Suggest that they each reread the story to themselves, to a partner, and to an older reader—you, a volunteer, an older student, or a classroom aide.

Ian and the Seed
By Delores Lowe Friedman

> **High-Frequency Words:** *in, out, plant, put, six, then*
>
> **Phonics/Decoding**   Final Consonants: *d, n, p, x*

Preview and Predict

- Display *Ian and the Seed* and have the title read aloud. Read the names of the author and illustrator. Briefly discuss the front and back cover illustrations. Ask children what they think this story will be about.
- **Picture Walk**   Encourage children to share their experiences with seeds and plants. Then page through the book and discuss the illustrations, incorporating story vocabulary as you do so. For example: Read the birthday banner on page 1, and have children find six candles in the picture; point out the flowerpot and the seed in Grandma's hand in the illustration on pages 2 and 3, noting that the seed is out of the pot; ask where the seed is on pages 4 and 5 (in the pot); explain that the pictures on pages 6 and 7 show Ian's plant over several days.

Read and Discuss

- Tell children you will read the story aloud together. Display page 1 and help children to name the story characters—Ian, Father, Mother, Grandma. Read page 1 with children. Then continue through the story.
- If children read *take* for *need* on page 3, say: *Take* makes sense, but look at this word. (Point to *need*.) What letter does it begin with? end with? Yes, it begins with *n* and ends with *d*. What word begins like *now* and ends like *seed*? Does *need* make sense?
- If children read *feed* for *fix* on page 7, say: *Feed* begins with the sound for *f*, but what letter does this word end with? (Point to *fix*.) Yes, *x*. What word begins like *feed* and ends with the sound *x* has in *six*? Does *fix* make sense?
- Remind children that the pictures on pages 6 and 7 show the plant over several days. Ask children to look for other picture clues that help to show that the plant needed time to grow. If necessary, encourage discussion of Ian's clothes.
- Ask: Why did Ian need to put the plant out?

Responding

Encourage children to compare Ian's experience to their own experiences with growing plants or watching them grow. How are they alike? How are they different?

> **Additional Support**
>
> If the children's responses indicate that they had difficulty decoding or reading high-frequency words, use the following lesson:
>
> **Phonics/Decoding (Final Consonants) and High-Frequency Words for Lesson 2, page 205**

Rereading for Fluency

Have children reread the story aloud at least three times. Suggest that they each reread the story to themselves, to a partner, and to an older reader—you, a volunteer, an older student, or a classroom aide.

Our Plants
By Jeannie W. Berger

High-Frequency Words: *do, here, it's, need, so, this, was, there*

Phonics/Decoding   Consonant Clusters with *r*

Preview and Predict

- Display *Our Plants* and have the title read aloud. Read the names of the author and illustrator. Briefly discuss the front and back cover illustrations. Ask children what they think this story will be about.
- **Picture Walk**   Ask children who have gardens or have seen gardens to share their experiences. Then page through the book and discuss the illustrations, incorporating story vocabulary as you do so. For example: ask what Dog will do with the rake and seeds on page 1; talk about pages 4 and 5, saying, "This ground looks so dry. Do you think plants will grow here?" For each picture, ask what Dog needs to do to make his garden grow.

Read and Discuss

- Tell children you will read the story aloud together. Read page 1 with children and continue through the story.
- If children read *Bird* for *Crow* on page 2, say: *Bird* makes sense, but look at this word. (Point to *Crow*.) What letters does it begin with? Yes, *cr*. What word begins with the sounds for *cr* and names a kind of bird? Yes, *Crow*.
- If children read *dirty* for *dry* on page 4, say: *dirty* makes sense, but this word begins with the sound for *dr* as in *dress*. What word begins with the sounds for *dr* and means "not wet"? Yes, *dry*. Does *dry* make sense?
- Ask why Cat and Crow thought the plants would not grow. Have them find the sentences that tell what Dog said, and use picture clues to figure out what Dog did so that the ground would not be too dry.
- Have volunteers reread page 8. Have children use word and picture clues to predict what Cat and Crow will do next.

Responding

Recall with children the things that Dog did to make his plants grow. Encourage them to use the story events to tell what might happen when Cat and Crow plant their seeds.

Additional Support

If the children's responses indicate that they had difficulty decoding or reading high-frequency words, use the following lesson:

Phonics/Decoding (Consonant Clusters) and High-Frequency Words for Lesson 3, page 205

Rereading for Fluency

Have children reread the story aloud at least three times. Suggest that they each reread the story to themselves, to a partner, and to an older reader—you, a volunteer, an older student, or a classroom aide.

A Walk in the City
By Tanner Ottley Gay

High-Frequency Words: *go, long, many, of, on, people, walk*

Phonics/Decoding   Consonant Clusters with *s, l*

Preview and Predict

• Display *A Walk in the City* and have the title read aloud. Read the names of the author and illustrator. Briefly discuss the front and back cover illustrations. Ask children what they think this story will be about.

• **Picture Walk**   Ask children to name things they might see on a walk in the city. Then page through the book and discuss the illustrations, incorporating story vocabulary as you do so. For example: On pages 2 and 3, talk about how many people children see; ask when the people know it is safe to walk across the street, pointing out the *go* sign; as needed, explain that on page 5, the children will take an elevator to the top of the Rose Building. For each picture, have children relate the illustrations to their own city experiences.

Read and Discuss

• Tell children you will read the story aloud together. Read page 1 with children and continue through the story.

• If children read *start* for *stop* on page 2, say: *Start* begins with the sounds for *st*, but look at this word. (Point to *stop*.) What letter does it end with? Yes, *p*. What word begins like *start* and ends with the sound for *p*? Does *stop* make sense? Can you find the word *stop* in the picture?

• If children read *big* for *small* on page 7, say: *Big* makes sense. But look at this word. (Point to *small*.) What letters does it begin with? end with? Think of a word that tells how something looks when you see it from far away—one that begins with the sounds for *sm* and ends like *ball* ? Does *small* make sense?

• Ask how the children got to the top of the Rose Building. Have children find and read the sentences that tell how.

Responding

Encourage children to tell what they would like to see and do if they took a walk in the city. Would they like to go to the top of a tall building? Why or why not?

Additional Support

If the children's responses indicate that they had difficulty decoding or reading high-frequency words, use the following lesson:

Phonics/Decoding (Consonant Clusters) and High-Frequency Words for Lesson 3, page 206

Rereading for Fluency

Have children reread the story aloud at least three times. Suggest that they each reread the story to themselves, to a partner, and to an older reader—you, a volunteer, an older student, or a classroom aide.

A Fish Trip
By Margo Lemieux

> **High-Frequency Words:** *call, eat, fish, say, to*
>
> **Phonics/Decoding** Consonant Clusters with *l, r, s*

Preview and Predict

- Display *A Fish Trip* and have the title read aloud. Read the names of the author and illustrator. Briefly discuss the front and back cover illustrations. Ask children what they think this story will be about.
- **Picture Walk** Invite children who have visited aquariums or pet shops with aquariums to share their experiences. Then page through the book and discuss the illustrations, incorporating story vocabulary as you do so. For example: On page 1, note the rainy weather, ask what sound raindrops make, and point to and read the words *drip, drip*; ask what Dad and Jed might say to each other during breakfast and what they might eat. For each aquarium scene, ask them to describe the kinds of fish and sea life they see.

Read and Discuss

- Tell children you will read the story aloud together. Read page 1 with children. Ask why Jed calls it a *drip drip day*. Then read page 2 with children. Continue through the story.
- If children read *turtles* for *fish* on page 4, say: *Turtles* makes sense, but look at this word. (Point to *fish*.) What letters does it begin with? Yes, *f*. What word begins with the sound for *f* and names animals that swim? Yes, *fish*.
- If children read *swimming* for *jumping* on page 5, say: *swimming* makes sense, and it has an *-ing* ending, but this word begins with the sound for *j*. (Frame *jump*.) Can you read this word now? What word begins with the sound for *j* and names something fish can do? Yes, *jump*. Does *jumping* make sense?
- Ask why Dad says it is a *drip drip* day at the end of the story.

Responding

Invite children to name other things Jed and Dad might see on a fish trip. Encourage them to tell what they think the best part of the fish trip was and why.

> ### Additional Support
>
> If the children's responses indicate that they had difficulty decoding or reading high-frequency words, use the following lesson:
>
> **Phonics/Decoding (Consonant Clusters) and High-Frequency Words for Lesson 3, page 206**

Rereading for Fluency

Have children reread the story aloud at least three times. Suggest that they each reread the story to themselves, to a partner, and to an older reader—you, a volunteer, an older student, or a classroom aide.

Where IS My Baby?

By Deborah Eaton

High-Frequency Words: *as, be, big, could, tree, under, when, your*

Phonics/Decoding Digraphs *sh, th*

Preview and Predict

- Display *Where IS My Baby?* and have the title read aloud. Read the names of the author and illustrator. Briefly discuss the front and back cover illustrations. Ask children what they think this story will be about.
- **Picture Walk** Invite children to tell what they do when they can't find something. Then page through the book and discuss the illustrations, incorporating story vocabulary as you do so. For example: On page 1, ask where Silly Milly's baby could be; have children use picture clues to tell where Silly Milly looked on pages 2 and 3 (in a big tree) and on pages 4 and 5 (under a bush); ask what Rae and Ruby Rabbit notice on page 6 that Silly Milly does not notice. For each picture, ask how children think Silly Milly is feeling.

Read and Discuss

- Tell children you will read the story aloud together. Read page 1 with children and continue through the story.
- If children read *tree* for *bush* on page 4, say: *Tree* makes sense, but look at this word. (Point to *bush*.) What letter does it begin with? Yes, *b*. Think of a word that names a very small tree—one that begins with the sound you hear at the beginning of *ball* and ends like *push*. Yes, *bush* has those sounds and makes sense.
- If children read *Then* for *When* on page 6, say: *Then* makes sense, but this word begins with the sound for *wh*. What word begins with the sound for *wh* and ends like *then*? Yes, *when*. Does *when* make sense?
- Ask what question is repeated several times in the story. Have volunteers read the question *Where IS my baby?* each time it appears.
- Ask children why Silly Milly couldn't find her baby.

Responding

Note that at the end of the story, Silly Milly has her baby, but forgets where she was going. Encourage children to tell where they think Silly Milly was going and why.

Additional Support

If the children's responses indicate that they had difficulty decoding or reading high-frequency words, use the following lesson:

Phonics/Decoding (Digraphs) and High-Frequency Words for Lesson 4, page 207

Rereading for Fluency

Have children reread the story aloud at least three times. Suggest that they each reread the story to themselves, to a partner, and to an older reader—you, a volunteer, an older student, or a classroom aide.

Fox and Chick
By Cass Hollander

High-Frequency Words: *at, back, come, her, house, how, more, over*

Phonics/Decoding Digraph *ch*

Preview and Predict

- Display *Fox and Chick* and have the title read aloud. Read the names of the author and illustrator. Briefly discuss the front and back cover illustrations. Ask children what they think this story will be about.
- **Picture Walk** Encourage children to share what they know about foxes and chicks. Then page through the book and discuss the illustrations, incorporating story vocabulary as you do so. (You may wish to explain the word *chat*.) For example: On pages 2 and 3, tell children that Fox wants Chick to come over to his house, but that Chick says Fox should come over to her house; ask what happens each time Fox comes to Chick's house and is sent away (Fox comes back.). For each picture, have children notice where the dog is.

Read and Discuss

- Tell children you will read the story aloud together. Note that there are no words on page 1, and have them tell what the picture shows. Then read page 2 with children. Continue through the story.
- If children read *talk* for *chat* on page 3, say: *Talk* makes sense, but it has different sounds. What letters does this word begin with? (Point to *chat*.) Think of a word that means "to talk"— one that begins with the sound for *ch* and ends like *hat*. Yes, *chat*. Does *chat* make sense?
- If children read *two* for *three* on page 5, say: *Two* makes sense, but this is a longer word. Think of another number—one that begins with the sounds for *th* and ends like *tree*. Yes, *three* has those sounds and makes sense.
- Ask children what sentences in the story tell when Fox came back. Have volunteers read the sentences.
- Ask why children think Chick kept asking Fox to come back.

Responding

Ask children if they think Fox will try to come back some other time. If they were Fox, what time would they choose to come back? Why?

Additional Support

If the children's responses indicate that they had difficulty decoding or reading high-frequency words, use the following lesson:

Phonics/Decoding (Digraphs) and High-Frequency Words for Lesson 4, page 207

Rereading for Fluency

Have children reread the story aloud at least three times. Suggest that they each reread the story to themselves, to a partner, and to an older reader—you, a volunteer, an older student, or a classroom aide.

Hank and Lin

By Stu Goodwin

> **High-Frequency Words:**   *down, had, him, his, if, she*
>
> **Phonics/Decoding**   Digraphs *ch, sh, th*

Preview and Predict

- Display *Hank and Lin* and have the title read aloud. Read the names of the author and illustrator. Briefly discuss the front and back cover illustrations. Ask children what they think this story will be about.
- **Picture Walk**   Encourage children to talk about silly animals they have read about. Then page through the book and discuss the illustrations, incorporating story vocabulary as you do so. For example: On page 1, identify Hank and Lin and discuss what they look like, using the words *he, she, his,* and *her* in the descriptions; on pages 2 and 3, discuss who is up and who is down. For each picture, encourage children to tell what they notice about the two animals.

Read and Discuss

- Tell children you will read the story aloud together. Read page 1 with children. Ask if children think *zanks* and *zins* are real animals or make believe animals. Then read page 2 with children. Continue through the story.
- If children read *he* for *she* on page 3, say: *He* makes sense for a boy animal, but Lin is a girl. Think of a word that can name a girl—one that begins with *sh* and ends like *he*. Yes, *she* makes sense and has those sounds.
- If children have trouble reading *thank* on page 8, say: Think of a word that people say after someone has helped them—one that begins with the sound for *th* and ends like *Hank*. Yes, *thank*. Does *thank* make sense?
- Ask children what Hank and Lin's problem was. Have volunteers read the sentences that tell how Hank and Lin solved their problem with each other's help.

Responding

Invite children to compare Hank and Lin. Ask: How are Hank and Lin alike? How are they different?

> **Additional Support**
>
> If the children's responses indicate that they had difficulty decoding or reading high-frequency words, use the following lesson:
>
> **Phonics/Decoding (Digraphs) and High-Frequency Words for Lesson 4, page 208**

Rereading for Fluency

Have children reread the story aloud at least three times. Suggest that they each reread the story to themselves, to a partner, and to an older reader—you, a volunteer, an older student, or a classroom aide.

I Like Cats
By Peggy Kahn

> **High-Frequency Words:** *before, can, each, from, good, like, made, they*
>
> **Phonics/Decoding**   Short *a*; Short *a* Phonograms: *-at, -ad, -ast*

Preview and Predict

- Display *I Like Cats* and have the title read aloud. Read the names of the author and illustrator. Briefly discuss the front and back cover illustrations. Ask children what they think this story will be about.
- **Picture Walk**   Invite children who have cats or know of cats to share their experiences. Then page through the book and discuss the illustrations, incorporating story vocabulary as you do so. For example: On pages 2 and 3, ask what each cat looks like; on page 5, ask what the hat is made from. For each picture, ask what the girls do to show they both like cats.

Read and Discuss

- Tell children you will read the story aloud together. Read page 1 with children, helping them to identify Pat and Jan. Then continue through the story.
- If children have trouble reading *Glad* on page 3, say: Look at this word. (Point to *Glad*.) What word part do you see at the end? Yes, *-ad*. Think of a word that begins with the sounds *gl* has in *glass* and ends with the sounds *-ad* has in *had*. Yes, *Glad*.
- Follow a similar procedure with *Hat* on page 5. Say: Think of a word that begins with the sound *h* has in *house* and ends with the sounds *-at* has in *cat*. Yes, *Hat*.
- If children read *first* for *fast* on page 8, say: *First* makes sense, but look at this word. What word part do you see? Yes , *-ast*. Now, think of a word that begins with *f* as in *first* and ends with the word part *-ast* as in *last*. Yes, *fast*.
- Ask what sentence is repeated several times in the story. Have volunteers read *But before she could say that, Jan said,* each time it appears.
- Ask children to find and read what Pat finally does say.

Responding

Encourage children to tell why they think Pat and Jan like cats.

> **Additional Support**
>
> If the children's responses indicate that they had difficulty decoding or reading high-frequency words, use the following lesson:
>
> **Phonics/Decoding (Phonograms) and High-Frequency Words for Lesson 5, page 208**

Rereading for Fluency

Have children reread the story aloud at least three times. Suggest that they each reread the story to themselves, to a partner, and to an older reader—you, a volunteer, an older student, or a classroom aide.

A Big Help
By Karen O'Donnell Taylor

High-Frequency Words: *day, did, help, little, make, there, were, who*

Phonics/Decoding Short *e*; Short *e* Phonograms: *-est, -elp, -et*

Preview and Predict

- Display *A Big Help* and have the title read aloud. Read the names of the author and illustrator. Briefly discuss the front and back cover illustrations. Ask children what they think this story will be about.
- **Picture Walk** Encourage children to share what they know about birds and where they live. Then page through the book and discuss the illustrations, incorporating story vocabulary as you do so. For example: On pages 2 and 3, ask why Bird needs help getting to her nest; have children name the animals on page 2 who will help–Skunk, Beaver, Deer, Snake. Have children look at page 4 and predict how the animals might use the little tree to help Bird.

Read and Discuss

- Tell children you will read the story aloud together. Read page 1 with children. Then continue through the story.
- If children read *cut* for *get* on page 4, say: *Cut* makes sense, but it has different sounds. Think of a word that begins with the sound *g* has in *game* and ends like *net*. Yes, *get* has those sounds and makes sense.
- If children have trouble reading *nest* on page 7, say: Think of a word that names a bird's home–one that begins with the sound *n* has in *net* and ends like *rest*. Yes, *nest* has the right sounds and makes sense.
- Ask what sentence is repeated several times in the story. Have volunteers read *If we all do a little, we can be a big help* each time it appears.
- Help children to recall the sequence of events in the story. Ask: How did each animal do a little to be a big help?

Responding

Ask children if they think Skunk made a good plan. Then encourage children to think of other ways the animals could all do a little to help Bird get into her nest.

Additional Support

If the children's responses indicate that they had difficulty decoding or reading high-frequency words, use the following lesson:

Phonics/Decoding (Phonograms) and High-Frequency words for Lesson 5, page 208

Rereading for Fluency

Have children reread the story aloud at least three times. Suggest that they each reread the story to themselves, to a partner, and to an older reader–you, a volunteer, an older student, or a classroom aide.

Great Frogs!
By Kathryn Riley

High-Frequency Words: *get, great, look, their, us*

Phonics/Decoding Short *o*; Short *o* Phonograms: *-og, -ob, -ot*

Preview and Predict

- Display *Great Frogs!* and have the title read aloud. Read the names of the author and illustrator. Briefly discuss the front and back cover illustrations. Ask children what they think this story will be about.
- **Picture Walk** Invite children to talk about and describe frogs they have seen in books or on walks. Then page through the book and discuss the illustrations, incorporating story vocabulary as you do so. For example: point out that the characters on page 1 are in their classroom; ask children to tell what the frogs on page 2 look like, mentioning that they are both great frogs; discuss the frogs on page 5 in a similar way. For each picture, ask children to find things in the story classroom that look like things in their classroom.

Read and Discuss

- Tell children you will read the story aloud together. Read page 1 with children and identify the story characters—Mr. Best, Ben, Maggie, and Robbie (at the table). Then read page 2 with children and continue through the story.
- If children read *little* for *lot* on page 3, say: *Little* makes sense, but this is a shorter word. (Point to *lot*.) Think of a word that means "very much"—one that begins like *little* and ends like *hot*. Yes, *lot* makes sense and has those sounds.
- If children read *what* for *where* page 5, say: *What* begins with the right sound, but doesn't make sense. Think of a question word that asks about a place—one that begins with the sound *wh* has in *what* and ends like *there*. Yes, *where*. Does *where* make sense?
- Ask children which sentence is repeated several times in the story. Have volunteers read *Great frogs!* each time it appears. Make sure they remember the title of the story.
- Ask children to find and read what Mr. Best, Ben, and Maggie say about Robbie's frogs.

Responding

Encourage children to tell what kind of frog they would like to make.

Additional Support

If the children's responses indicate that they had difficulty decoding or reading high-frequency words, use the following lesson:

Phonics/Decoding (Phonograms) and High-Frequency Words for Lesson 5, page 209

Rereading for Fluency

Have children reread the story aloud at least three times. Suggest that they each reread the story to themselves, to a partner, and to an older reader—you, a volunteer, an older student, or a classroom aide.

Try, Try Again
By Debbie Dillar

High-Frequency Words:	*again, no, off, some, sun, try, very*
Phonics/Decoding	Short *i*; Short *i* Phonograms: *-it, -in, -is, -ip, -ig, -ith*

Preview and Predict

- Display *Try, Try Again* and have the title read aloud. Read the names of the author and illustrator. Briefly discuss the front and back cover illustrations. Ask children what they think this story will be about.
- **Picture Walk**   Encourage children to share times when they have tried to do something again and again. Then page through the book and discuss the illustrations, incorporating story vocabulary as you do so. For example: identify Cricket and Beetle on page 1 and discuss what kind of day it is (*a very good day to be out in the sun*); mention that Beetle has a problem he's trying to solve: he wants to learn how to jump: ask what happens when Beetle does *try* to jump on page 5; help children name the other story characters–Spider, Worm–and point to the words. Ask if children think Beetle will learn to jump.

Read and Discuss

- Tell children you will read the story aloud together. Read page 1 with children. Then continue through the story.
- If children read *hop* for *flip* on page 5, say: *Hop* makes sense, but it has different sounds. Look at this word. (Point to *flip*.) What letters does this word begin with? Yes, *fl*. What word part do you see? Yes, *-ip*. Now read the word. Does *flip* make sense?
- If children read *crawl* for *spin* on page 7, say: *Crawl* makes sense, but it has different sounds. Look at this word. (Point to *spin*.) What letters does this word begin with? Yes, *sp*. What word part do you see? Yes, *-in*. Now read the word. Does *spin* make sense?
- Ask what sentence Beetle says over and over again in the story. Have volunteers read *I have to try, try, again* each time it appears.
- Ask who finally helped beetle to jump. Have them read the sentence that tells how.

Responding

Encourage children to tell if they think Beetle would be able to jump by himself if he kept trying. Ask them to explain their thinking.

Additional Support

If the children's responses indicate that they had difficulty decoding or reading high-frequency words, use the following lesson:

Phonics/Decoding (Phonograms) and High-Frequency Words for Lesson 6, page 209

Rereading for Fluency

Have children reread the story aloud at least three times. Suggest that they each reread the story to themselves, to a partner, and to an older reader–you, a volunteer, an older student, or a classroom aide.

Grasshopper and Ant
By Alex Haber

High-Frequency Words: *any, much, now, than, that, way*

Phonics/Decoding Short *u*; Short *u* Phonograms: *-un, -ump, -uch*

Preview and Predict

- Display *Grasshopper and Ant* and have the title read aloud. Read the names of the author and illustrator. Briefly discuss the front and back cover illustrations. Ask children what they think this story will be about.
- **Picture Walk** Encourage children to share what they know about grasshoppers and ants. Then page through the book and discuss the illustrations, incorporating story vocabulary as you do so. For example: On page 1, ask if children like to have fun in any of the ways that Grasshopper does; ask if they think Ant is going to play or to work on pages 2 and 3, and why; discuss how much work Ant does in the garden. Have children look at page 9 and predict what will happen at the end of the story.

Read and Discuss

- Tell children you will read the story aloud together. Read page 1 with children. Then continue through the story.
- If children read *play* for *run* on page 2, say: *Play* makes sense, but it has different sounds. Look at this word (*run*). What letter do you see at the beginning? Yes, *r*. What word part do you see at the end? Yes, *-un*. Now read the word. Does *run* make sense?
- If children read *saw* for *met* on page 6, say: *Saw* makes sense, but it has different sounds. Think of a word that begins with the sound for *m* and ends like *net*. Does *met* make sense?
- Ask children to talk about what Grasshopper likes to do for fun and what Ant likes to do for fun. Have children read the sentences that tell about both kinds of fun.
- Ask children where they think Ant got all the food shown on pages 10 and 11. Have them find the sentences and the pictures that tell where. (See pages 5 or 6)

Responding

Invite a volunteer to read the question on page 12. Encourage children to tell whether or not they think Ant helped Grasshopper and why.

Additional Support

If the children's responses indicate that they had difficulty decoding or reading high-frequency words, use the following lesson:

Phonics/Decoding (Phonograms) and High-Frequency Words for Lesson 6, page 209

Rereading for Fluency

Have children reread the story aloud at least three times. Suggest that they each reread the story to themselves, to a partner, and to an older reader—you, a volunteer, an older student, or a classroom aide.

All in Fun
By Suzy Kline

High-Frequency Words: *after, are, by, other, side, thought, why*

Phonics/Decoding   Short Vowels; Double Final Consonants

Preview and Predict

- Display *All in Fun* and have the title read aloud. Read the names of the author and illustrator. Briefly discuss the front and back cover illustrations. Ask children what they think this story will be about.
- **Picture Walk**   Invite children to share times they have played funny tricks on their friends. Then page through the book and discuss the illustrations, incorporating story vocabulary as you do so. For example: display page 1 and explain that Harry and Song Lee are friends; ask why Harry is pointing to Song Lee's bag on pages 2 and 3, and why Song Lee is looking at the side of her dress on page 4; note that on page 9, Harry is looking from one side to the other. Ask children to predict what trick the two friends are playing on one another.

Read and Discuss

- Tell children you will read the story aloud together. Read page 1 with children. Then continue through the story.
- If children read *hall* for *hill* on page 4, say: *Hall* has the right sounds, but doesn't make sense. (Point to *hill*.) Think of a word that names something you might climb—one that begins like *hall* and ends like *will*. Yes, *hill* makes sense and has those sounds.
- If children read *yard* for *grass* on page 6, say: *Yard* makes sense, but has different sounds. Think of a word that names what grows in a yard—one that begins like *grow* and ends like *glass*? Yes, *grass* has those sounds and makes sense.
- Ask children how they know there wasn't a bug on Song Lee's bag or dress. Have them read *Made you look….* each time it appears.
- Ask if children think Harry really thought there was a bug on him. At what point did Harry figure out it was a trick?

Responding

Ask if children think Harry and Song Lee are good friends. Have them tell why, pointing out as needed that good friends don't get mad at one another when a trick is "all in fun."

Additional Support

If the children's responses indicate that they had difficulty decoding or reading high-frequency words, use the following lesson:

Phonics/Decoding (Phonograms) and High-Frequency Words for Lesson 6, page 210

Rereading for Fluency

Have children reread the story aloud at least three times. Suggest that they each reread the story to themselves, to a partner, and to an older reader—you, a volunteer, an older student, or a classroom aide.

A Great Place for Llama

By Virginia Mueller

> **High-Frequency Words:**   *door, has, ran, stop, them*
>
> **Phonics/Decoding**   Long *a*: CVC*e*

Preview and Predict

- Display *A Great Place for Llama* and have the title read aloud. Read the names of the author and illustrator. Briefly discuss the front and back cover illustrations. Ask children what they think this story will be about.
- **Picture Walk**   Encourage children to talk about the kinds of clothes they wear for different activities, such as swim suits for swimming and pajamas for sleeping. Then page through the book and discuss the illustrations, incorporating story vocabulary as you do so. For example: ask what they think Mama Llama said to Llama as he ran out the door in his pajamas on page 1; have children name the animals on pages 2 and 3 and tell what Llama might say to them; ask if Llama is dressed for the party on pages 4 and 5 or the game on page 7. Ask children to predict what will happen at the Bears' house on page 9.

Read and Discuss

- Tell children you will read the story aloud together. Read page 1 with children. Then continue through the story.
- If children read *pool* for *place* on page 2, say: *Pool* makes sense, but has different sounds. Look at this word. What letters does this word begin with? Yes, *pl*. What vowel sound does this word have? Yes, long *a*. Now read the word. Does *place* make sense?
- If children read *whack* for *wake* on page 9, say: *Whack* doesn't make sense. Look at this word. (Point to *wake*.) What vowel sound does this word have? Yes, long *a*. Now read the word. Does *wake* make sense?
- Ask what sentence is repeated several times in the story to tell what Llama said as he left each place.
- Ask why Little Bear thought his house was a great place for Llama to stop.

Responding

Ask children which place in the story they would most like to visit and why. Encourage children to tell what they would do at this place.

> ### Additional Support
>
> If the children's responses indicate that they had difficulty decoding or reading high-frequency words, use the following lesson:
>
> **Phonics/Decoding (Long Vowels) and High-Frequency Words for Lesson 7, page 210**

Rereading for Fluency

Have children reread the story aloud at least three times. Suggest that they each reread the story to themselves, to a partner, and to an older reader—you, a volunteer, an older student, or a classroom aide.

Never Wake a Sleeping Snake

By Bonnie Larkin Nims

> **High-Frequency Words:** *even, just, never, or, saw, sleep, thing*
>
> **Phonics/Decoding**   Long *i*: CVCe; Compound Words

Preview and Predict

- Display *Never Wake a Sleeping Snake* and have the title read aloud. Read the names of the author and illustrator. Briefly discuss the front and back cover illustrations. Ask children what they think this story will be about.
- **Picture Walk**   Ask children to tell how they would behave if they didn't want to wake a sleeping snake. Then page through the book and discuss the illustrations, incorporating story vocabulary as you do so. For example: point out Mike on page 1, explaining that he never just says things, he yells them; have children speculate about what Mike is yelling about on pages 2–5; for pages 6 and 7, ask what mother saw that made her say "Sh-sh" (a sleeping snake). Ask children to predict what will happen when Mike sees the snake.

Read and Discuss

- Tell children you will read the story aloud together. Read page 1 with children. Then continue through the story.
- If children read *tire* for *bike* on page 3, say: *Tire* makes sense, but it has different sounds. Look at this word. What letter does it begin with? Yes, *b*. What vowel sound does it have? Yes, long *i*. Now read the word. Does *bike* make sense?
- If children have trouble reading *asleep* on page 6, say: Look closely at this word. What two smaller words do you see? Yes, *a* and *sleep*. Now put the words together. Does *asleep* make sense?
- Ask what happened that helped Mike to stop yelling all the time.
- Ask children to find and read what mother thinks about sleeping snakes, *never wake a sleeping snake*, each time it appears in the story. Why do children think mother might say that?

Responding

Encourage children to suggest other ways Mike's mother and father might have stopped Mike from yelling all the time.

> **Additional Support**
>
> If the children's responses indicate that they had difficulty decoding or reading high-frequency words, use the following lesson:
>
> **Phonics/Decoding (Long Vowels) and High-Frequency Words for Lesson 7, page 211**

Rereading for Fluency

Have children reread the story aloud at least three times. Suggest that they each reread the story to themselves, to a partner, and to an older reader—you, a volunteer, an older student, or a classroom aide.

A Tune for My Mother

By Tim Johnson

High-Frequency Words: *ask, give, mother, old, show*

Phonics/Decoding   Long *o*: CVCe

Preview and Predict

- Display *A Tune for My Mother* and have the title read aloud. Read the names of the author and illustrator. Briefly discuss the front and back cover illustration. Ask children what they think this story will be about.
- **Picture Walk**   Invite children to share special things they have done for their mothers, or other special people, on Mother's Day, such as make breakfast or put on a show. Then page through the book and discuss the illustrations, incorporating story vocabulary as you do so. For example: ask what Jo, the girl on page 1, will give her mother for Mother's Day; ask what she might be writing on page 2; explain that the thought balloons on pages 6 to 9 show what Jo is dreaming about; point out the musical notes on page 9, explaining that these symbols show a song. Ask children to predict what will happen when Jo puts on her Mother's Day show.

Read and Discuss

- Tell children you will read the story aloud together. Read page 1 with children. Then continue through the story.
- If children read *jack* for *joke* on page 5, say: *Jack* has some of the right sounds, but doesn't make sense. Look at this word. What vowel sound does it have? Yes, long *o*. Think of a word that begins and ends like *jack* and has a long *o* sound. Does *joke* make sense?
- If children read *wake* for *woke* on page 10, say: *Wake* makes sense, but has a different vowel sound. What letters are in this word? Yes, *w-o-k-e*. Think of a word that begins and ends like *wake* and has a long *o* sound. Yes, *woke* has those sounds and makes sense.
- Ask children how the author shows the tune Jo wrote for her mother. Have volunteers read the tune each time it appears.
- Ask how the dogs ended up helping Jo with her show.

Responding

Encourage children to tell about a special person in their lives.

Additional Support

If the children's responses indicate that they had difficulty decoding or reading high-frequency words, use the following lesson:

Phonics/Decoding (Long Vowels) and High-Frequency Words for Lesson 7, page 211

Rereading for Fluency

Have children reread the story aloud at least three times. Suggest that they each reread the story to themselves, to a partner, and to an older reader—you, a volunteer, an older student, or a classroom aide.

Not Too Big
By John Wilson

High-Frequency Words: *about, always, build, new, read, take, work*

Phonics/Decoding   Long *e: e, ee*

Preview and Predict

- Display *Not Too Big* and have the title read aloud. Read the names of the author and illustrator. Briefly discuss the front and back cover illustrations. Ask children what they think this story will be about.
- **Picture Walk**   Ask children which they prefer, big things or little things and why. Then page through the book and discuss the illustrations, incorporating story vocabulary as you do so. For example: display page 1 and tell children that Dee always likes her things big; then ask what kind of tower Dee will build on page 2, which muffin she will take on page 3, what kind of book she will read on page 4, and which new fish she will buy on page 5; explain that page 8 shows the big cat Dee worked on to give to her Aunt. Ask children to predict what will happen when Aunt Jenny tries to take the big cat home.

Read and Discuss

- Tell children you will read the story aloud together. Read page 1 with children. Then continue through the story.
- If children read *good* for *sweet* on page 3, say: *Good* makes sense, but has different sounds. Look at this word. What letters does this word begin with? What vowel letters do you see? Now think of a word that tells how good something tastes—one that begins like *swim* and ends like *meet*? Yes, *sweet* makes sense and has the right sounds.
- If children read *have* for *keep* on page 9, say: *Have* makes sense, but has different sounds. Look at this word. What letters does it begin and end with? Yes, *k* and *p*. What vowel sound does it have? Yes, long *e*. Now read the word. Does *keep* make sense?
- Ask children to find and read the sentence that tells what Dee always says.
- Ask what happened to make Dee change her mind and say, *"I like my things to be big, but not too big!"*

Responding

Encourage children to find and name things in the classroom that Dee would like, such as Big Books, posters, wall murals, a large stuffed animal, and so on.

Additional Support

If the children's responses indicate that they had difficulty decoding or reading high-frequency words, use the following lesson:

Phonics/Decoding (Long *e: e, ee;* Vowel Pairs) and High-Frequency Words for Lesson 8, page 211

Rereading for Fluency

Have children reread the story aloud at least three times. Suggest that they each reread the story to themselves, to a partner, and to an older reader—you, a volunteer, an older student, or a classroom aide.

A Boat for Toad
By Anne W. Phillips

> **High-Frequency Words:**   *brother, father, found, home, play, room, water*
>
> **Phonics/Decoding**   Vowel Pairs: *ea, oa, ow*

Preview and Predict

- Display *A Boat for Toad* and have the title read aloud. Read the names of the author and illustrator. Briefly discuss the front and back cover illustrations. Ask children what they think this story will be about.
- **Picture Walk**   Ask children to share what they know about boats. Then page through the book and discuss the illustrations, incorporating story vocabulary as you do so. For example: ask how many boats toad found on page 2; point out the thought balloon that shows Toad's father on page 4 and the one that shows his baby brother on page 6; discuss the picture on pages 8 and 9, asking what will happen when the boat fills with water; ask children what they think will happen now that Toad is at home on page 11.

Read and Discuss

- Tell children you will read the story aloud together. Read page 1 with children. Then continue through the story.
- If children have trouble reading *floating* on page 2, say: This word has an *ing* ending. (Frame *float*.) Now look at the word. Think of a word that names what boats do—one that begins like *fly* and ends like *boat*. Yes, *float*. Say the word with the ending. Does *floating* make sense?
- If children read *run* for *row* on page 8, say: *Run* makes sense, but doesn't have the right ending sounds. Think of a word that tells how people can make a boat go—one that begins like *run* and ends like *show*. Yes, *row* makes sense and has those sounds.
- Have children find and read what Toad said when he was in the big boat and what he said when he was in the little boat.
- Ask: What did Toad's little brother want to play?

Responding

Ask children if they thought the end of the story was funny. Encourage them to explain their feelings.

> **Additional Support**
>
> If the children's responses indicate that they had difficulty decoding or reading high-frequency words, use the following lesson:
>
> **Phonics/Decoding (Long *e: e, ee*; Vowel Pairs) and High-Frequency Words for Lesson 8, page 212**

Rereading for Fluency

Have children reread the story aloud at least three times. Suggest that they each reread the story to themselves, to a partner, and to an older reader—you, a volunteer, an older student, or a classroom aide.

Old Sky
By Philemon Sturges

High-Frequency Words: *because, bring, find, friend, morning, start*

Phonics/Decoding Vowel Pairs: *ay, ai*

Preview and Predict

- Display *Old Sky* and have the title read aloud. Read the names of the author and illustrator. Briefly discuss the front and back cover illustrations. Ask children what they think this story will be about.
- **Picture Walk**   Invite children to discuss how big the sky is and how its size compares to the sun, the moon, and the earth. Then page through the book and discuss the illustrations, incorporating story vocabulary as you do so. For example: ask children to find the sun on page 3; discuss how the sun brings each morning to start the day; ask what the two friends are doing on pages 4 and 5. For each picture, note that the words the boy says are in special type, while the words the man says are in normal type.

Read and Discuss

- Tell children you will read the story aloud together. Display page 1, noting with children that there are no words on this page. Discuss what the man and boy are doing. Then turn to page 2. Read the sentences with children. Continue through the story.
- If children have trouble reading *beside* on page 3, say: Look closely at this word. What two smaller words do you see? Yes, *be* and *side*. Now put the words together. Does *beside* make sense?
- If children read *snake* for *snail* on page 11, say: *Snake* has the right beginning sounds, but doesn't make sense. Look at this word. What letter do you see at the end? Yes, *l*. Think of a word that names a small animal—one that begins like *snake* and ends like *pail*. Does *snail* make sense?
- Ask children to find and read the sentence that tells what Father Sun does each day. Ask them to find and read the sentence that tells what Sister Moon does.
- Ask volunteers to find and read each sentence that the boy says.

Responding

Invite children to help you arrange the items mentioned in the story in size order, from largest to smallest. Encourage them to add other things from nature to their list.

Additional Support

If the children's responses indicate that they had difficulty decoding or reading high-frequency words, use the following lesson:

Phonics/Decoding (Long *e: e, ee;* Vowel Pairs) and High-Frequency Words for Lesson 8, page 212

Rereading for Fluency

Have children reread the story aloud at least three times. Suggest that they each reread the story to themselves, to a partner, and to an older reader—you, a volunteer, an older student, or a classroom aide.

Looking After Billy
By Claire Masurel-Schumacher

High-Frequency Words: *children, first, gave, lived, next, together, would*

Phonics/Decoding   Sounds for *y*: Long *i*, Long *e*

Preview and Predict

- Display *Looking After Billy* and have the title read aloud. Read the names of the author and illustrator. Briefly discuss the cover illustration. Ask children what they think this story will be about.
- **Picture Walk**   Have children share their experiences watching little brothers or sisters or other small children. Then page through the book and discuss the illustrations, incorporating story vocabulary as you do so. For example: explain that the two children on page 1 are Cal and Lucy, good friends who live next to each other and do many things together; note that on pages 4 and 5, Cal's mother asks the children to watch Billy while she works in the next room; for pages 6–11, ask what the children do to try to stop Billy from crying, then ask what they would do.

Read and Discuss

- Tell children you will read the story aloud together, but fade out your lead so that they have the lead voice. Read page 1 with children and continue through the story.
- If children read *crawl* for *cry* on page 4, say: *Crawl* begins with the right sounds, but doesn't make sense. Look at this word. What sounds can *y* have at the end of a word? Yes, long *i* or long *e*. Think of a word that names something a baby might do–one that begins like *crawl* and ends with a sound for *y*? Yes, *cry* makes sense and has the right sounds.
- If children read *silly* for *funny* on page 10, say: *Silly* makes sense, but has the wrong sounds. Look at this word. It has a *y* ending. (Frame *fun*.) If I take off the ending can you read the word? Yes, *fun*. Now put the ending back on the word. Does *funny* make sense?
- Ask children what Cal and Lucy did to try to stop Billy from crying. Have volunteers read the sentences that tell what the children tried.
- Ask: What did Cal and Lucy do that finally stopped Billy from crying?

Responding

Recall that Cal and Lucy stopped Billy from crying by reading to him. Have children brainstorm a list of storybooks they might read to a little brother or sister.

Additional Support

If the children's responses indicate that they had difficulty decoding or reading high-frequency words, use the following lesson:

Phonics/Decoding (Sounds for *y*: Long *i*, Long *e*) and High-Frequency Words for Lesson 9, page 212

Rereading for Fluency

Have children reread the story aloud at least three times. Suggest that they each reread the story to themselves, to a partner, and to an older reader–you, a volunteer, an older student, or a classroom aide.

Ned's New Old Sled

By Robin Bloksberg

High-Frequency Words: *afraid, every, head, right, school, throw, turn*

Phonics/Decoding   Vowel Pairs: *ew, oo, ou, ue*

Preview and Predict

- Display *Ned's New Old Sled* and have the title read aloud. Read the names of the author and illustrator. Briefly discuss the front and back cover illustrations. Ask children what they think this story will be about.
- **Picture Walk**   Encourage children to share their sledding experiences. Then page through the book and discuss the illustrations, incorporating story vocabulary as you do so. For example: point out the hat on Ned's head on page 1; explain that Ned's school friends are taking turns sledding down the hill on page 2, and note how every one of their sleds is newer than Ned's; discuss whether or not the children might be afraid to sled down the hill. Continue to develop vocabulary and story line through pictures.

Read and Discuss

- Tell children you will read the story aloud together, but fade out your lead so that they have the lead voice. Read page 1 with children and continue through the story.
- If children read *word* for *wood* on page 4, say: *Word* has some of the right sounds, but doesn't make sense. Look at the vowels in this word. Think of a word that names something we get from trees—one that begins like *word* and ends like *good*. Does *wood* make sense?
- If children read *toss* for *throw* on page 16, say: *Toss* makes sense, but doesn't have the right sounds. Think of another word that can mean "toss"—one that begins like *three* and ends like *show*. Yes, *throw* makes sense and has those sounds.
- Ask what Ned and his friends thought about his father's sled. Have volunteers find and read the sentences that tell what they thought.
- Ask: How did Ned and his friends feel after they took a turn on the sled?

Responding

Encourage children to discuss how Ned's father's old sled could be new to Ned. Ask them to share old things that belonged to parents or other family members that seemed new to them.

Additional Support

If the children's responses indicate that they had difficulty decoding or reading high-frequency words, use the following lesson:

Phonics/Decoding (Sounds for *y*: Long *i*, Long *e*) and High-Frequency Words for Lesson 9, page 213

Reading for Fluency

Have children reread the story aloud at least three times. Suggest that they each reread the story to themselves, to a partner, and to an older reader—you, a volunteer, an older student, or a classroom aide.

A Moon for Ana Gracia
By Anne Sibley O'Brien

High-Frequency Words: *hand, keep, kind, sister, want*

Phonics/Decoding Base Words and Endings

Preview and Predict

- Display *A Moon for Ana Gracia* and have the title read aloud. Read the names of the author and illustrator. Briefly discuss the front and back cover illustrations. Ask children what they think this story will be about.
- **Picture Walk**   Invite children to tell how they got their names—were they named after a family member? Then page through the book and discuss the illustrations, incorporating story vocabulary as you do so. For example: on page 1, explain that Grandma is taking Ana Gracia out for her birthday and that the other people are her father, mother, and sister; explain that on page 5, Grandma and Ana Gracia will take a boat ride; ask what Ana Gracia is holding in her hand on page 8; explain that on page 11, the picture shows Grandma when she was six. Ask children why they think Grandma is giving the moon to Ana to keep.

Read and Discuss

- Tell children you will read the story aloud together, but fade out your lead so that they have the lead voice. Read page 1 with children and continue through the story.
- If children read *walking* for *waiting* on page 5, say: *Walking* begins with the right sounds and ends with *ing*, but doesn't make sense. (Frame *wait*.) Think of a word that means "to stay until someone or something comes"—one that begins like *walk* and has a long *a* sound. Yes, *wait*. Now add the *ing* ending. Does *waiting* make sense?
- If children have trouble reading *greatest* on page 14, say: Look closely at this word. What ending do you see? Yes, *-est*. (Frame *great*.) Now what word do you see? Yes, *great*. Read the word with the *-est* ending. Does *greatest* make sense?
- Ask children who Ana Gracia is named after. Have a volunteer find and read the sentence that tells this (page 10).
- Ask children to find and read the sentence that tells where the necklace came from.

Responding

Ask children to tell about any special gifts they have ever given or received.

Additional Support

If the children's responses indicate that they had difficulty decoding or reading high-frequency words, use the following lesson:

Phonics/Decoding (Sounds for *y* : *Long i*, *Long e*) and High-Frequency Words for Lesson 9, page 213

Rereading for Fluency

Have children reread the story aloud at least three times. Suggest that they each reread the story to themselves, to a partner, and to an older reader—you, a volunteer, an older student, or a classroom aide.

Fishing with Grandpa
By Rita V. Partridge

High-Frequency Words: *air, hard, only, same, tell, until, which*

Phonics/Decoding Base Words and Endings: *-es, -ies*

Preview and Predict

- Display *Fishing with Grandpa* and have the title read aloud. Read the names of the author and illustrator. Briefly discuss the front and back cover illustrations. Ask children what they think this story will be about.
- **Picture Walk** Invite children who like to fish or have family members who like to fish to share their experiences. Then page through the book and discuss the illustrations, incorporating story vocabulary as you do so. For example: ask children to tell what they see on page 1; explain that Grandpa says *"fishing is very hard work"*; ask children to use picture clues on pages 2–13 to tell what might be hard about it (getting up early, carrying things, waiting until a fish bites, knowing which fish to keep, keeping only the big fish).

Read and Discuss

- Tell children you will read the story aloud together, but fade out your lead so that they have the lead voice. Read page 1 with children and continue through the story.
- If children read *cold* for *cool* on page 5, say: *Cold* makes sense, but ends with the wrong sound. This word ends with *l*. Think of a word that means almost the same as *cold*—one that begins like *cold* and ends like *pool*? Yes, *cool* makes sense and has the right sounds.
- If children read *baby* for *babies* on page 11, say: *Baby* makes sense, but this word has an *ies* ending. What happens to words when the *ies* ending is added? Yes, we drop the *y* first. (Frame *bab*.) What word would this be if it had a *y* at the end. Yes, *baby*. Now say a word that means more than one *baby*. Does *babies* make sense?
- Ask children to find and read the sentences that tell why fishing is hard work.
- Ask why Janie is making a face on page 15. Have volunteers find and read the sentences that tell why. Why might cleaning a fish not be fun?

Responding

Encourage children to tell what they learned about fishing from reading the story. Ask if they, too, would like to go fishing and to explain why or why not.

Additional Support

If the children's responses indicate that they had difficulty decoding or reading high-frequency words, use the following lesson:

Phonics/Decoding (*r*-Controlled Vowels) and High-Frequency Words for Lesson 10, page 214

Rereading for Fluency

Have children reread the story aloud at least three times. Suggest that they each reread the story to themselves, to a partner, and to an older reader—you, a volunteer, an older student, or a classroom aide.

Three Wishes for Buster

By Andrew Clements

High-Frequency Words:	*around, know, must, surprise, took, wait, what*
Phonics/Decoding	Base Words and Endings: *-ed, -er, -est, -ing*

Preview and Predict

- Display *Three Wishes for Buster* and have the title read aloud. Read the names of the author and illustrator. Briefly discuss the front and back cover illustrations. Ask children what they think this story will be about.
- **Picture Walk**   Display page 1 and discuss the fish family around the baby fish. Ask children what wish each family member might make for the baby. Then page through the book and discuss the illustrations, incorporating story vocabulary as you do so. For example: point out that on pages 2–5, the family makes their wishes, and must now wait for Buster to grow up to see what happens; ask what Buster is doing on pages 8–13 (swimming around fast, helping an older fish, going to school). Ask if children think the family's wishes will come true.

Read and Discuss

- Tell children you will read the story aloud together, but fade out your lead so that they have the lead voice. Briefly discuss page 1. Then read page 2 with children and continue through the story.
- If children have trouble reading *everywhere* on page 4, say: This word is made up of two smaller words. (Frame *every*.) What is this word? Yes, *every*. (Frame *where*.) Now read this word. Yes, *where*. Now put the two words together. Does *everywhere* make sense?
- If children read *swimming* for *zipping* on page 9, say: *Swimming* makes sense, but doesn't have the right sounds. Let's look at the word without the ending. (Frame *zip*.) Can you read the word now? Yes, *zip*. Now read the word with the ending. Does *zipping* make sense?
- Ask what the three wishes were that Buster's family made. Have volunteers read what each family member wished.
- Ask what surprise Buster had for his family. Call on a volunteer to read what Buster did.

Responding

Ask children if the wishes Buster's family made were good wishes for a fish. Discuss with children what wishes their parents might have for them when they grow up.

Additional Support

If the children's responses indicate that they had difficulty decoding or reading high-frequency words, use the following lesson:

Phonics/Decoding (*r*-Controlled Vowels) and High-Frequency Words for Lesson 10, page 214

Rereading for Fluency

Have children reread the story aloud at least three times. Suggest that they each reread the story to themselves, to a partner, and to an older reader—you, a volunteer, an older student, or a classroom aide.

What Seahorse Saw
By Robin Bernard

> **High-Frequency Words:** *away, happy, own, place, think*
>
> **Phonics/Decoding** *r*-Controlled Vowels: *ar, or*

Preview and Predict

- Display *What Seahorse Saw* and have the title read aloud. Read the names of the author and illustrator. Briefly discuss the front and back cover illustrations. Ask children what they think this story will be about.
- **Picture Walk**   Invite children to name things a seahorse might see in the ocean. Then page through the book and discuss the illustrations, incorporating story vocabulary as you do so. For example: have children identify Seahorse on page 1; explain that on pages 2 and 3, Seahorse swims away to a new place to see more things; have children describe the animals Seahorse sees on pages 3–13, naming each animal for them—Cowfish, Porcupinefish, Dogfish, Ribbonfish, Sawfish, Starfish.

Read and Discuss

- Tell children you will read the story aloud together, but fade out your lead so that they have the lead voice. Read page 1 with children. Explain that *Seahorse* is a compound word, or a word that is made up of two smaller words. Then continue through the story.
- If children read *shake* for *shark* on page 6, say: *Shake* doesn't make sense. Think of a word that names a kind of big fish—one that begins like *shake* and has the same vowel sound and ending sound as *bark*. Yes, *shark* makes sense and has the right sounds.
- If children read *legs* for *arms* on page 13, say: *Legs* makes sense, but doesn't have the right sounds. Think of a word that names another part of the body—one that has the same sound *ar* has in *star* and ends like *farms*. Yes, *arms* makes sense and has the right sounds.
- Ask what sentences are repeated several times in the story. Have volunteers find and read these sentences. (The first and last two sentences on pages 2, 5, 6, 9, and 10.)
- Ask children how Seahorse felt when he got back home.

Responding

Ask children which of the many animals Seahorse saw was their favorite. Encourage them to explain their choices.

> ### Additional Support
>
> If the children's responses indicate that they had difficulty decoding or reading high-frequency words, use the following lesson:
>
> **Phonics/Decoding (*r*-Controlled Vowels) and High-Frequency Words for Lesson 10, page 214**

Rereading for Fluency

Have children reread the story aloud at least three times. Suggest that they each reread the story to themselves, to a partner, and to an older reader—you, a volunteer, an older student, or a classroom aide.

PART 2 Accelerating Literacy Development Through Easy-Reading Materials

In addition to receiving support to read and respond to on-level materials, it is important that children receive frequent and consistent opportunities to read at their independent level. This section includes ideas for building a library of easy-reading materials and suggests activities that will increase children's fluency and enthusiasm for reading.

Building a Library of Easy-Reading Materials

Books listed on the bibliography of easy-reading books on page 178 will offer your children easy and high-interest reading experiences. This list includes both fiction and nonfiction titles. Each book is leveled according to difficulty. Books that are categorized as Easy are approximately one level below children's grade level. Books categorized as Very Easy are approximately two levels below.

Several criteria were used to decide on the appropriate category for each book. These same criteria can be used when choosing additional books for your easy-reading library.

- **The amount of text** on the page is approximately the amount of text found in books that are one to two levels below grade level.
- **The appearance of the book** is consistent with on-level books children are reading. It is important that children do not feel that a book "looks too easy."
- **The subject matter** is likely to be interesting and appealing to children at this grade level.
- **The background concepts** needed to understand each book are consistent with ideas and information that children reading at one or two grades below grade level are likely to be familiar with.
- **The number of difficult words and concepts** contained in each book has also been taken into consideration.

In addition, each book has been evaluated for specific elements that might cause difficulty, such as unusual methods of text presentation, art that may be too abstract, sentence structures or word referents that may cause confusion, and use of symbolism or figurative language that may interfere with comprehension.

Bibliography of Easy-Reading Books

Books available from libraries and bookstores:

Very Easy Books

Afro-Bets 123 Book by Cheryl Willis Hudson.
Just Us Books 1987 (24p) paper
The Afro-Bet kids present the numbers from one to ten.

★ **Beach Ball—Left, Right** by Bruce McMillan.
Holiday 1992 (32p)
A colorful beach ball journeys through the surf back to its
young owner.

Cars! Cars! Cars! by Grace Maccarone Scholastic 1995 (28p)
Humorous dogs show off their favorite cars.

Do You Want to be My Friend? by Eric Carle.
HarperCollins 1971 (32p) also paper
A lonely little mouse goes off looking for a friend.

First Snow by Emily McCully. HarperCollins 1985 (32p)
also paper
After the storm the family shovels out and drives off for a
wonderful sledding adventure.

I Can by Susan Winter. Dorling Kindersley 1993 (24p)
A boy can do most things better than his little sister.

I Went Walking by Sue Williams. Harcourt 1989
also paper
A boy meets a wonderful assortment of animals on his walk.

Kipper's Book of Colors by Mick Inkpen. Harcourt 1995 (24p)
Identify and name colors with the playful dog Kipper.

My Book by Ron Maris. Puffin 1986 paper
A child's book is special to him.

★ **Tabby: A Story In Pictures** by Aliki. HarperCollins 1995
A young girl loves sharing her playful kitten's first year.

Yellow Ball by Molly Bang. Morrow 1991 (24p) Puffin paper
A ball goes off shore for a sea adventure and returns to a
young boy.

Where's the Fish? by Taro Gomi. Morrow 1986 (32p)
Find the fish who's hiding somewhere in the pictures.

Who's Counting? by Nancy Tafuri. Greenwillow 1986 (24p)
also paper
Mother keeps close watch over her playful puppies.

Easy Books

Big Long Animal Song by Mike Artell. HarperCollins/
Good Year 1994 (8p)
Presents a simple look at size. **Available in Spanish as *Gran
cancion de los animales.***

Brown Bear, Brown Bear, What Do You See? by Bill Martin,
Jr. Holt 1983 (24p)
This all-time favorite features animals and colors.

Cat On the Mat by Brian Wildsmith.
Oxford U. Press (16p) paper
Simple rhyming words present a cat's activities.

Five Little Ducks by Raffi. Crown 1988 (32 p) also paper
Ducks are found and counted in this familiar song.

Have You Seen My Duckling? by Nancy Tafuri.
Greenwillow 1984 (24p) also paper
Readers will spot the missing duckling before mother
duck does.

Have You Seen My Cat? by Eric Carle.
Picture Bk Studio 1991 paper; Scholastic 1991 paper
In this story with few words a child searches for a lost cat.

★ **Joshua James Likes Trucks** by Catherine Petrie.
Childrens 1982 (32p) also paper
Joshua James is fascinated with trucks in this simple explo-
ration of size, colors, and opposites. **Available in Spanish as
*A Pedro Pérez le gustan los camiones.***

★ **Jump, Frog, Jump!** by Robert Kalan. Morrow 1981 (32p)
Scholastic paper
In this cumulative tale, a frog tries to catch a fly without getting
caught himself. **Available in Spanish as *Salta, ranita, salta.***

Machines by Ann Morris. HarperCollins/GoodYear 1995 (8p)
Machines can do many kinds of jobs.

My Puppy by Inez Greene. HarperCollins/GoodYear 1994 (8p)
A young girl has fun with her frisky puppy. **Available in
Spanish as *Mi perrito.***

Pancakes, Crackers, and Pizza: A Book of Shapes by
Marjorie Eberts and Margaret Gisler. Childrens 1984 (32p) also
paper
Eddy sees triangles, squares, and circles in the food he loves
to eat.

Rain by Robert Kalan. Greenwillow 1978 (24p) also paper
Simple text describes a rainstorm.

★ **Who Is Who?** by Patricia McKissack. Childrens 1983 (32p)
also paper
Lively twin boys always make opposite choices.

KEY ★ Multicultural

The following Guided Reading books from Rigby's Literacy Tree Program are suggested for additional Easy Reading. They are available from Rigby, (800) 822-8661.

Emergent Reading Bibliography

WELCOME TO MY WORLD

Topic Books
The Treasure Hunt
My Magnet
I Am Climbing
Show and Tell
The Machine
Tubes Can Be Fun
In the Sand
Whiskers

Guided Reading

Set A
Fruit Salad
The Farm
A Scrumptious Sundae
A Zoo
The Circus
Who Likes Ice Cream?
A Toy Box
Sometimes

Set B
Buffy
Dressing Up
Too Many Clothes
What Are You?
Signs
Sharing
Miss People's Pets
Let's Build a Tower

Set C
Teeny Tiny Tina
Who's Coming for a Ride?
Getting Ready for the Ball
Wheels
Dancing Shoes
Tommy's Tummy Ache
Blue Day

FOOD AND FUN

Topic Books
Hands, Hands, Hands
Who Ate the Lettuce?
Cat Food
Beaks
The Surprise Party
Cat and Mouse
Milk
Oh, Fiddlesticks!

Guided Reading

Set A
Mud Pie
Our Baby
Kittens
What Has Spots?
Who Made These Tracks?
The Birthday Cake
On the Farm
I Spy

Set B
Here's What I Made
Hungry Horse
Look Out!
Don't Wake the Baby
I Can Do It Myself
Hat Trick
Hello, Goodbye
Ants Love Picnics, Too

Set C
The Bike Parade
Filbert the Fly
Don't Leave Anything Behind
I Paint
Dad's Garden
Our Garden
Water
Koalas

WORK AND PLAY

Topic Books
Our Shadows
Hiding
Our House
Jump Into Bed
In a Minute
After the Rain
Going to Work
A Piece of Paper

Guided Reading

Set A
Ben the Bold
Dear Santa
In My Bed
The Scarecrow
Sunrise
Giant's Breakfast
What Is Red?
The Train Ride

Set B
Chew Chew Chew
Camping
Climbing
Happy Birthday!
Woof!
I Like
What Goes in the Tub?
Yellow

Set C
Pet Parade
Nests
When I Was Sick
In My Room
Our Dog Sam
Surprise Cake
Guess What!
Have You Seen?

Emergent Reading Bibliography (continued)

ANIMAL ANTICS

Topic Books
My Little Dog
Let Me In!
I Am a Cat
Good and Ready
Buzz Off, Bee
Wanda's New Bed
The Pirate and the Parrot
Look Out for Bears!

Guided Reading

Set A
All Join In
The Circus Clown

When I Pretend
Hands
Pets
Green Footprints
Visitors
What Did Kim Catch?

Set B
Noses
Tails
Sitting
In Went Goldilocks
The Storm

The Boogly
I Saw a Dinosaur
Noises

Set C
The Puppet Show
Shadows
Shopping
Grandpa Snored
Timmy
Go Back to Sleep
Henry and the Helicopter
The Wedding

Early Reading Bibliography

LET'S GET TOGETHER

Topic Books
Lost
Amy Goes to School
What About Bennie?
Sarah's Seed
Our Soccer Team
Names and Games
Carrot Soup
Lunchtime

Guided Reading

Set A
Wrinkles
Talk, Talk, Talk
Legs
Trucks
Screech
Sleepy Bear
Moonlight
Row Your Boat

Set B
Goodnight, Little Brother
Words Are Everywhere
Monkey's Friends
Bruno's Birthday
Just Like Grandpa
Secret Soup

Sally's Picture
Can I Play Outside?

Set C
Dad's Bike
Countdown
Riddles
Christmas Shopping
Sneezes
At Night
Bang
Water Falling

SAFE AND SOUND

Topic Books
Stop, Look, Listen
Sending Signals
Jumper
I Saw a Sign
Out of Reach
Don't Forget
The Secret Message
The Wolf and the Seven Little Kids

Guided Reading

Set A
In the Garden
Waiting

Family Photos
If You're Happy
Inside or Outside?
Grandma's Memories
Odd Socks
Roll Over

Set B
If You Like Strawberries, Don't Read
   This Book
My Monster Friends
What's Around the Corner?
Pete's New Shoes
The Grump
Patterns
The Printing Machine
Sleeping

Set C
The Wobbly Tooth
Woolly, Woolly
The Wide-Mouthed Frog
What Tommy Did
Mrs. Bold
Skin
T.J.'s Tree
Lilly Lolly Little Legs

Early Reading Bibliography (continued)

OUT AND ABOUT

Topic Books
- Footprints
- The King's Pudding
- The Never Told Story
- The Fishing Contest
- Fascinating Faces
- Postcards from Pop
- Sally's Surprise Garden
- The Cat and the Dog

Guided Reading

Set A
- In the Park
- Bossy Betina
- Pizza for Dinner
- Dad Didn't Mind at All
- Goodness Gracious
- The Hungry Chickens
- No Extras
- BMX Billy

Set B
- Dad's Bathtime
- Gregor the Grumblesome Giant
- Ten Little Caterpillars
- Boxes
- A Brand New Butterfly
- Emma's Problem

- Only an Octopus
- Hippo's Hiccups

Set C
- The Crab at the Bottom of the Sea
- Buffy's Tricks
- When I'm Older
- Making Caterpillars and Butterflies
- Just My Luck
- Phillipa the Dragon
- What Is Bat?
- Whatever Will These Become?

TIMES AND SEASONS

Topic Books
- Lizzie's Lunch
- Time for Family
- Rainbow Parrot
- Tall Tales
- Happy Birthday, Duckling
- Rice
- Little Half Chick
- How Lizard Lost His Colors

Guided Reading

Set A
- A Friend
- Daniel
- Wind and Sun
- The Fastest Gazelle
- The Two Little Mice
- Why Elephants Have Long Ears
- The Frog Princess
- The Dinosaur's Cold

Set B
- Papa's Spaghetti
- The Queen's Parrot
- I Have a Question, Grandma
- How Fire Came to Earth
- Vagabond Crabs
- How Turtle Raced Beaver
- Too Much Noise
- Monkey and Fire

Set C
- Half for You, Half for Me
- Gallo and Zorro
- Trees
- The Deer and the Crocodile
- Rice Cakes
- My House
- The Barnaby's New House
- Mice

Cost-Effective Ways to Obtain Reading Materials

Following are some ideas for obtaining books and other reading material that will help you develop and enhance your classroom library.

Environmental Print

- **Recipes** Children can collect recipes for favorite treats and follow a simple recipe in class.

- **Advertisements** Find interesting ads or fliers in newspapers and magazines. Encourage children to figure out the best deals on items that interest them.

- **Greeting Cards** Ask family members to recycle greeting cards they receive by giving them to the classroom. Children can learn the spellings of holiday names, interpret jokes and greetings, and use the cards as models for creating their own greeting cards.

- **Catalogs** Children can use catalogs in a variety of ways: for the fun of browsing, for reading about products that appeal to them, for making a wish list, or for finding out about new or unusual products.

  - Ask parents to send catalogs to school. Place them in a box and let children go through and find their favorites.

  - Check your local library or bookstores to obtain books that describe and give mailing information and costs for a variety of catalogs. Send for the catalogs that you think will entice children to browse and read.

- **Travel Brochures and Road Maps** Travel brochures, maps, and itineraries are available free of charge from many travel agencies. Children can map routes and trips they have taken, calculate distance, and find out more about places they'd like to visit.

- **Health and Public Service Information** The "Consumer Information Catalog" published by the U.S. Government Printing Office offers free and low-cost publications on a variety of topics such as food and nutrition, health, travel and hobbies, and emergency preparedness. Booklets such as "Why Save Endangered Species" may be of interest to primary-age children. To obtain the free catalog, call or visit the nearest U.S. Government Bookstore or write to Consumer Information Center, P.O. Box 100, Pueblo, CO 81002.

- **Menus** Request copies of menus from children's favorite restaurants. Children can learn to recognize menu items, and learn about different kinds of food.

- **Newspapers** You might post a daily comic strip for children to enjoy, or encourage children to browse through the newspaper to find articles about topics that interest them. The Sunday edition of many newspapers contains sections designed especially for children.

Books, Magazines, and Newspapers

- Seek assistance from the public library. Some libraries are willing to lend large numbers of books to schools that have no libraries. Many libraries extend special privileges to teachers and will allow them to check out books and videos for extended periods. Also check with libraries to find out when they are planning used book sales. Books are often sold for under 25¢ at these sales.

- Involve children and their parents in various types of sales to generate funds for purchasing books. Enlist the services of the PTA or Parent Club to sponsor a book fair and donate proceeds for the purchase of books.

- Contact new and used book stores, and ask them to donate overstocked books and remainders.

- Ask friends, neighbors, and family members to save magazines and provide them for classroom use. Be sure to screen magazines before adding them to the library.

- Contact community service and local professional organizations, such as the Lions or Rotary Club, and Phi Delta Kappa, which often provide donations and assistance to schools.

- Seek funding through private and public grants to purchase books. *The Catalog of Federal Domestic Assistance* provides information about federal grants and is available through the Superintendent of Documents, U.S. Government Printing Office, Washington, DC 20401. Contact your state department of education for information regarding state funds that may be available to fund literacy programs. Private grants are available through such organizations as the Wal-Mart Foundation, TEL: 1-501-273-6504.

- Seek assistance from Reading Is Fundamental (RIF), a national nonprofit organization that provides help with fundraising, book ordering and discounts, and volunteer recruitment. Any public agency or private nonprofit group may apply to RIF. To obtain a proposal form, write to Reading Is Fundamental, Inc., 600 Maryland Ave., SW, Suite 600, Washington, DC 20024. TEL: 1-202-287-3220

- On children's birthdays during the school year, ask parents to donate a new book in the child's name. Use your book club "free books" for children who may not be able to bring a new book. You might place a bookplate with the child's name inside the book cover. Then celebrate the honored child and book with a "dedication ceremony."

- Conduct a book drive. Ask parents, teachers, and community organizations to donate used paperbacks. Trade these in for children's books at bookstores that trade and sell used books.

- Trade your student-made big books with other classrooms to build variety and interest.

Materials Free to Teachers

The reference section of your local library is a great source of information about free materials. Your librarian can help you. Listed below is a sampling of free books and other materials available to teachers.

- *Teaching Tolerance* is a free twice-yearly magazine available to educators. The magazine provides teachers of all levels with articles, ideas, and resources for promoting interracial and intercultural understanding in the classroom. To receive the magazine, send a written request on school letterhead to *Teaching Tolerance*, 400 Washington Ave., Montgomery, AL 36104. FAX: 1-334-264-3121

- *Free (and Almost Free) Things for Teachers* by Susan Osborn. © 1993. Publisher: Perigee Books, imprint of The Putnam Publishing Group, 200 Madison Ave., New York, NY 10016. TEL: 1-800-631-8571. $8.95

  This resource book lists more than 200 items that can be ordered for the cost of a postage stamp, or for no more than five dollars. It provides names and addresses of publishers, manufacturers, government agencies, and others that offer booklets, posters, catalogs, maps, teaching guides, and other materials.

- A free resource kit with posters and pamphlets on various topics, such as African American, Latino, and Asian/Pacific history, is available from the American Federation of Teachers, 555 New Jersey Ave., NW, Washington, DC 20001. TEL: 1-800-238-1133

- *Magazines for Kids and Teens* by Donald R. Stoll. © 1994. Educational Press Assn. of America, Rowan College of New Jersey, 201 Mullica Hill Road, Glassboro, NJ 08028, TEL: 1-609-256-4610/International Reading Assn., 800 Barksdale Road, P.O. Box 8139, Newark, DE 19714, TEL: 1-302-731-1600. $8 (IRA members)/$10 (non-members)

This resource guide lists more than 200 magazines serving children. Request sample copies of the magazines of interest by writing to the editorial addresses provided. There may sometimes be a charge, but most of the samples will be free.

Sources of Audiocassettes and Books in Other Languages

Call or write to these organizations and request a catalog to find out what they have to offer.

▶ Audiocassettes and Books

Khmer (Cambodian), Korean, Spanish, Vietnamese
Binet International
P.O. Box 1429
Carlsbad, CA 92018
TEL: 1-619-941-7929
FAX: 1-619-941-5717

Chinese*, Khmer, Korean, Spanish, Vietnamese
Children's Book Press
246 First St.
San Francisco, CA 94105
TEL: 1-415-995-2200
FAX: 1-415-995-2222

Chinese*, Hmong, Japanese, Khmer, Korean, Lao, Spanish, Tagalog, Thai, Vietnamese
Multicultural Distributing Center
800 N. Grand Ave.
Covina, CA 91724
TEL: 1-818-859-3133
     1-800-537-4357 (outside CA)
FAX: 1-818-859-3136

Arabic, Chinese*, Hindi, Hmong, Lao, Portuguese, Somali, Spanish, Urdu, and more
Multi-Cultural Books and Video, Inc.
28880 Southfield Rd., Ste. 183
Lathrup Village, MI 48076
TEL: 1-800-567-2220
FAX: 1-810-559-2465

Spanish
Sundance Publishing
P.O. Box 1326
Littleton, MA 01460-9936
TEL: 1-800-343-8204
FAX: 1-800-456-2419

Recorded Books, Inc.
270 Skipjack Road
Prince Frederick, MD 20678
TEL: 1-800-638-1304
FAX: 1-410-535-5499

▶ Video

Spanish
Multi-Cultural Books and Video, Inc.
28880 Southfield Rd., Ste. 183
Lathrup Village, MI 48076
TEL: 1-800-567-2220
FAX: 1-810-559-2465

*These companies offer audiocassettes in Mandarin and Cantonese.

Setting Up the Classroom Library

A well-designed classroom library helps encourage students to read. The library should be attractive and highly visible, making it obvious that it is an important part of the classroom. Here are some things to keep in mind when setting up your classroom library.

Library Area Provide an environment that encourages reading. You might design comfortable seating using carpet, donated easy chairs, or pillows. Use bookshelves, movable bulletin boards, or other dividers to partition the area for privacy and quiet, and to set the area apart from the rest of the classroom. Ideally, the area should be large enough for four to six children to use at one time.

Books Include many different types of books as well as other print materials. A classroom collection may include mysteries, folktales, myths, legends, realistic fiction, poetry, picture books, informational books, series books, and so forth. Magazines and real-world resources (phone book, catalogs) are also appropriate. As your collection grows, select titles that represent the cultural and ethnic diversity of society. Many teachers gradually obtain four to six copies of favorite titles so that small groups can read the same book at the same time.

Display and Organization Displaying books with the faces rather than the spines showing is a good way to "sell" books to readers. You can display some books on the tops of tables and shelves. You might also ask drugstores or supermarkets about used display racks they might be willing to donate for classroom use. Although shelf space is usually limited, you can have a rotating display to draw reader's attention to specific titles. The rest of the collection can be organized into baskets, into boxes, or on shelves by a number of categories such as type of book, theme, topic, author, reading level, content area, or some combination of these features. The organization should be simple and one that allows the children to manage the collection.

There are two ways to use the library: for instruction and for independent reading to develop children's fluency.

Using the Library for Instruction

Plan for Additional Instruction in Reading and Writing

Additional instruction in reading and writing can help those children who are experiencing difficulty in tracking print, in developing their phonemic awareness, and in developing adequate decoding and spelling strategies. Following is a basic plan that can be used with additional reading materials to provide this instruction. This plan, which is intended for use with small groups, follows a predictable sequence that takes 25–30 minutes daily.

Five Day Plan:

Day 1	Day 2	Day 3	Day 4	Day 5
Rereading Familiar Books	Rereading Familiar Books	Rereading Familiar Books	Rereading Familiar Books	Rereading Familiar Books
First Reading Picture Walk/ Book Preview and Shared Reading	Coached Reading	Coached Reading	Independent Reading	Independent Reading
Making Words or Rounding Up the Rhymes	Writing Sentences	Making Words or Rounding Up the Rhymes	Writing Sentences	Word Wall

A description of each of the activities shown above follows.

(5–10 minutes) Rereading Familiar Books

This is an opportunity for children to practice reading books that they have already read and to allow you time to coach children who need individual support. Children may practice reading independently, with a partner, with an adult, or with a small group.

Regardless of whether it is an adult or another child listening to a reader, if the reader gets stuck on a word, the listener helps him or her by providing various hints. (See Hints, page 190.)

(10 minutes) First Reading: Picture Walk/ Book Preview and Shared Reading

Early in first grade, the teacher should first read a new book aloud in order to provide a model of a fluent reading. Then a shared reading can take place. Eventually, however, it is important for children to succeed in independent reading. As the year goes on and children develop strategies and confidence, they should take over the initial reading. By observing the development of the children, you will be the best judge of when to begin to fade out your lead and let children try their developing strategies on the first reading. It is important that by the spring of first grade, children try reading the book individually before they read it aloud as a group.

In Grade 2, the first reading is often guided or independent. The fading of teacher support should happen more quickly than at Grade 1.

Picture Walk/Book Preview

Engage children in a picture walk or help them preview the book. In a picture walk, before reading anything, you and children go through the pages. On each page, ask questions so that children will tell about what they see in the pictures. As you do this, you can lead them to use certain key words. Also, in order to provide an opportunity for children to hear words that they do not have in their listening vocabulary, you can voice those words by using them in the discussion.

Shared Reading

Shared reading allows children the chance to hear the teacher's fluent reading and to gradually join in. In the first shared reading, your voice is in the lead, the children chiming in as they can. In subsequent shared readings of the same book, you should drop back so that the children can take the lead. Your voice is now a little behind the children's voices. If the group struggles or misreads a word, model strategies for reading new words.

To help children who have difficulty tracking text, the first shared reading or two should be from your copy of the book. As the children focus on it, point to the text during the shared reading. It may be necessary to do this for up to as much as half a year in first grade. It may also be necessary for the beginning of second grade.

(10 minutes) Making Words or Rounding Up the Rhymes

Making Words is a hands-on, manipulative activity that will help children learn how letters go together to make words, and how small changes make different words. From a list you have predetermined, you should ask children to make from six to nine words with a given group of letters. The last word should be a word from the book the children are reading. After making the words, children can sort them by patterns. Example:

> Give each child the letters [*a, e, u, l, m,* and *s*]. Have children form the following words one at a time, each time instructing them to add, change, and/or rearrange letters as necessary: [*Sam, same, lame, meal, seal, seam, slam, Samuel*]. When words are homonyms or may not be in children's listening vocabularies, use them in a quick sentence.

(10 minutes) **Making Words or** **Rounding Up** **the Rhymes** continued	Have the words written on index cards. Now have children say the words aloud. Ask them to sort out the rhyming words. Point out the spelling pattern that is the same in each rhyming pair. Then have children identify the two words that begin with a capital letter because they are names. **Rounding Up the Rhymes** is an alternative activity. Using books that have many rhyming words in them, direct children to a page where there are two or more rhyming words that have the same spelling pattern. Have children identify those rhyming words. Write down the words and point out to children the spelling pattern that is the same in each rhyming pair. Tell them that thinking of rhyming words can sometimes help them spell words. Ask them to spell one or two more words with the same spelling pattern, and write those down so that children can see the pattern. It is important to tell children that thinking of a rhyme will often but not always help them spell words because some rhymes have more than one spelling, for example, *pause/cause, claws/paws.*

DAY 2

(10 minutes) **Rereading** **Familiar Books**	[Same as Day 1]
(5–10 minutes) **Coached Reading**	Coaching children in their development of reading strategies is one of the most valuable things you can do. In addition to coaching individual children while others are rereading with partners, you can coach them during group readings. The group may all try reading the book to themselves, and then individuals might read pages aloud. It is essential that the children know that when the reader comes to an unknown word or misreads a word, the teacher will not simply tell but will "give a hint." The teacher's hints should be similar to those given on page 190 for use by partners as they practice rereading for fluency. Prompt children to learn and use decoding strategies. A list of general suggestions (Teacher Prompts) appears on page 191. Most important, perhaps, to a child struggling to read, is the praise and reinforcement provided by coaching. Comments such as the following encourage children and help them see how they can use strategies to figure out words on their own. *"That was excellent. You realized that what you had read didn't make sense so you reread. You figured out that the word can't be [dives], but you know that [Grandma drives a car]. Then you checked the first letters, [d-r]. They match the sounds you hear at the beginning of [drives].* *"You thought of a word that made sense and had the right letters when you figured out that word. You were really using what you've learned."* *"Good, you looked at the picture to help you remember what we talked about— [something that looks like a lizard and has a name that begins with the sounds for s-a-l. A salamander!"]*

(10 minutes) **Writing Sentences**	Through writing sentences in response to reading, children learn how to write. As they write and are coached by the teacher, they develop the phonemic awareness and letter-sound patterns essential to continued progress in reading.
	Guided Writing Guided writing ensures that children think about the correct order and spelling of a word's sound-letter associations. Pose a question about the book to help the group come up with a sentence, which everyone then writes. Children write, and you write the sentence yourself on a pad or chart. Children themselves should decide how to represent each sound, unless you know that it is an irregular spelling or a phonic element with which they are not yet familiar. As you write, it is important for you to stay a word behind most of the children so that they are not copying you but are first trying to spell the words independently before looking at what you have written. As children write the sentence, they should use the Word Wall for the spelling of any words that are on it.
	Individual Sentences Later, after children have acquired more knowledge of phonic elements, they should write their sentences individually so that they begin developing their independent writing. They will use invented or temporary spellings, and they need opportunities to develop in their use of them. For that reason, you need to check each child's sentence. If a particular sound is not represented in a word, help the child to say the word and listen for that sound, and to add a letter or two to represent it. Again, remind children to use the Word Wall for the spelling of any words that are on it.

DAY 3

(5–10 minutes) **Rereading Familiar Books**	[Same as Day 1]
(10 minutes) **Coached Reading**	[Same as Day 2]
(10 minutes) **Making Words or Rounding Up the Rhymes**	[Same as Day 1]

DAY 4

(5–10 minutes) **Rereading** **Familiar Books**	[Same as Day 1]
(10 minutes) **Independent** **Reading**	By the end of the week, the children should be able to read the book fluently and successfully. On the last two days of the week, children should read on their own, either silently or softly to themselves. Continue to check the progress of individual children and coach them as necessary. After having the whole group read the book to themselves, you might ask individuals to read it aloud, or you may wish to have children read in pairs. Then as each pair reads, you can move among them and provide support and coaching as needed.
(10 minutes) **Writing** **Sentences**	[Same as Day 2]

DAY 5

(5–10 minutes) **Rereading** **Familiar Books**	[Same as Day 1]
(10 minutes) **Independent** **Reading**	[Same as Day 4]
(10 minutes) **Word Wall**	The Word Wall is a place to display high-frequency words. Teachers attach the letters of the alphabet to a bulletin board or large paper mural that is close to the area in which the children meet. Words are then placed below the letter with which they begin. (To help differentiate the words, you may wish to put each word within a letter group on different colored paper. It doesn't matter what color a word is on, but try not to have two words that begin with the same letter on the same color paper.) Encourage children to use the wall whenever they write to help them spell those words correctly.

Name _____

Hints for Helping Your Partner Read

What makes sense?

Are there word parts you know?

What letter sounds do you know?

Now what do you think the word is?

    Look at that word again.
    Does it begin with the letter __?

    Look at the end of that word.
    It rhymes with _____.

Is there a picture?
Does that word go with it?

Look at the picture.
That thing is in the picture.

Read the sentence again.
Does that word make sense?

Teacher Prompts to Teach Decoding Strategies

Self-Monitoring

Were there enough words? *(child tracking during early stages)*

Why did you stop? What did you notice?

Good checking. How did you know it wasn't _____ ?

Let's look at what you said here. Does it make sense?

Let's look at what you said here. Does the word on the page look like what you said?

Decoding Words

Good job! How did you figure that word out?

What word starts with the letter __ and would make sense here?

Is there a familiar rhyming part you recognize?

Can you sound out the word and think of what would make sense here?

Can you read the rest of the sentence and then go back to the word?

Can you get any clues from the pictures?

Why don't you start again at the beginning of the sentence? *(after the child has paused and attempted a word)*

Cross-Checking

Check it. *(after correct and incorrect attempts)*

Does it make sense? *(after sounding out)*

Does the word you said look like the word on the page? *(after using context)*

Using the Library for Independent Reading

Motivating Children to Read

These ideas can help you motivate children to read for pleasure and to be involved in meaningful, enjoyable reading experiences.

Interest Inventory Create an interest inventory to find out what topics children are interested in and what types of books they would most like to read. Duplicate copies of the inventory for each child to complete.

- In the top half of the inventory, have each child list topics that he or she is interested in learning more about.
- In the bottom half, list several categories of books, such as stories about real people, make-believe animal stories, books about real animals, funny stories, folktales or fairy tales, joke and riddle books, and so on from which children can choose.
- Tally the information and then have children help gather books about the most requested categories.
- Conduct the inventory at different times throughout the year.

Library Cards Encourage use of the library to obtain books by helping children obtain their own library cards. Perhaps ask the local librarian to visit your classroom, bringing forms that children can use to obtain cards. If possible, visit the library with children and show them how to use the card catalog. You might post the library hours in the classroom as well as a listing of upcoming events held at the library, such as read-alouds or puppet performances.

Advertise Books Take time during the school routine to advertise books by giving a synopsis and showing a few illustrations in each book. Encourage children to tell about books they have read and enjoyed. Then provide time for children to read, discuss, and swap books.

Favorite Author/Topic Focus on a favorite author or topic for a week. Check out a collection of books by a favorite author or on a favorite topic for the classroom. You might have a festival in honor of the author or topic of the week.

Guest Readers Invite guest readers to come to the classroom to read to children. Guest readers might include parents, grandparents, older children, community leaders, local TV personalities, a local sports figure, a doctor, or a police officer. You might tie the guest readers to units of study in the classroom. Guest readers can show children how people from all walks of life find practical and pleasurable reasons for reading.

Pen Pals Arrange for children to write letters to and receive responses from children in other classrooms about books they are reading or have read. A pen pal might also be an older person living in a nursing home, a "book buddy" (child or adult) in the hospital, or a friend or relative who lives far away. You might also pair university students who are taking elementary-education courses with elementary children. This kind of experience would provide benefits to both.

How Did It End? Read aloud a story almost to the end. For a longer book, read one or two chapters. Then put the book on display for children to finish reading the story on their own. Have more than one copy of the book available if possible.

Tape-Record Stories Have children tape-record their favorite stories. Allow time for children to practice reading aloud their stories several times before taping themselves. This will help them be fluent readers on tape. Set up a listening center where small groups of children can listen to the tapes.

- You might have different readers tape-record stories and have children guess who the "mystery reader" is.
- Have children tape-record themselves reading at various times throughout the year so that they can hear their progress.

Cross-Age Reading Help children establish "reading buddies" with other children who are younger or older. Each week, have reading buddies bring books to share and read to each other. Have them meet at specific times and days on a regular basis.

Helping Children Select Books

Use the following suggestions to help children select books to read independently.

Have individual children gather books they are interested in reading. Ask the child to determine a purpose for reading a book in which he or she is interested. If children wish to read a challenging book about a nonfiction topic they want to learn more about, help them clarify this purpose and explain that they should read to find the information they want even though they may not understand all of the concepts and vocabulary. If children wish to read a longer or more challenging book because their friends have promoted it, encourage them to do so. Children can talk with their friends about the book to help clarify concepts and events.

If children wish to read for pleasure and relaxation, encourage them to select books that are easy for them to read. Help children understand that the best way for them to improve their reading is to increase the number of minutes they read each day, and to spend most of their time reading at a comfortable level.

Here is a procedure you can teach children to help them determine whether a book may be too difficult.

- Help children select a passage that is approximately 50 words long in the book they chose.
- As the child reads the text silently, have him/her raise a finger for each word not known.
- If the child counts five or more unknown words, the book may be too difficult. Encourage the child to choose an easier story. If the child wants to read the book anyway, you might offer to read it together or suggest that the child read it with a partner.

Making Easy Books Acceptable

The following suggestions apply to children in second grade and beyond.

Audio Cassette Project Help your children create an audio cassette library of pattern books and rhyming books for the enjoyment of listeners of all ages. You can model reading aloud folktales such as *The Little Red Hen* and rhyming books such as *The New Kid on the Block* by Jack Prelutsky.

Reading Aloud Reading aloud is one of the most effective techniques for promoting children's literacy growth. Reading stories aloud can

- motivate children to read the stories themselves
- expand children's appreciation of literature and literary styles
- expose children to enjoyable literature that they are not yet able to read independently
- provide a model for fluent reading

Research supports a daily 20-minute period (or longer) for reading aloud. Choose quality literature to share, such as Newbery Medal and Caldecott Award winners, Children's Choices selections, and winners of other children's book awards. Ask the school or public librarian for award listings. The American Library Association publishes lists; lists are also found in *Children's Books in Print*. Also consult books containing annotated lists of recommended read-aloud books.

Encourage parents to read aloud and share books with their children at home. One of the best ways to make easy books appealing is to model your own enjoyment of books that, although simple, appeal to readers of all ages. For example, read aloud from books such as *Go, Dog, Go* by P. D. Eastman or any of the easy Dr. Seuss books, and encourage children to read the rest of the book to find out what happens. Make sure to include read-alouds that are easy enough for children to pick up and read on their own some of the time. Also read aloud rhyming poems from books such as *Where the Sidewalk Ends* by Shel Silverstein and tell children why you like each poem. Describe entertaining easy books for children and encourage them to describe books they have read and enjoyed.

Series Books Utilize book series that contain appealing characters and lively, humorous situations that engage children's interest. Children are motivated to read and master the book, despite the difficulty they may at first have in reading it. Since the sequels typically present familiar characters, similar vocabulary, and related plots, children find reading each successive book easier and more appealing. Each time children begin a new book in a series, encourage them to predict something about the characters and events, using knowledge they have gained reading other books in the series.

Suggested Series Books to Use in Grades 1 and 2

Amanda Pig series by Jean Van Leeuwen
Amelia Bedelia series by Peggy Parish
Arthur series by Marc Brown
Babar the Elephant series by Jean and Laurent Brunhoff
Clifford series by Norman Bridwell
Commander Toad series by Jane Yolen
Cut-Ups series by James Marshall
D. W. series by Marc Brown
First Grade series by Joanne Ryder
Fox series by James Marshall
Frances books by Russell Hoban
Frog and Toad series by Arnold Lobel
George and Martha series by James Marshall
Golly Sisters series by Betsy Byars
Harold series by Crockett Johnson
Harry series by Gene Zion
Henry and Mudge series by Cynthia Rylant
Jamaica series by Juanita Havill
Little Bear series by Else Holmelund Minarik
Petunia series by Roger Duvoisin
Sheep books by Nancy Shaw

Suggested Series Books to Use in Grades 2 and 3

Adam Joshua Capers by Janice Lee Smith
Brian and Pea Brain series by Elizabeth Levy
Horrible Harry series by Suzy Kline
Janetta stories by Helen Griffith
Julian series by Ann Cameron
Mrs. Piggle Wiggle series by Betty MacDonald
Nate the Great series by Marjorie Weinman Sharmat
Peachstreet Mudders series by Matt Christopher
Polk Street Kids series by Patricia Reilly Giff
Sebastian Super Sleuth series by Mary Blount Christian
Sophie series by Dick King-Smith

Making Difficult Books Accessible

Use the following suggestions to make difficult but enticing books more accessible to children.

Buddy and Mini-Group Reading Have less able readers read with partners for whom the books are less difficult. Children might also read together in small mixed-ability groups of about four to six children. Have available multiple copies of several quality books representing a variety of topics, authors, and writing styles from which children in each group can choose. The books children choose can be the basis for forming the mini-groups. If necessary, model for children such cooperative skills as active listening, taking turns, and providing encouragement.

Tape Recordings and Audio Cassettes Instead of a live reading, a tape recording or commercial audio cassette of a *difficult* book can be substituted to provide a model for children to listen to one or more times before they read the book themselves. Libraries frequently lend audio cassettes of well-known books. A great variety of children's books is available on audio cassette.

Videos Find out which of your children's favorite stories are available as films or visual presentations on videocassettes. You might read aloud the text version to children, and then check out the video from a store or the public library and show it to children. Or, show the video version first and then read the book aloud. Alternately, encourage children to read the book on their own. Discussions comparing text and video versions can promote critical thinking and comprehension.

Television and Radio Programs Encourage children to view programs that promote literature and reading. These include the following:

▶ *Reading Rainbow,* the award-winning public television series, encourages children (ages 5–8) to read and introduces them to the wonders of books. Each episode is built around specific books and takes viewers on location to explore further the books' themes. Contact your local public television station to obtain (for a nominal fee) a booklist, schedule, and Teacher's Guide of the *Reading Rainbow* programs to be featured during the year.

▶ *Storytime,* another award-winning weekday series, welcomes children (ages 3–7) to the world of stories and outstanding children's literature. Three hosts introduce each of the books read aloud in the series. Together with celebrity guest readers, they discuss the stories with a small group of children.

▶ *Read to Me!* (on public radio in some locations) encourages children to get involved with books. *Read to Me!* reviews books for children of all ages.

If there is a television or radio in your school, you might watch or listen to these programs in class. Otherwise, bring in a local radio and TV guide from the newspaper and help children locate programs such as these to listen to or to view at home. You might post listening or viewing times in the classroom. Plan a time for discussing the books presented on radio or TV. Bring those books to class and encourage children to read them.

Responding to Books

The ideas listed below can be used to help children express their insights and understanding of any book they read. Suggestions for responding to both fiction and nonfiction books are given.

Discussion After children have read the same text or related texts, hold small-group or whole-class discussions on the material read. If children meet to discuss in small groups, you or an aide might circulate from group to group to guide and facilitate discussion.

Posters Invite children to create posters about fiction and nonfiction books they have read. Have them design a poster to encourage others to read the book.

Mini-Presentations Have children give one-minute presentations or thumbnail sketches to tell about or "sell" selections they have read. Help children time themselves as they prepare and practice their presentations.

Fiction

Retell the Story Invite children to retell a favorite story in a small group, using the book as a prompt. You might begin telling the story and then have children add sentences to complete the story.

Story Strips As children retell a story, write the key events on sentence strips. Have children rebuild the story on the floor or in a pocket chart by arranging the events in sequence.

Dramatize Have children use simple props to act out or pantomime a story. Small groups of children can work together to plan and organize the dramatization and decide on roles. Allow time for children to gather materials and rehearse.

Story Boards Give small groups of children each a large sheet of paper folded into quarters, or four sheets of paper that they can tape together. Explain to children that they will use each frame to highlight a different part of the story. Ask group members to draw a representation of an important moment in the story in each frame, and write a sentence or two in the frame telling about the event.

Big Books Create a big book version of the story. You might write the text for each page of the story on large sheets of paper. Then distribute the pages and have children draw illustrations to go with each one. Once the drawings or paintings are done, have children put the pages in correct sequence. Make a front and back cover out of sturdy paper. Punch holes at the top or sides and use binder rings or lace yarn to hold the book together.

Story Variations/Innovations Use a story as a stimulus for writing a new story. The new story might spring from a pattern or idea in the original, or be a further adventure of one of the story characters.

Story Maps Write these headings on a large sheet of paper: Setting, Characters, Problems, Events, Ending. Help children complete the story map using words, phrases, or pictures. They can use the completed story map to retell the story.

Reader's Theater Have children read the story aloud as if it were a play. Have one child read the narrative parts and others read the words and thoughts of various characters. Explain that they will not act out the story, but will read their parts while standing or sitting. They will use their voices and the expressions on their faces to make the story interesting to the audience. Before they make their presentation, allow children time to practice reading the story once aloud as a group. You might want to duplicate copies of the story so that each child can mark the lines he or she is to read. Remind children to read loudly and clearly, and with expression.

Comic Frames Partners or small groups can illustrate key scenes from a story in comic frames and write dialogue in speech balloons.

Letters to Characters Children can write or dictate a letter to their favorite story character telling what they thought of the story and why.

Nonfiction

Collage Pairs of children who have read the same nonfiction books can create a collage of pictures and words related to the topic.

Questions and Answers Partners or small groups of children who have read the same selection might each write or dictate questions for the others to answer.

Did You Know That . . . Make a list of facts learned from reading a nonfiction book. This may be done initially as a group endeavor, and later as an independent activity when children have gained experience with the process.

PART 3 Communicating Students' Successes to Parents

All children benefit from knowing that their families are aware of and proud of their achievements. All parents want to see their children succeed. But sometimes success is difficult to offer to the parents of students who are reading below their grade level. This section will provide you with a number of ideas for sharing students' successes with their families.

The activities in this section can be used with all students but will be particularly beneficial in increasing the self-esteem of students who are experiencing reading difficulties.

> *Home/Community Connections,* the home-school component of *Invitations to Literacy* provides a comprehensive program for communicating with parents, making parents and teachers partners, using volunteers in the classroom, and moving beyond the classroom to the community. This section, along with *Home/Community Connections,* will provide you with a variety of resources for addressing the needs of all of your students and their families.

Highlighting Successes

Brag Bag A brag bag alerts parents to work that their child is proud of. Brag Bags can be made from recycled gift bags, shopping bags, canvas tote bags, or small backpacks.

Along with the child's work, include a message to the child's parents telling why the work is special. Ask for a reply.

Success Balloon On a small piece of paper, write a note that describes a success that a student has experienced. Fold the paper and stick it inside a balloon. Blow up the balloon and send it home with the child.

Photograph Successes Using your own camera or a disposable one, take photographs of students reading, performing, working on a project, or involved in some other activity. Send home the photographs and have children explain to their families what is happening.

Videotape Students' Successes Use a camcorder to record students reading aloud or participating in a group discussion or some other activity that will show parents their children participating successfully. Send the video home to families on a rotating basis.

HappyGram Send home a HappyGram to tell families about something positive that their child has done. Copy and complete the form on page 201 and send it home with the child.

Create Something Special Create a plaque, magnet, or some other special item to send home each week. Discuss who has done something well and have students vote on the classmate who should receive the award. Make sure that each student gets a chance to take the plaque home at least once before any student gets a second chance. Allow the student who receives the award to keep the special plaque or magnet at home for one week. To make the plaque or magnet, do the following:

- Obtain a sheet of Styrofoam (about 1/8" thick) or heavy cardboard from an art supply store. Spray paint it gold or silver. Add a fancy border or other decorations.

- Attach a magnet or hanging tab to the back side so it can be used as a plaque or as a magnet to put on the refrigerator door.

- With metallic or permanent marker, print a message such as "For a Job Well Done."

Instead of a plaque or magnet, you might purchase an inexpensive picture frame and insert a certificate with a similar message. Print the certificate in a fancy script.

Phone Calls Make a plan for making positive phone calls to the families of each child on a regular basis throughout the year. Mention specific and positive behavior and news about their child.

Weekly Learning Goals At the beginning of each week, work with each student to make a list of one or two specific and realistic goals for the coming week. At the end of the week, meet again briefly with each student. Put a sticker or checkmark by the goals that have been met. Discuss any that have not been met. Discuss a plan for how they might be achieved. Have children take home the list to share with their families.

Letter Dialogue Have each student work with a peer partner or aide to write or dictate a weekly letter to their parents describing what they are doing in school. Students can use questions such as these to help them write informative letters:

- What story did I read this week?
- Did I like it? Why or why not?
- What is one interesting thing I learned this week?
- What was my favorite school activity this week?

Ask parents to write a letter to their child in response to the child's letter to them.

Sharing Students' Reading Progress

It is important that all students be encouraged to show off the reading progress they are making to their families. This is especially beneficial for students who are receiving extra support for their reading. Use the suggestions below to help students share their reading progress.

Organize a Home Reading Program

Identify Which Books Can Go Home Set aside a bookshelf especially for the books that students may take home. Include books on a variety of topics, and spanning several levels of difficulty.

Set Up a Check-Out System Create a pocket chart to hang near the shelf. Include a pocket for each student. Write the title and author of each book in your take-home library on a 3 x 5 index card. Place the card in the inside cover of the book. Then explain and demonstrate the following process to students: Each time a student checks out a book, that student places the book's index card in the pocket with his or her name on it. When the student returns the book, he or she places the card in the inside cover of the book before returning it to the shelf.

Document Reading Progress

At the beginning of the school year, tape-record students reading a book that is slightly above their instructional level. Midway through the year tape-record them reading the same book. Label and date each recording and send the audio cassettes home so that parents can hear the difference in their child's reading fluency.

Make the Home Reading Experience Successful

Plan for successful reading experiences in the following ways:

- Encourage students to practice reading the books they wish to take home with a partner until they feel comfortable with their reading.

- Redirect the purpose of the reading activity and suggest that students bring home easy books to read aloud to younger siblings.

- If a student selects a particularly challenging book, have him or her meet with another student who has read the same book and have the two of them read the first part of it together. The student who has already completed the book can offer help with character names, events, and new vocabulary.

- Encourage students to bring home books the class has read together and reread them for a family member. Rereading familiar books will help students build reading fluency and confidence—and give them a sense of pride and accomplishment as they share their reading progress with parents and friends.

Get Family Members Involved

Give students a bookmark from the master on page 202. Each time a student takes a book home, have him or her write the title and author's name on one side of the bookmark. After reading the book at home, each family member who shared the reading experience can sign the back side of the bookmark.

After students have collected a certain number of bookmarks, provide them with a reward. The reward might be one of the following:

- **A "Bag of Fun."** A bag of fun is a special tote bag which is allowed to go home only on very special occasions. The bag would hold a book and some or all of the following: a stuffed animal, an audio cassette of the story, puzzles, games, or other activities related to the book.

- **A "No-Cost Reward."** A no-cost reward might be a reward that allows a student to pick the read-aloud story, to be the teacher's assistant, to be first in line, or any other activity that students might consider a privilege.

Monitor Students' Reading

On a poster, create a class chart to keep track of the group's home-reading efforts. Periodically set aside time to discuss with each student his or her book choices. Discuss which books were the family's favorites and why.

CLASS HOME-READING CHART			
STUDENT'S NAME			
FICTION BOOKS			
NONFICTION BOOKS			
FOLKTALES			
POETRY			

Acknowledge Success

Every two or three weeks have a "Home-Reading Awards" ceremony in which students are acknowledged for their efforts. You might recognize all students for the number of minutes read by giving cut-out ribbon or stick awards.

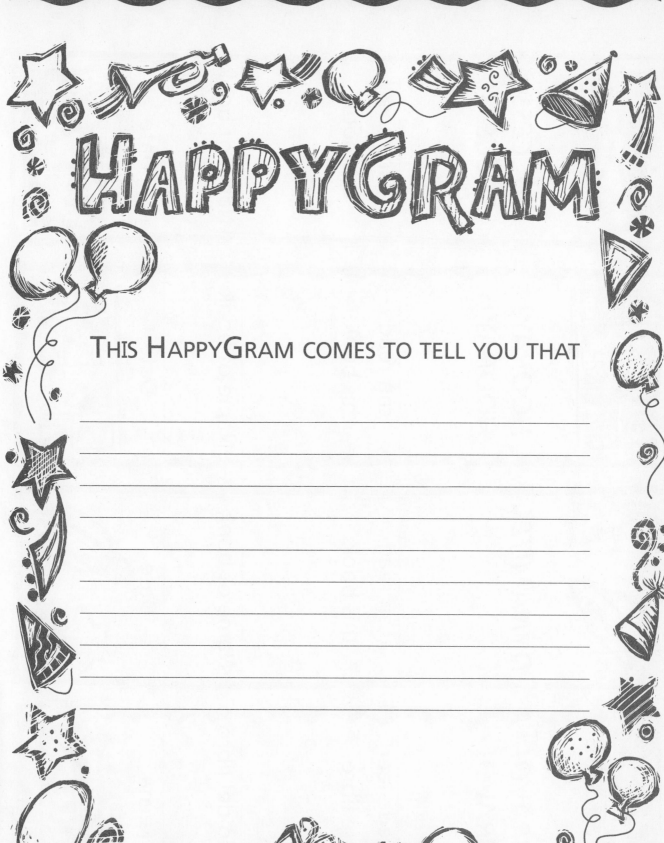

HappyGram

THIS HappyGram COMES TO TELL YOU THAT

_____
_____
_____
_____
_____
_____
_____
_____

SUCCESS! SUCCESS!

_____ can read this book.

Name of book

Date

HOORAY! HOORAY!

_____ can read this book.

Name of book

Date

DYNAMITE!

_____ can read this book.

Name of book

Date

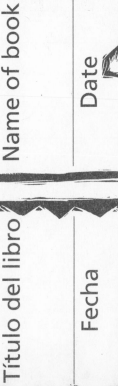

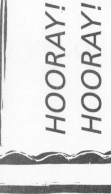

¡BRAVO! ¡BRAVO!

_____ puede leer este libro.

Título del libro

Fecha

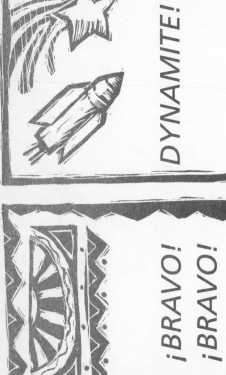

PART 4 Phonics/Decoding

Lesson 1: Initial Consonants

Wake Up!

Initial Consonants:
t, b, g, k, m, z, v

High-Frequency Words: *all, I, jump, run, the, time, up*

Write the following sentence from *Wake Up!* on the chalkboard. Have children read it aloud with you.

I wake up all the <u>time</u>.

Point to the word *time*. Repeat *time*, asking children to listen for the beginning sound. Remind them that *t* stands for the /t/ sound they hear at the beginning of *time*.

Have children sit where you can see their feet. Tell them that you will say some words and that they should tap their feet softly each time they hear a word that begins with the sound for *t*. Say the following words: *tap, table, house, dog, tire, rest, tomorrow, light*. Record each word that begins with *t* on chart paper.

Have children brainstorm other words that begin with *t*. If children have difficulty thinking of words, encourage them to look for objects in the classroom whose names begin with the sound for *t*. Record the words children suggest on charts, and add them to the Word Wall.

Have children read the words in each list aloud with you. Then invite volunteers to use the words in oral sentences.

Follow a similar procedure to review other consonants, using the following sentences and word groups:

b: The rabbit would not get out of <u>bed</u>.   *ball, bag, horn, bat, map, bounce, bake*

g: The turtle wanted to <u>go</u> to the race.   *get, walk, gate, tip, lift, give, game*

k: The sheep <u>kicked</u> up his legs.   *keep, kind, pen, key, race, fit, kit*

m: The turtle <u>made</u> the rabbit run and jump.   *melt, fun, mix, mother, soap, cat, meat*

z: I <u>zip</u> up all the time.   *zebra, mouse, net, sock, zigzag, play, zoo*

v: The rabbit was <u>very</u> tired.   *vine, tooth, vet, bat, vacation, lick, voice*

For the next two lessons, follow the same procedure as above, using the sentences and word groups provided. You may wish to vary children's responses by having them clap or hop when they hear the target sound.

The Hen Sat

Initial Consonants:
c, d, j, n, p, r, y

High-Frequency Words: *and, cat, dog, fast, one, three, two, went*

Follow the procedure for *Wake Up!* using these sentences and word groups.

c: Two <u>cat</u>s went fast.   *cape, go, me, cut, cap, sun, coat*

d: Three <u>dog</u>s went fast.   *day, dust, lip, here, deer, sat, dark*

j: The hen did not <u>jump</u>.   *jelly, fast, time, jug, joke, long, junk*

n: The rat was <u>near</u> the hen.   *neat, big, plant, nickel, nice, tree, night*

p: The animals ran <u>past</u> the hen.   *paper, down, put, said, peek, house, pack*

r: One <u>rat</u> was going fast.   *race, call, run, house, rag, raft, rabbit*

y: The hen was in the <u>yard</u>.   *yell, help, yo-yo, year, friend, yesterday, yogurt*

Snuffy, Fluffy and the Mice

Initial Consonants:
f, h, l, s, w, qu

High-Frequency Words: *a, baby, have, my, our, see, we, with*

Follow the procedure for *Wake Up!* using these sentences and word groups.

f: My mice run <u>fast</u>.   *food, came, find, fun, dog, my, five*

h: I <u>have</u> a baby mouse.   *help, baby, hide, heat, girl, house, do*

l: We <u>laugh</u> at the pets.   *life, time, for, lick, lake, lock, send*

s: I <u>see</u> the dog jump up.   *sun, soap, big, fish, sip, deep, sell*

w: See our Fluffy <u>with</u> a rose.   *wish, toy, well, wipe, ball, want, coat*

qu: The pet show is not <u>quiet</u>.   *quarter, top, quilt, quart, star, quite, jug*

Lesson 2: Final Consonants

Jump, Jill, Jump

Final Consonants:
f, l (ll), r, s, t

High-Frequency Words: *but, for, is, it, not, will, you*

Write the following sentence from *Jump, Jill, Jump* on the chalkboard. Have children read it aloud with you.

Jump with <u>Bill</u>.

Point to the word *Bill*. Say *Bill* several times, asking children to listen for the ending sound. Remind them that the letters *ll* stand for the /l/ sound they hear at the end of *Bill*.

Tell children that you will say some words and that they should wiggle their fingers each time they hear a word that ends with the sound for *l*. Say the following words: *tell, send, take, call, sell, find, ball*. As children identify the correct words, record them on chart paper, listing *sell* under *tell* and *ball* under *call*.

Have children brainstorm other words that end with the sound for *l*. If children have difficulty, encourage them to think of words that rhyme with the words already recorded. Add the words children suggest to the chart, listing rhyming words in columns. Add the lists to the Word Wall.

Have children read the listed words aloud with you. Then invite volunteers to use the words in oral sentences.

Use a similar procedure to review other final consonant sounds, using the following:

f: It is not <u>safe</u> for Jill to jump with Bill and Kit.   *chief, like, leaf, stop, play, roof, loaf*

r: It is time <u>for</u> you.   *car, say, door, pear, how, more, your*

s: Kit <u>jumps</u> with Bill.   *hiss, plays, pail, had, this, pass, beep*

t: All three will <u>fit</u>.   *sit, meat, home, beat, mend, fit, cat*

Me Too!

Final Consonants:
b, k, g, m

High-Frequency Words: *am, came, he, me, said, too*

Follow the procedure for *Jump, Jill, Jump,* using these sentences and word groups.

b: After the race, he got in the <u>tub</u>.   *web, came, pig, rub, grab, cube, hop*

k: I will <u>sneak</u> under the finish line.   *joke, seat, bike, feel, hook, rake, miss*

g: Pam is fast and <u>big</u>.   *dig, read, plant, rug, hug, lid, bag*

m: He <u>came</u> for the run too.   *am, fly, start, dime, ham, sun, team*

Ian and the Seed

Final Consonants:
d, n, p, x

High-Frequency Words: *in, out, plant, put, six, then*

Follow the procedure for *Jump, Jill, Jump,* using these sentences and word groups.

d: Ian put the <u>seed</u> in the pot.   *braid, pig, feed, weed, six, sad, bird*

n: The plant was <u>green</u>.   *then, fish, cone, had, bean, thin, grow*

p: The plant came <u>up</u>.   *cap, hop, bear, grape, find, clap, sweep*

x: Ian is <u>six</u> years old.   *fix, tax, me, will, mix, log, box*

Lesson 3: Consonant Clusters

Our Plants

Consonant Clusters with *r*

Write the following sentence from *Our Plants* on the chalkboard, underlining as shown. Have children read the sentence aloud with you.

> Cat and <u>Crow</u> came out too.

Point out the word *crow* and have children repeat it, listening for the beginning sounds. Remind them that when the letters *c* and *r* come together in a word their sounds are so close together they almost seem like one sound.

Remind children that *r* is often paired with other consonants too. Write the *r* clusters *br, cr, dr, fr, gr, pr,* and *tr* across the top of the chalkboard. Then, as you say some words that begin with *r* clusters, have children repeat each word. Call on a volunteer to go to the chalkboard and stand under the cluster that stands for the beginning sounds in the word. If everyone agrees that the child has chosen the correct cluster, record the word below it on the chalkboard. Say the following words: *dry, grow, creep, try, drive, friend, green, break, present, Friday, tricycle, crisp, frog, bright, dress, brown, print.*

Have children read each word on the board aloud with you. Invite a volunteer to use the word in an oral sentence. Finally, have children reread pages 4 and 5 in *Our Plants* and find four words that begin with *r* clusters. *(grow, dry, crow, try)*

A Walk in the City

Consonant Clusters with *l, s*

Follow the procedure in the *Our Plants* lesson for the clusters *bl, cl, fl, gl, pl,* and *sl,* using the following sentence and words.

> Many people in the city walk past the <u>flag</u>.
> *black, glass, clay, fly, play, slip, sliver, glad, clip, floor, blame, please, flower, blue, place, sleep*

Repeat the procedure for the clusters *sk, sm, sn, sp,* and *st.*

> Up here, the city is so <u>small</u>.
> *skunk, skate, sneak, space, stop, smell, spot, smart, snail, sky, snow, spin, stir, step*

A Fish Trip

Consonant Clusters with *r, l, s*

Assign each child one or more of the consonant clusters with *l, r,* or *s.* Have children look through the three WATCH ME READ Books in the theme for words that begin with the assigned clusters. Have children use small self-sticking notes to mark the words they find. Then have them take turns reading to the group the words found and identifying the two letters that stand for the beginning sounds.

Lesson 4: Digraphs

Where IS My Baby?

Digraphs *sh, th*

High-Frequency Words: *as, be, big, could, tree, under, when, your*

Write the following sentence from *Where IS My Baby?* on the chalkboard. Have children read it aloud with you.

> "Where is my baby?" <u>she</u> said.

Point to the word *she*. Remind children that two letters together sometimes stand for one sound. Say *she* several times, asking children to listen for the sound at the beginning of the word. Underline the *sh* and remind children that these letters stand for the sound they hear at the beginning of *she*.

Next, write this sentence on the chalkboard: "Could he be under this <u>bush</u>?"
Have children read the sentence with you. Then ask where they hear the /sh/ sound in the word *bush*. (at the end of the word)

Tell children that you will say some words and that they should make the /sh/ sound each time they hear a word that has that sound. Say the following words: *dish, send, sharp, run, plate, lash, shell, stop, rush.* Record on chart paper each word that has the digraph *sh*.

Have children brainstorm other words that have the digraph *sh*. Record the words children suggest on charts, and add them to the Word Wall.

Use a similar procedure to review the digraph *th*, using the following sentences and words:

> "Could he be up in <u>this</u> big tree?"
> "He was <u>with</u> you all the time," said Ruby.
> *that, thin, like, sip, they, note, thorn, bath, mouth, boat, path, think, rain, tooth*

Have children read the words in each list aloud with you. Then invite volunteers to use the words in oral sentences.

Fox and Chick

Digraph *ch*

High-Frequency Words: *at, back, come, her, house, how, more, over*

Follow the procedure above for the digraph *ch,* using the following sentences and words:

> <u>Chick</u> went to her house.
> The dog will <u>teach</u> Fox a lesson.
> *teach, loud, chirp, hide, touch, cheese, rich, road, chill, chase, jump, chew*

Hank and Lin

Digraphs *ch, sh, th*

High-Frequency Words: *down, had, him, his, if, she*

Assign each child or pair of children one of the consonant digraphs *ch, sh,* or *th*. Have children look through the three WATCH ME READ Books in the theme for words containing their assigned digraphs. Have children use small self-sticking notes to mark the words they find. Then have them take turns reading the words found and identifying each digraph.

Lesson 5: Phonograms

I Like Cats

Short *a*, Short *a* Phonograms

High-Frequency Words: *before, can, each, from, good, like, made, they*

Write the following sentence from *I Like Cats* on the chalkboard, underlining as shown. Have children read it aloud with you.

> "You can see my two <u>cats</u>."

Point to the word *cats*. Ask children to listen for the short *a* sound as you say *cats* several times.

Have children build words that have the short *a* sound by using phonograms. Start by writing the following sentences on the chalkboard, underlining as shown.

> "I <u>am</u> glad to have her, so I call her <u>Glad</u>."
> "I made him a hat from a <u>bag</u> <u>and</u> he likes it."
> This time Pat was <u>fast</u>.

Have children brainstorm words that rhyme with the underlined words. List the words children suggest on charts, and add them to the Word Wall. (Possible responses: *am: ham, jam, cram, Sam, ram; Glad: sad, Dad, bad, had, lad; bag: drag, rag, flag, tag, sag; and: band, hand, land, stand; fast: last, blast, past*)

Have children read the words in each list aloud with you. Then invite volunteers to use the words in oral sentences.

A Big Help

Short *e*, Short *e* Phonograms

High-Frequency Words: *day, did, help, little, make, there, were, who*

Follow the procedure in *I Like Cats,* using these sentences:

> I need to <u>rest</u>.
> "I'll <u>get</u> the little tree down," said Beaver.
> Bird wants to get <u>well</u>.
> You all did a little, and you were a big <u>help</u>.

(Possible responses: *rest: best, test, nest, west; get: bet, set, wet, net; well: sell, bell, yell, tell, shell; help: yelp, kelp*)

Great Frogs!

Short *o*, Short *o* Phonograms

High-Frequency Words: *get, great, look, their, us*

Follow the procedure for *I Like Cats,* using these sentences:

"Mr. Best, loot my <u>frog</u>," said Ben.
"They look a <u>lot</u> like the frogs that we see on our walks. Great frogs!"
Frogs like to <u>hop</u>.

(Possible responses: *frog: dog, log, bog, clog; lot: cot, blot, tot, trot, hot, spot; hop: mop, cop, hop, slop, top*)

Lesson 6: Phonograms

Try, Try Again

Short *i*, Short *i* Phonograms

High-Frequency Words: *again, no, off, some, sun, try, very*

Write the following sentence from *Try, Try Again* on the chalkboard. Have children read it aloud with you.

<u>It</u> was a very good day to be out.

Point to the word *it*. Ask children to listen for the short *i* sound as you say *it* several times.

Have children build words that have the short *i* sound by using phonograms. Write the following sentences from *Try, Try Again* on the chalkboard, underlining as shown.

Beetle sat <u>in</u> the sun.
So Beetle <u>did</u> a little <u>flip</u>, but he came down on his back.
"I can <u>dig</u>, but I can't jump."

Have children brainstorm words that rhyme with the underlined words. List the words children suggest on charts, then add them to the Word Wall. (Possible responses: *in: bin, pin, thin, din, spin, chin, grin; did: kid, lid, rid, hid; flip: sip, rip, dip, slip, zip, skip; dig: fig, big, rig*)

Have children read the words in each list aloud with you. Then invite volunteers to use the words in oral sentences.

Grasshopper and Ant

Short *u*, Short *u* Phonograms

High-Frequency Words: *any, much, now, than, that, way*

Follow the procedure used for *Try, Try Again,* using these sentences.

Grasshopper had to have <u>fun</u>.
"It's a day for me to <u>jump</u> and run!"
Ant was <u>snug</u> inside her house.

(Possible responses: *fun: sun, run, bun; jump: pump, bump, dump; snug: rug, dug, bug*)

All in Fun

Short Vowels, Double Final Consonants

High-Frequency Words: *after, are, by, other, side, thought, why*

Assign each child or pair of children one of the vowel letters, *a, e, i, o,* or *u.* Have children look through the three WATCH ME READ Books in the theme for words that have the short sound for their assigned vowel. Have children attach small self-sticking notes to the words they find. Then have them share their findings with the group as you record the words.

(Possible responses: *a: bag, grass, back; e: dress, yell, get, then, when; i: big, it, is, in, sit; o: on, off; u: bug, jump, up, fun*)

Finally, ask children which words have double final consonants. Invite volunteers to use those words in oral sentences.

Lesson 7: Long Vowels CVC*e*

A Great Place for Llama

Long *a:* CVC*e*

High-Frequency Words: *door, has, ran, stop, them*

Write the following sentence from *A Great Place for Llama* on the chalkboard. Have children read it aloud with you.

> This isn't a good <u>place</u> for me.

Point to the word *place.* Ask children to listen for the long *a* sound as you repeat *place* several times. Remind children that words with the consonant-vowel-*e* pattern often have a long vowel sound.

Have children build words that have the long *a* sound by using phonograms. Start by writing the following sentences from *A Great Place for Llama* on the chalkboard, underlining as shown.

> "I couldn't <u>wake</u> them up!"
> "This is a great <u>place</u> for you to stop, Llama," said Little Bear.
> Pig was there too, and they were playing a <u>game</u>.

Have children brainstorm words that rhyme with the underlined words. List the words children suggest on charts, then add them to the Word Wall. Have children read the words in each list aloud with you. Then invite volunteers to point to a word, read it, and use it in an oral sentence.

(Possible responses: *wake: cake, bake, take, rake; place: space, race, chase, lace, trace; game: same, blame, lame, came*)

Never Wake a Sleeping Snake

Long _i_: CVCe

High-Frequency Words: _even, just, never, or, saw, sleep, thing_

Follow the procedure used for _A Great Place for Llama_, using these sentences.

> Mike never just said things.
> He even yelled when things were fine.
> Mike never yelled, not even one time.

(Possible responses: _Mike: like, spike, bike; fine: dine, line, pine; time: dime, lime, grime_)

A Tune for My Mother

Long _o_: CVCe

High-Frequency Words: _ask, give, mother, old, show_

Have children go on a "word hunt" through _A Tune for My Mother_. Have them use self-sticking notes to mark words that have the long _o_ or the long _u_ sound and the vowel-consonant-_e_ pattern. Have children read aloud the sentences containing these words. (page 1: _cute_; page 5: _joke_; page 10: _tune_)

Lesson 8: Long _e: e, ee_; Vowel Pairs

Not Too Big

Long _e: e, ee_

High-Frequency Words: _about, always, build, new, read, take, work_

Write the following sentence from _Not Too Big_ on the chalkboard. Have children read it aloud with you.

> "Nothing is too big for me."

Point to the word _me_. Ask children to listen for the long _e_ sound as you say _me_ several times. Explain that the letter _e_ at the end of _me_ stands for the long _e_ sound. Then ask children to find the word _Dee_ on page 9. Ask what letters stand for the long _e_ sound in _Dee_. (ee) Then ask children to find another word on page 9 that has the long _e_ sound. (keep)

Write _keep_ on chart paper. Then pose the following "riddles." Write the answer to each riddle under _keep_. Have children read all the words aloud with you.

> This word names the sound a car horn makes. _(beep)_
> This word tells what you do at night. _(sleep)_
> This word tells about water in the ocean. _(deep)_

A Boat for Toad

Vowel Pairs *ea, oa, ow*

High-Frequency Words: *brother, father, found, home, play, room, water*

Write the following sentences from *A Boat for Toad* on the chalkboard, underlining as shown.

> Toad walked all the way to the <u>beach</u>.
> "I can't <u>row</u> this <u>boat</u>," he said.

Point to the word *beach*. Say *beach* several times, asking children to listen for the long *e* sound. Explain to the children that the letters *ea* stand for the long *e* sound in the word *beach*. Follow the same procedure for the words *row* and *boat*, having the children listen for the long *o* sound.

Have children turn to pages 8–9 in *A Boat for Toad*. Have them find two words in which the letters *ea* stand for the long *e* sound. (page 8: *creaked, leaked*) Then have them find three words in which *oa* stands for the long *o* sound. (page 9: *float, boat, toad*)

Old Sky

Vowel Pairs *ay, ai*

High-Frequency Words: *because, bring, find, friend, morning, start*

Write the following sentences on the chalkboard, underlining as shown.

> Beside you that <u>snail</u> is very, very small.
> If he went as fast as he could, it would take all <u>day</u> just for him to get down from the tree.

Review the long *a* sound in the words *snail* and *day*, calling attention to the vowel pairs *ai* and *ay*.

Take children on a "word hunt" through the three WATCH ME READ Books in the theme. Have them find and read aloud the words in which the vowel pairs *ay* and *ai* stand for the long *a* sound. *(Not Too Big: always, day; A Boat for Toad: day, play; Old Sky: day, way, snail)*

Lesson 9: Sounds for *y*: Long *i*, Long *e*

Looking After Billy

Sounds for *y*: Long *e* and Long *i*

High-Frequency Words: *children, first, gave, lived, next, together, would*

Write the following sentence from *Looking After Billy* on the chalkboard. Have children read it aloud with you.

> At first the <u>baby</u> was sleeping, so Cal and <u>Lucy</u> played a game together.

Point to the words *baby* and *Lucy*. Say *baby* and *Lucy* several times, asking children to listen for the long *e* sound. Explain that in these words, the *y* stands for the long *e* sound.

Next, write the following sentence on the board and have children read it with you.

And when he saw the children playing, he started to <u>cry</u>.

Point to the word *cry*. Say *cry* several times, asking children to listen for the long *i* sound in *cry*. Explain that sometimes the letter *y* stands for the long *i* sound.

Write the following headings on the chalkboard.

Long e   Long i

Then say the word *sky* and ask children whether they hear the long *e* sound or the long *i* sound. Write *sky* under the heading *Long i*. Continue with the following words: *spy, chilly, try, lucky, fry, gravy, windy, jelly, by, penny, sly, baby, fly, dry, happy, Billy, funny*. As children respond, list each word under the appropriate heading.

Have children read aloud the words in each list. Then invite volunteers to use the words in oral sentences. Finally, have children read page 1 in *Looking After Billy* and find three words in which *y* stands for the long *e* sound. (*Lucy, very, many*)

Ned's New Old Sled

Vowel Pairs *oo, ew, ue, ou*

High-Frequency Words: *afraid, every, head, right, school, throw, turn*

Write the following sentence from *Ned's New Old Sled* on the chalkboard, underlining as shown.

It was made of <u>wood</u>.

Read the sentence aloud with children. Point to the word *wood*. Say *wood* several times, asking children to listen for the /oo/ sound. Remind children that the letters *oo* sometimes stand for the vowel sound heard in the word *wood*.

Next, write these sentences on the board:

He put on one <u>boot</u> and then the other.
Ned didn't have a <u>new</u> sled, so he went back into the house.
"Would <u>you</u> like to take a turn with us?"

Read each sentence aloud with children and point to the underlined word. Have children tell what vowel sound they hear in the words (/o͞o/) and what letters stand for that sound. (*oo, ew, ou*)

Have children find and read aloud the word with the /o͞o/ vowel sound on page 2 of *Ned's New Old Sled*. (*school*) Ask a volunteer to name the letters that stand for the /o͞o/ sound in *school*. Then have children find and read aloud the two words with the /oo/ vowel sound on page 4, and name the vowel letters in those words. (*took, wood*)

A Moon for Ana Gracia

High-Frequency Words: *hand, keep, kind, sister, want*

Take children on a "word hunt" through the two books *Ned's New Old Sled* and *A Moon for Ana Gracia*. Have children look for words that have the *y* as in *by* and the *y* as in *baby*. (*Ned's New Old Sled: many, every, my, funny, try; A Moon for Ana Gracia: very, my*)

Lesson 10: *r*-Controlled Vowels

Fishing with Grandpa

> **High-Frequency Words:**   *air, hard, only, same, tell, until, which*

Write the high-frequency words on the chalkboard. Have children read through *Fishing with Grandpa,* searching for the high-frequency words. Invite children to read aloud those sentences that contain the high-frequency words.

Three Wishes for Buster

> **High-Frequency Words:**   *around, know, must, surprise, took, wait, what*

Follow the procedure used for *Fishing with Grandpa* to review the high-frequency words in *Three Wishes for Buster.*

What Seahorse Saw

r-Controlled Vowels: *ar, or*

> **High-Frequency Words:**   *away, happy, own, place, think*

Write the following sentence from *What Seahorse Saw* on the chalkboard, underlining as shown. Have children read it aloud with you.

Seahorse was happy to see Starfish.

Point to the letters *or* in the word *seahorse* and explain that these letters stand for the /or/ sound in *seahorse.* Review the /ar/ sound in the word *starfish.*

Tell children that you will say some words that contain either the /ar/ or the /or/ sound. If the word has the /ar/ sound as in *star*, children should point into the air towards the stars. If the word has the /or/ sound as in *horse*, they should "gallop" like a horse with their feet.

Say the following words: *car, sports, mark, snore, park, shore, corn, large, fork, arm, horn.*

Invite children to think of other words that have the /ar/ and the /or/ vowel sounds. Record children's responses and ask them to use the words in oral sentences.

Next, have children read each of the following pages from *Fishing with Grandpa* and *Three Wishes for Buster*, and have them read aloud the sentences containing each word.

Fishing with Grandpa	*Three Wishes for Buster*
Page 1: *hard*	Page 4: *hard*
Page 3: *before*	Page 14: *for*
Page 5: *starting*	Page 15: *before, more*
Page 14: *more*	
Page 16: *harder*	

Description of Teaching Strategies and Techniques

A number of strategies and techniques are suggested in the selection plans in this *Extra Support Handbook*. Following is a description of some of the strategies and techniques used.

Language Experience Approach

Description: The language experience approach is a way of teaching reading in which children's own experiences and language are used as a springboard for instruction. Articulating thoughts, feelings, and experiences encourages children to be active, creative participants in the learning process.

This approach can be used with the whole class, small groups, or individuals, and includes the following steps:

- **Identify an experience.** The teacher and/or children bring up a topic or experience for discussion. The discussion might involve an experience such as a field trip, a story, a retelling of a news item, a comment on a current event, or anything of interest at the moment.

- **Record children's words.** As children tell about the topic or experience, the teacher writes down their words on the board or on chart paper.

- **Read the experience story.** The teacher or child reads back the story, pointing to words while children repeat. The teacher and children might also do a choral reading.

- **Select and utilize words for instruction.** Sometimes the teacher and children pick out difficult or meaningful words from the experience story. These are written on individual index cards and used for matching activities, as sight words, and other vocabulary activities.

- **Utilize it in a variety of ways.** The experience story can also be used in the following ways: Write each sentence on sentence strips and use for sequencing practice; introduce phonic word-attack skills, structural analysis, and linguistic patterns using story words; duplicate the experience story for each child for reading practice; and so on.

Before Reading Activities

Picture Walk

Description: A picture walk prepares children for reading a selection by giving them advance information about the selection. It involves guiding children through the pictures, photographs, or other visuals in the selection. Basically, the picture walk tells children what they will read before they read it.

- A picture walk might be done with fiction or nonfiction to help children get a sense of the selection or to introduce them to the characters. In some cases, the pictures can be used to tell the story or to help children predict what will happen in the story, or to get an idea of what they might learn from informational text.

- The picture walk should be an interactive discussion among teacher and children and should promote student discovery, rather than teacher telling. Whenever possible, important vocabulary should be incorporated into the discussion.

Concept Map

Description: A concept map is a visual representation of ideas related to a key concept. Mapping serves to organize these ideas and helps children see the relationship between the key concept and their own knowledge.

- **Before Reading** A key concept is written on the board. Children brainstorm what they know about that concept. While individual children may have little knowledge about a concept, children collectively often have a great deal of information. Through brainstorming, you can determine children's prior knowledge and can build on that knowledge to prepare children for reading the selection.

- **During Reading** The concept map helps children process and understand what they are reading. It helps them to see how the information fits together. Children can stop periodically during reading to add information they learn to the map.

- **After Reading** Children can add to the map and use it to review or to summarize what they read.

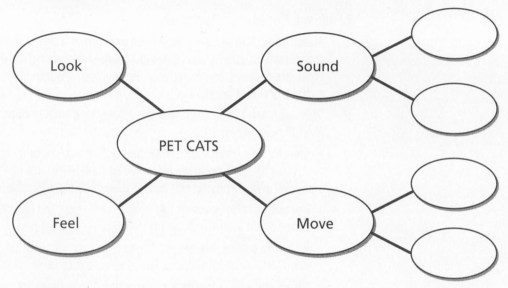

Semantic Map

Description: Like a concept map, a semantic map presents a graphic display of words in categories and shows how words are related to one another. A semantic map focuses on words rather than ideas.

- This technique can be used in small groups or as a whole-class activity. If this activity is done in small groups, a Recorder might be chosen in each group to record the group's efforts. If this activity is done as a whole class, the teacher can record words on the map and simultaneously lead a discussion.

Making Predictions

Description: Making predictions involves using story information and children's own experience to predict what might happen in a story, or what a selection might be about. Predicting helps children set a purpose for reading and enables them to be active participants in the reading process.

- **Before Reading** Children preview the story or selection by reading the title and any headings, captions, or introduction and looking at the illustrations and other graphic aids. Based on this preview, children make their predictions.

- **During Reading** Children think about, monitor, and modify their predictions, based on what they read. They can stop at designated points to make predictions about the next section or sections they will be reading, or to explain their reasons for certain predictions (*Why do you think so?*).

- **After Reading** Children review, evaluate, confirm, or modify their predictions. They can discuss why they think some predictions were confirmed and why others were not.

Story Map Prediction

Description: Story map prediction is a variation of the prediction strategy. Story map prediction may be used with narrative text and focuses on the setting, characters, problem/events, and resolution (ending) of a story. Before reading, children preview, make predictions about as many of the elements as they can, and add information to the story map. During reading, children revise their predictions as they discover new information. After reading, they complete the story map.

During Reading Activities

Self-Question

Description: Self-questioning is a reading comprehension strategy in which children ask themselves questions about the content as they read, and then read on to find their answers. When reading nonfiction, children can identify important ideas, pose a question related to those ideas, and then read to answer the question. Questions generated from this process help the child asking the question to set a purpose for reading by focusing on text that answers the question.

Monitor Comprehension

Description: Monitoring is a strategy that children can apply during reading to evaluate how well they understand the text. They can check their comprehension by asking themselves questions such as *Do I understand this? Is this making sense? What are the important ideas?* If children find they are not understanding the selection, they take steps to remedy the situation:

- They can use context clues, adjust reading rate, reread, or read ahead.
- If children are unable to resolve the problem and ask for help, they should be asked to state the cause of their problem and explain the steps they have taken to remedy it.

Clarify and Get Feedback

Description: Clarifying is a strategy that helps children focus on confusing parts of the text by identifying what they do not understand. For example, they may bring up a word or concept or an unclear referent that is confusing them. There are several strategic actions children can take to clarify the text:

- Read parts that are unclear more slowly, and review any illustrations that might help clear up the confusion.
- Read ahead in the text to see whether new information will clarify the text.
- Consult a dictionary.
- Ask someone for help if confusion still exists.

Provide feedback and support as children attempt to get clarification.

Evaluate

Description: Evaluating involves making a judgment about something. Children can do this by asking questions such as the following about selections they read:

- How do I feel about what I read? Why?
- Could these things really happen? Why or why not?
- Do I like the story so far? Why?
- What is this character like?
- What are the most important ideas I have read? What have I learned?

Summarize

Description: Summarizing is a strategy through which children find the most important ideas in a story or article and then restate those ideas in their own words. During reading, children periodically pause to sum up important ideas or events, thereby constructing meaning from the text and improving their comprehension. After reading, summarizing provides a means for reviewing and remembering what was read.

- In narrative text, children can summarize by focusing on story elements and retelling the major events in order.
- In expository text, children can summarize effectively by focusing on the topic and main ideas.

After Reading Activities

Assisted Reading

Description: Assisted reading is an oral reading technique that involves children in listening to and reading along with a more fluent reader. It helps children with poor decoding skills read grade-level texts fluently and with confidence. This technique can be used in a variety of ways.

- Children can repeat after hearing sentences read, or read simultaneously with an adult, another child, or an audio cassette. Some children may want to take audio cassettes home and make them part of the home reading experience.
- This technique can be used with individual children or with small groups.
- The kind and level of assistance provided should be individualized. When reading simultaneously with children, your voice should be loud and strong for those parts that children are having difficulty with, but only barely audible for the parts that children are able to read without assistance. When serving as a model for children to echo or repeat, the more competent reader can read entire sentences when necessary. But when less support is required, assist only with the pronunciations of short phrases and individual words.
- Since this technique is difficult for children to do, limit the time for doing the assisted reading to no more than five to eight minutes.

Echo Reading

Description: Echo reading provides another model for reading and helps build reading fluency. In this technique, you read aloud one line at a time. The child or children read the same line aloud immediately afterward, using the same intonation and expression. As children become proficient, gradually increase the amount of text children echo from a line to a paragraph to a page.

Choral Reading

Description: Choral reading is an easy, effective method that allows resistant or anxious children to read aloud without being put on the spot by being asked to read alone. Choral reading may be done in several ways.

- Small groups or the whole class, with or without teacher help, can read the text together.
- You or another capable reader can read certain portions of the text with small groups chiming in for designated parts.
- Small groups can be assigned paragraphs of a selection or stanzas of a poem and, in turn, read them aloud.

Radio Reading

Description In radio reading, one child reads as other children listen to the reading of a selection, with books closed, as they would listen to a radio broadcast. Emphasis is placed on the message, not on word-perfect reading. Following the reading, the listeners summarize what was read. If any portion was unclear, everyone opens their books to the section in question and rereads it.

Repeated Reading

Have children reread selected pieces of literature. They might reread in a variety of ways: echo, choral, with a partner, individually, or along with an audio cassette of the book.

Paired Reading

In this procedure, children read orally in pairs by taking turns. Pair groupings may be as follows:

- Two children with uneven literacy skills may be paired. The more capable reader can assist the less able reader, who may be unable to read the text independently. Similarly, children with the same language background but differing literacy skills or knowledge of English can support one another as they read.

- Older children can be paired with younger ones. As they read together, one child can move a finger under the words in a sentence. The two switch roles for the next sentence.

- Paired reading might take place with a special reading partner—a stuffed animal. These special partners are always willing to listen and are available at any time.

Small-Group Reading Small-group reading is similar to paired reading, but involves more than two readers.

Name _____

Citybook

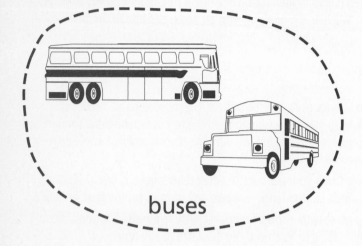

buses

taxis

window

signs

statues

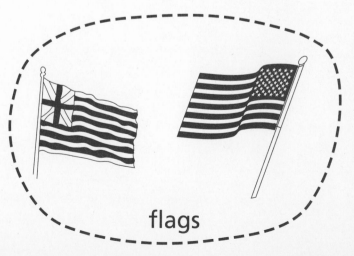

flags

Name _____

Listen to the Desert/Oye al desierto

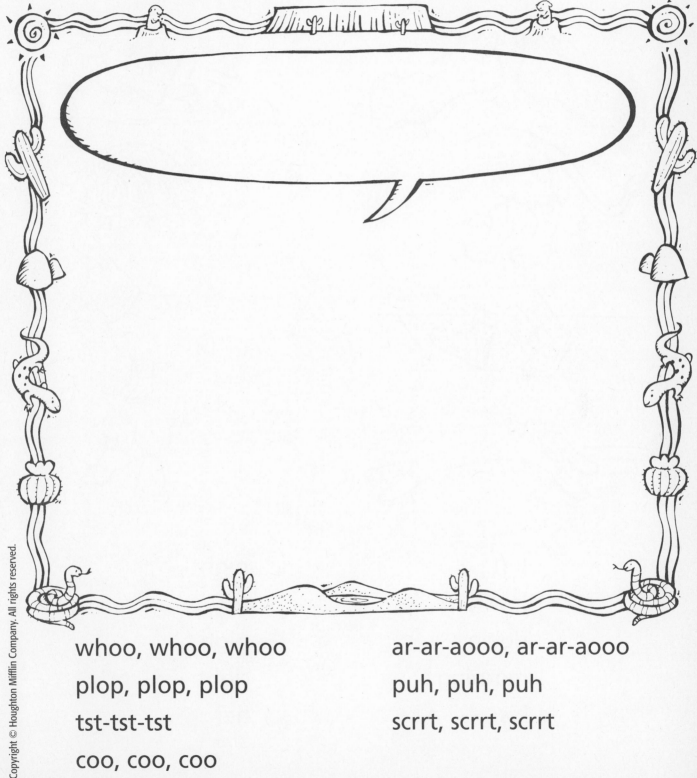

whoo, whoo, whoo

plop, plop, plop

tst-tst-tst

coo, coo, coo

ar-ar-aooo, ar-ar-aooo

puh, puh, puh

scrrt, scrrt, scrrt

Name _____

The Foot Book

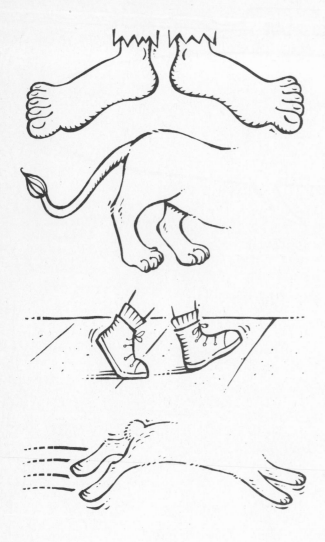

left	night
low	up
down	high
morning	right
his	her

Name _____

The Lady with the Alligator Purse

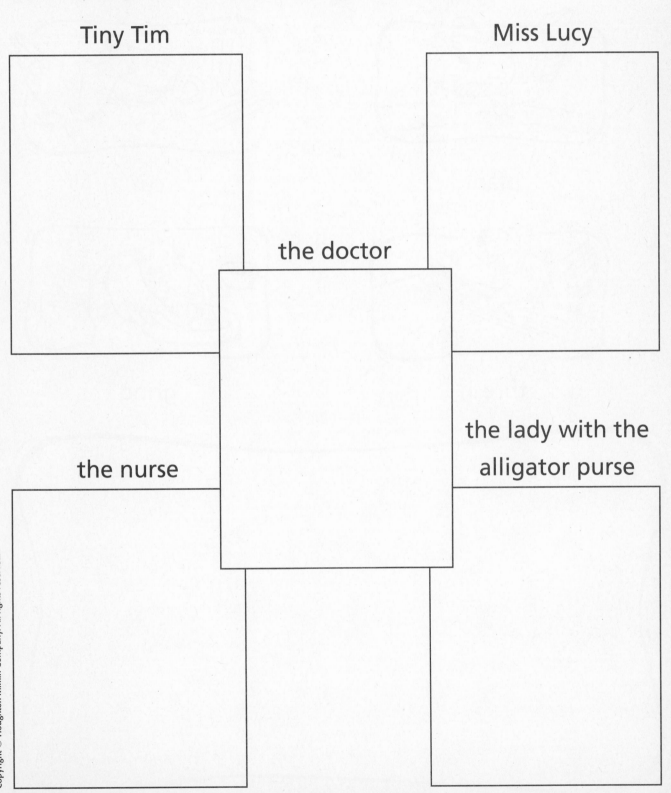

Tiny Tim

Miss Lucy

the doctor

the nurse

the lady with the
alligator purse

Name _____

The Little Red Hen

1.

plant

2.

cut

3.

thresh

4.

grind

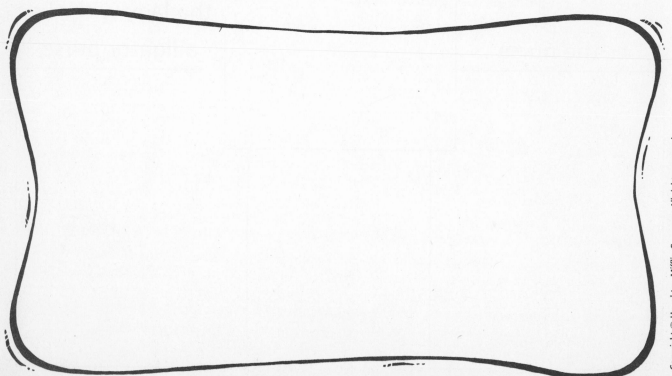

Name _____

Flower Garden

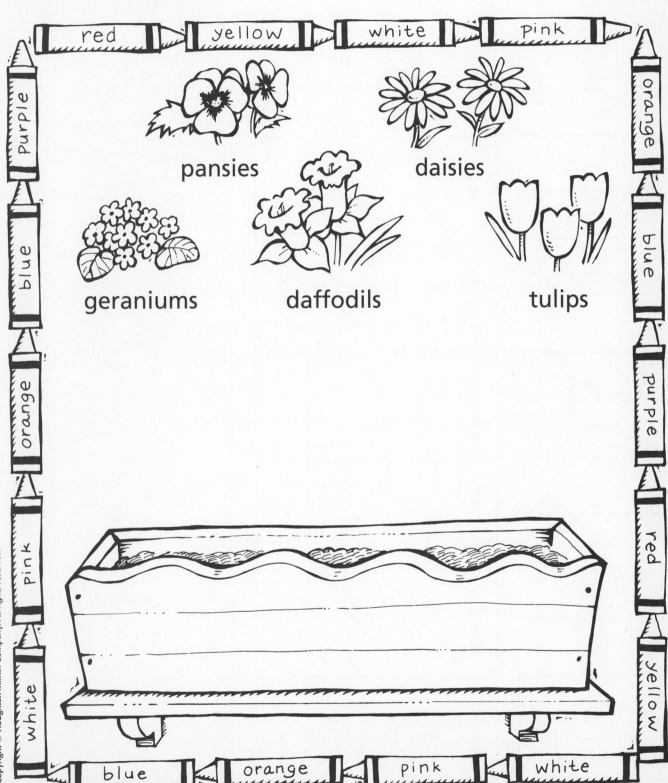

pansies

daisies

geraniums

daffodils

tulips

Name _____

The Very Hungry Caterpillar

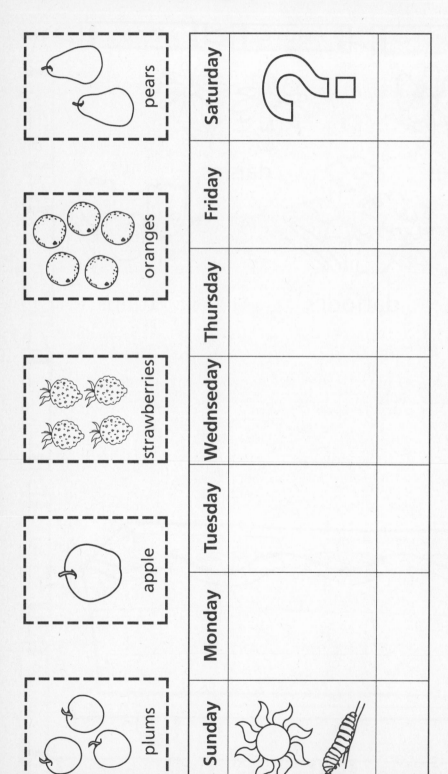

Sunday	Monday	Tuesday	Wednseday	Thursday	Friday	Saturday	

pears

oranges

strawberries

apple

plums

Name _____

A Color of His Own

1.

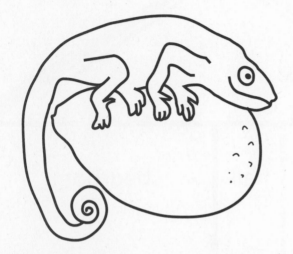

A chameleon is yellow on a lemon.

2.

The chameleon climbed onto the greenest leaf.

3.

In autumn, the leaf and the chameleon turned yellow.

4.

Now the chameleons will always be alike.

Name _____

There's an Alligator Under My Bed

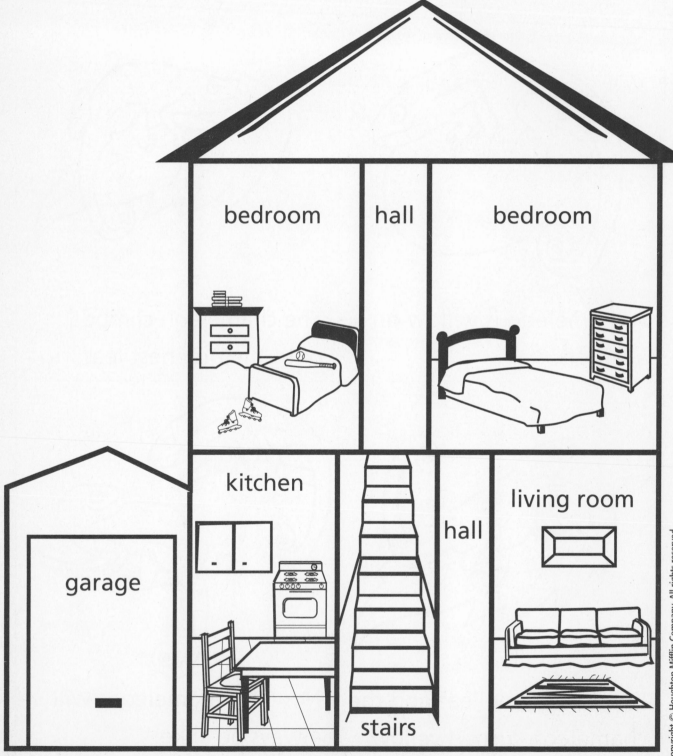

bedroom   hall   bedroom

kitchen   living room

garage   hall

stairs

Name _____

If You Give a Moose a Muffin

What the Moose Asked For ⇨	What the Moose Made
(socks) ⇨	_____
(paper and paints) ⇨	_____
(pillow/sheet) ⇨	_____

muffin pages 86, 87	scenery pages 100, 101	sock puppets page 98
sheet page 103	ghost pages 104, 105	sweater page 93
needle and thread page 95	cardboard and paints page 99	blackberry jam page 89

Name _____

George Shrinks

make his bed

clean his room

wash the dishes

take out the garbage

water the plants

feed the fish

check the mail

Name _____

The Tug of War

Tug of War
Problem: Tapidou's friends, the mighty Elephant and the mighty Hippo, tease him all the time because he is so small.

How Tapidou Might Solve His Problem	How Tapidou Solves His Problem

Name _____

Something from Nothing

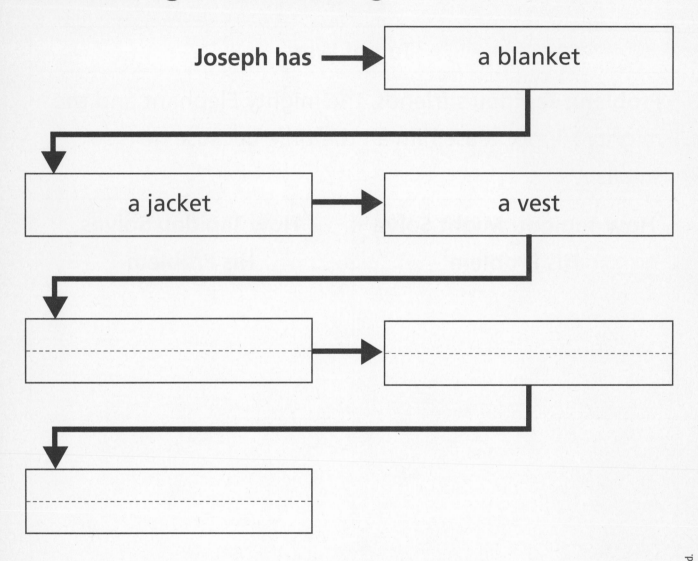

Joseph has ➡ a blanket

a jacket ➡ a vest

```
GLOSSARY
```

needle	a small, thin piece of steel with a sharp point and a hole for thread, used for sewing: *My mother used a **needle** and thread to sew my button on my shirt.*
material	cloth or fabric: *I chose a soft, blue **material** for my new robe.*

Name _____

One of Three

	What I Do	What the Sisters Do
Playing Together		play dress-up
Playing Alone		play with a doll

Name _____

Enzo the Wonderfish

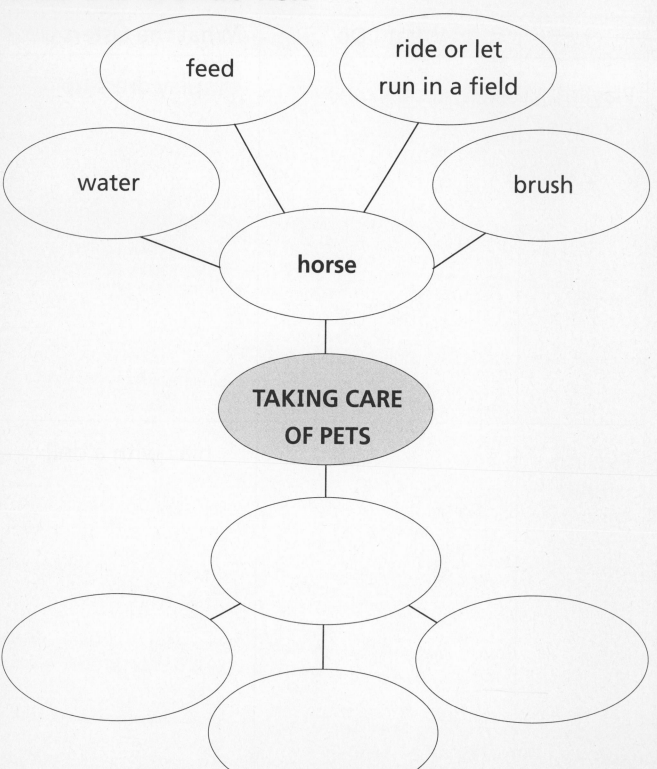

feed

ride or let run in a field

water

brush

horse

TAKING CARE OF PETS

Name _____

Swimmy

FISH IN SCHOOLS AND CHILDREN IN GROUPS	
How They Are Alike	**How They Are Different**
have friends	fish hunt for food
safer	children play games

GLOSSARY

creatures living people or animals: *Swimmy saw many different* **creatures.**

marvel a wonderful thing: *Swimmy thought the things he saw under the sea were* **marvels.**

school (of fish) a large group of fish swimming together: *Swimmy and his friends swam together as a* **school** *of fish.*

Title _____

Setting	**Characters**

Story

Problem	**Events**

Solution _____

Title _____

Topic or Title

Main Idea

Details